A Concise
German
Grammar

A Concise German Grammar

TIMOTHY BUCK

OXFORD

UNIVERSITY PRESS

OXFORD
UNIVERSITY PRESS

Great Clarendon Street, Oxford OX2 6DP
Oxford University Press is a department of the University of Oxford.
It furthers the University's objective of excellence in research, scholarship,
and education by publishing worldwide in

Oxford New York

Athens Auckland Bangkok Bogotá Buenos Aires Calcutta
Cape Town Chennai Dar es Salaam Delhi Florence Hong Kong Istanbul
Karachi Kuala Lumpur Madrid Melbourne Mexico City Mumbai
Nairobi Paris São Paulo Singapore Taipei Tokyo Toronto Warsaw

and associated companies in Berlin Ibadan

Oxford is a registered trade mark of Oxford University Press
in the UK and certain other countries

Published in the United States
by Oxford University Press Inc., New York

British Library Cataloguing in Publication Data
Data available

Library of Congress Cataloging in Publication Data
(Data applied for)

ISBN 019 870022 9 (P/b)
ISBN 019 870027 X (H/b)

1 3 5 7 9 10 8 6 4 2

Typeset by Graphicraft Limited, Hong Kong
Printed in Great Britain
on acid-free paper by
Bookcraft (Bath) Ltd., Midsomer Norton

Preface

This book aims to equip undergraduates with a reliable, readable, and accessible source of information on German grammar which meets the widely-felt need for a comprehensive yet concise guide to the language. It is hoped that, in addition to serving as a reference grammar, it may also be found useful as a 'reading grammar' that a user may gradually work his or her way through. A special feature is the inclusion of supplementary sections dealing with individual prepositions and conjunctions—areas in which students may be glad to have detailed guidance.

The book uses the new spelling system introduced in August 1998.

I am greatly indebted to the late Professor Paul Salmon (Edinburgh University) and Dr Jeffrey Ashcroft (St Andrews University), who read the text in its original version, and Dr Charles Russ (York University), who went through the final draft of the book, for their helpful comments and suggestions; the responsibility for the printed text is, of course, mine.

University of Edinburgh   T.B.
1999

Contents

Pronunciation Guide

PHONETIC SYMBOLS

VOWELS

[a]	a *Mann*	[o]	o *Drogist*
[aː]	a *Vater*, aa *Maat*, ah *Sahne*	[oː]	o *Sog*, oh *Bohne*, oo *Boot*
[ɛ]	ä *lächeln*, e *setzen*	[ŏ]	(in *oi*, *oy*) *Memoiren*, *loyal*
[ɛː]	ä *Mädchen*, äh *zählen*	[ʊ]	u *lustig*
[e]	e *Demokrat*	[u]	u *Duell*
[eː]	e *eben*, ee *Schnee*, eh *gehen*	[uː]	u *Fuß*, uh *Kuh*
[ə]	e *Sonne*	[ŭ]	u *Suite*
[ɐ]	er *Fenster*, r *mehr*	[œ]	ö *fördern*
[ɪ]	i *Zimmer*	[ø]	ö *Zölibat*
[i]	i *direkt*	[øː]	ö *böse*, öh *Söhne*
[iː]	i *gib*, ie *lief*, ieh *sieh*, ih *ihr*	[ʏ]	ü *Lücke*
[ĭ]	i *Australien*	[y]	ü *Büro*, y *dynamisch*
[ɔ]	o *Motte*	[yː]	ü *Küken*, üh *Mühe*, y *typisch*

NASAL VOWELS: [ãː] am, an, em, en (*Elan*, *Amüsement*), [ɛ̃ː] aim, ain, ein, en (after *i* or *y*), im, in (*Terrain*, *Teint*, *Bassin*), [ɔ̃ː] om, on (*Affront*), [œ̃ː] um (*Parfum*). (They are shortened in unstressed syllables, e.g. *Enquete* [ã-].)

DIPHTHONGS

[aɛ] ai *Mai*, ei *reich*   [ɔø] äu *Häuptling*, eu *Reue*   [aʊ] au *auch*

CONSONANTS

[b]	b *haben*, bb *Ebbe*	[ks]	chs *Lachs*, cks *Klecks*,
[ç]	ch *Licht*, g (in *-ig*) *zwanzig*		ks *Koks*, x *Lexikon*
[d]	d *Ding*, dd *Widder*	[kv]	qu *Quelle*
[ʤ]	dsch *Dschungel*, g *Gin*,	[l]	l *lachen*, ll *voll*
	j *jetten*	[m]	m *amüsant*, mm *hämmern*
[f]	f *fünf*, ff *Affe*, v *vier*,	[n]	n *Sohn*, nn *Henne*
	ph *Phobie*	[ŋ]	ng *Klingel*, n *krank*
[g]	g *gehen*, gg *Dogge*	[p]	p *Pilz*, -b *Dieb*
[h]	h *Humor*	[r]	r *rosa*, rh *Rhabarber*
[j]	j *jung*	[s]	s *Haus*, ss/ß *hassen*, *Maß*
[k]	k *König*, ck *backen*,	[ʃ]	sch *Wunsch*, sk *Ski*,
	kk *Akkord*, c *Café*,		ch *Branche*, s (in *sp-*, *st-*)
	ch *Charakter*, -g *trug*		*Sport*, *stehen*

[t]	t *Zeit*, th *Thema*, dt *Stadt*, -d *Land*	[ʧ]	tsch *Quatsch*, ch *Couch*
[ts]	z *Zahn*, zz *Skizze*, ts *Lotse*, tz *benutzen*, ds *Landsmann*, c *Cäsar*, t *Aktion*	[v]	w *Wald*, v *Version*
		[x]	ch *lachen*
		[z]	s *so*
		[ʒ]	g *Regime*, j *Journalist*

OTHER SYMBOLS

[ʔ] glottal stop ['] stress mark [ˌ] indicates a syllabic consonant

THE GERMAN ALPHABET

The names of the letters of the German alphabet are pronounced as follows:

A	[aː]	H	[haː]	O	[oː]	V	[faʊ]
B	[beː]	I	[iː]	P	[peː]	W	[veː]
C	[tseː]	J	[jɔt, *Aust.* jeː]	Q	[kuː, *Aust.* kveː]	X	[ɪks]
D	[deː]	K	[kaː]	R	[ɛr]	Y	['ʏpsilɔn]
E	[eː]	L	[ɛl]	S	[ɛs]	Z	[tsɛt]
F	[ɛf]	M	[ɛm]	T	[teː]		
G	[geː]	N	[ɛn]	U	[uː]		

ADDITIONAL SYMBOLS: Ä [ɛː], Ö [øː], Ü [yː], (lower case) ß [ɛs'tsɛt].

PRONUNCIATION GUIDE

Stress falls on the first syllable—with certain exceptions, notably:

(*a*) **lebéndig** *alive*, **die Forélle** *trout*, **die Hornísse** *hornet*, **der Holúnder** *elder*, **der Wachólder** *juniper*; (*b*) most words of foreign origin, e.g. **die Geographíe** *geography*, **der Theológe** *theologian*, **der Patiént** *patient*, **die Existénz** *existence*, **romántisch** *romantic*, **europäisíeren** *to Europeanize*, and nouns ending in -ei, e.g. **die Heucheléi** *hypocrisy*; (*c*) inseparable verbs, e.g. **begínnen** *to begin*, **entdécken** *to discover*; (*d*) (with the prefix ab-) **abschéulich** *abominable*, **die Abtéilung** *department*; (with the prefix un-) **unéndlich** *infinite*, as well as some adjectives which may also have initial stress, e.g. **unerréichbar** *unattainable*; (*e*) certain compounds, e.g. **das Jahrhúndert** *century*, **die Apfelsíne** *orange*, **die Zweidríttelmehrheit** *two-thirds majority*, **willkómmen** *welcome*, **beiséite** *aside*, **zusámmen** *together*; (*f*) some place-names, e.g. **Bayréuth, Bremerháven, Hannóver** *Hanover*, **Heilbrónn, Paderbórn**, also names in -in (with final stress), e.g. **Schwerín**; (*g*) most abbreviations in which the names of the letters are pronounced (the final letter being stressed), e.g. **der BH́** *bra*, **die DNŚ** *D.N.A.*

Compound adjectives of the type **stéinált** *as old as the hills*, **stóckfínster** *pitch-dark* take level stress.

An important feature of German speech is the phenomenon known as the glottal stop (as heard, for example, in Cockney *wa'er* for *water*—or indeed sometimes in standard English speech, reinforcing a stressed vowel: *he | IS lying!*). It occurs before vowels in initial position or following a prefix as well as at the junction of compounds in which the second element begins with a vowel, e.g. **der | Arzt** *doctor*, **ver|achten** *to despise*, **die Hoch|ebene** *plateau*; here a consonant must not be carried over to the vowel that follows, as happens in English: contrast **für | Eva** with *for‿Eve*, **ein | Eis** with *an‿ice*.[1]

VOWELS

Vowels are pure and never diphthongized as in Southern English (e.g. *say*, *boat*). They are usually *short* before a double consonant or consonantal cluster, or **ch**, **sch**, or **ng** (e.g. **der Mann** *man*, **hart**[2] *hard*, **die Kunst** *art*, **der Geruch** *smell*), and *long* before a single consonant or silent **h** (e.g. **der Rat** *advice*, **die Kuh** *cow*), if doubled (e.g. **das Boot** *boat*) or if final and stressed (e.g. **das Büro** *office*); a long stem vowel as in **loben** *to praise* remains long in derived forms, e.g. **lobt, lobte**.

Spelling is not, however, an infallible guide to vowel length in German. Exceptions—and they are fairly numerous—to the general rules above include:

(i) WITH LONG VOWEL: **die Art** *kind*, **der Bart** *beard*, **die Jagd** *hunt*, **nach** *after*, *towards*, **der Papst** *pope*, **sprach** *spoke*, **die Sprache** *language*, **zart** *tender*; **die Gebärde** *gesture*, **das Gemälde** *painting*, **das Gespräch** *conversation*, **das Rätsel** *riddle*; **die Beschwerde** *complaint*, **die Erde** *earth*, **erst** *first*, **der Herd** *cooker*, **die Herde** *herd*, **der Krebs** *crustacean*, *cancer*, **das Pferd** *horse*, **das Schwert** *sword*, **stets** *always*, **werden** *to become*, **der Wert** *value*, **wert** *dear*, *worth*; **das Obst** *fruit*, **Ostern** *Easter*, **hoch** *high* (but **die Hochzeit** *wedding*), **der Mond** *moon*, **der Trost** *consolation*; **Österreich** *Austria*, **die Behörde** *authority*, **trösten** *to console*; **das Buch** *book*, **die Buche** *beech*, **der Fluch** *curse*, **fluchen** *to swear*, **die Geburt** *birth*, **der Husten** *cough*, **husten** *to cough*, **der Kuchen** *cake*, **die Suche** *search*, **suchen** *to look for*, **das Tuch** *cloth*, **wusch** *washed*; **düster** *gloomy*, **die Wüste** *desert*.

(ii) WITH SHORT VOWEL: **ab, an, bis, das, des, es, hin, in, man, mit, ob, um, ur-** in **das Urteil** *judgement* and **urteilen** *to judge*, **von, was, weg; am, im, vom, zum; das Kap** *cape* (geog.), **der Chef** *boss*, **der Lorbeer** (o short) *laurel*, **der Klub** *club*; **die Grammátik** *grammar*, **die Metápher** *metaphor*, **der Apríl**, **das Kapítel** *chapter* (stressed vowels pronounced short).

Vowels in words of foreign origin are generally *short* in unstressed final syllables ending in a consonant, e.g. **der Tábăk** *tobacco*, **Jápăn**, **der Átlăs**,

---

[1] In English it has been possible, for example, for *an ewt* to evolve into *a newt*; such developments are phonetically impossible in German.
 The glottal stop is *not* sounded in certain compounds, e.g. **allein, einander, vollenden**, also such adverbs as **darauf, heraus, hinein, vorüber**.
[2] Words containing a *short vowel + r + consonant* are often mispronounced by English speakers, who tend to substitute a long vowel and drop **r; hărt** then sounds like Southern English *heart* (haht), **mŏrgen** *tomorrow* like *Morgan* (mawgan), and so on.

das Réquiĕm, Aristóphanĕs, die Téchnĭk *technology, technique*,[3] das Fázĭt *conclusion (drawn)*, das Stádiŏn *stadium*, das Épŏs *epic*. (Exceptions include: der Bálkān *the Balkans*, das Plátīn *platinum*, der Álkohōl *alcohol*, words in -ian e.g. der Thýmiān *thyme*, -iv e.g. der Kónjunktīv *subjunctive*.) Those in unstressed non-final syllables ending in a vowel are also short (while retaining the quality of the long vowel), e.g. *e*legánt, das R*i*tuál, der Gor*í*lla.

CONSONANTS

Consonants calling for special care are: (*a*) l (the 'clear' l used initially as in lang—similar to initial English *l*—must also be used in other positions, e.g. in halten, Ball; the 'dark' *l* (approaching *u*) used by English speakers in e.g. *hold, ball* is quite out of place in German);[4] (*b*) r (the 'uvular' r—pronounced much like French *r* as in *la rue*—is, despite the shared symbol, entirely different from English *r*; after a long vowel r is vocalized, i.e. reduced to a vowel); (*c*) the two types of ch, viz. the 'hard' *Achlaut* akin to Scots *ch* as in *loch*, used after a, o, u, au, and the 'soft' *Ichlaut*, a sound like that of *H* in *Hugh* used after other vowels and diphthongs as well as consonants, e.g. in lächeln, Brecht, ich, Milch, durch.

A striking feature of the German consonant system is the devoicing of b, d, g—i.e. their realization as p, t, k—at the end of a word or element of a compound, or before a suffix, e.g. gab *gave*, die End/station *terminus*, mög/lich *possible* (exception: the suffix -ig, pronounced as if -ich); also in the prefixes ab-, ob-, sub- (b pronounced p, e.g. ab/surd, das Ob/jekt, der Sub/kontinent) and ad- (d pronounced t, e.g. das Ad/jektiv).

AUSTRIAN AND SWISS STANDARD GERMAN

Both Austrian and Swiss standard German differ in their pronunciation from the (North) German standard in a number of ways. For instance, 'front' r (produced with the tip of the tongue) is used in Austrian and Swiss (as well as southern German) speech instead of uvular r; in native words 'hard' [x] replaces 'soft' [ç] for ch altogether in Swiss German and after r (e.g. durch [dʊrx]) in Austrian German; vowel length may be different.

Some of the more striking differences are found in the pronunciation of words of foreign origin:

(i) for initial ch before e, i [k] is used in Austria (and southern Germany), e.g. die Chemie [keˈmiː] *chemistry*, China [ˈkiːna], der Chirurg [kiˈrʊrk] *surgeon* (= German standard [ç]).

(ii) final -e is often silent in Austrian German, e.g. die Clique [klɪk], die Nuance [nyˈãːs], die Sabotage [zaboˈtaːʒ].

---

[3] Cf. die Informátik *computer science*, die Klássik *classicism*, die Romántik *romanticism*, die Lýrik *lyric poetry*, die Symbólik *symbolism*. Some words, however, have final stress and long i, e.g. die Musík *music*, die Fabrík *factory*, die Physík *physics*.

[4] Inevitably, differences noted between German and English pronunciation will not always be valid for all English-speaking areas. Irish English, for example, always has 'clear' *l*.

(iii) -**ment** is generally pronounced [-mɛnt] in Swiss German, e.g. **das Reglement** [reglə'mɛnt] *regulations* (= *German standard* [-'mãː]).

(iv) -**on** is [-oːn] in Austria and (commonly) Switzerland (also in southern Germany), e.g. **der Balkon** [bal'koːn] *balcony* (= *German standard* [-ɔŋ]).

(v) the stress falls on the final syllable in Austrian **der Kaffee** [ka'feː], **das Platin** [pla'tiːn] *platinum*, **das⁵ Sakko** [za'koː] *sports jacket*, **der Tabak** [ta'bak] *tobacco* (= *initial stress in the German standard*); in **die Mathematik** [mate'maːtɪk] *mathematics*, however, it is placed—contrary to German practice ([-ma'tiːk])—on the penultimate. Swiss German tends to shift the stress to the first syllable, e.g. **das Büro** ['byːro] *office*.

(vi) other words, e.g. Austrian **das Billard** [bi'jaːr] *billiards*, **die Taille** ['tae̯ljə] *waist*, **die Medaille** [me'dae̯ljə] *medal*, **der Chef** [ʃeːf] *boss*; Swiss **der Komfort** [kɔm'fɔrt] *comfort, luxury* (= *German standard* ['bɪljart], ['taljə], [me'daljə], [ʃɛf]; [kɔm'foːɐ]).

SPELLINGS AND SOUNDS

SPELLING	SYMBOL	EXAMPLES	REMARKS
a 1 long	[aː]	s**a**gen	like *a* in *father*
2 short	[a]	M**a**nn, **a**kut	like Southern English *u* in *fun*, Northern English *a* in *man*
aa, ah	[aː]	A**a**l, n**a**h	= **a** 1
ai	[ae̯]	M**ai**	like *y* in *my* (but with the mouth open wider for the first component than for that of the English diphthong)
au	[ao̯]	H**au**s	like *ou* in *house* (but with the mouth open wider for the first component than for that of the English diphthong)
ä 1 long	[ɛː]	M**ä**dchen	as **ä** 2, but with the vowel lengthened; similar to *ai* in *hair* (in North Germany **e** 1 is widely used instead)
2 short	[ɛ]	h**ä**tte	like *e* in *set*
äh	[ɛː]	w**äh**len	= **ä** 1
äu	[ɔø̯]	Fr**äu**lein	like *oi* in *noise*
b 1	[b]	**B**är, ha**b**en	as in English
2	[p]	Kal**b**, Hu**b**-raum, lie**b**-lich; a**b**strakt, O**b**jekt, Su**b**jekt; lie**b**t, hü**b**sch, Gelü**b**de	like English *p*; **b** is unvoiced when final, at the end of an element in a compound, or before a suffix; also in the prefixes **ab-, ob-, sub-,** and before an unvoiced consonant or **d, g**

⁵ In Germany the word is usually masculine.

SPELLING	SYMBOL	EXAMPLES	REMARKS
c 1	[k]	**C**lou	(before **a, o, u** and **l, r**) = **k**
2	[ts]	**C**äsar	(elsewhere) = **z**
ch 1	[x]	au**ch**	(after **a, o, u, au**) like *ch* in Scots *loch*
2	[ç]	lä**ch**eln, Bü**ch**er, Ei**ch**e; Mil**ch**, man**ch**e, dur**ch**; **Ch**emie; Mäd**ch**en	(after other vowels and diphthongs; after consonants; at the beginning of words when followed by **e** or **i**; also in the suffix **-chen**) like the *h* in *hue*
3	[k]	**Ch**arakter	(in words of Greek origin before **a, o** and **l, r**) = **k**
chs	[ks]	Fu**chs**	(if the **s** is part of the stem) like English *x* (but **ch** and **s** are articulated separately in e.g. (des) **Loch-s**, (du) **lach-st**)
ck	[k]	Bo**ck**	= **k**
d 1	[d]	**d**u, la**d**en	as in English
2	[t]	run**d**, Wan**d**-uhr, freun**d**-lich, Mä**d**-chen; A**d**jektiv; Wo**d**ka, wi**d**men	like English *t*; **d** is unvoiced when final, at the end of an element in a compound, or before a suffix; also in the prefix **ad-**, and before an unvoiced consonant or **g, m, n, v, w**
dt	[t]	Sta**dt**, san**dt**e	like English *t*
e 1 long	[eː]	L**e**ben	like *ay* in Scots *say* or *eh* in Northern English *eh lad*
2 short	[e]	M**e**dizin	(in words of foreign origin in unstressed syllables) as **e** 1 but shortened
3 short	[ɛ]	B**e**tt	like *e* in *set*; the prefixes **er-, ver-,** and **zer-** are also pronounced with this vowel
4 neutral	[ə]	Lieb**e**, b**e**ginnen	(in unstressed syllables) like *a* in *ago*; in the unstressed endings **-el, -eln, -em, -en** the **e** is generally dropped in ordinary speech after certain consonants, e.g. **Nebel, betteln, messen** (cf. the pronunciation of *petal, dozen* as *pet'l, doz'n*)
			-er: this ending is pronounced [-ɐ], a short vowel close to the *u* in *fun*, e.g. **ein guter Lehrer**; similarly **-ern** [-ɐn], e.g. **wandern**
ee, eh	[eː]	S**ee**, s**eh**en	= **e** 1

SPELLING	SYMBOL	EXAMPLES	REMARKS
ei	[ae̯]	m*ei*n	like *y* in *my*
eu	[ɔ̯ø]	h*eu*te	like *oi* in *noise*
f	[f]	*f*liegen	as in English
g 1	[g]	*g*ehen, Geolo*g*ie	as in English ('hard' *g*)
2	[k]	Ta*g*, We*g*-weiser, tra*g*-bar; sa*g*t, Ja*g*d	like English *k*; **g** is unvoiced when final, at the end of an element in a compound, or before a suffix; also before an unvoiced consonant or **d** (NOTE: in North German speech **g** is generally pronounced here like **ch** instead, e.g. la*g* [laːx], Ber*g* [bɛrç]—see **ch** 1 and 2)
3 -ig	[-ɪç]	Köni*g*, zwanzi*g*	**g** is here pronounced like **ch** 2, except in the South which uses [-ɪk]; similarly before a consonant (e.g. **König**s and, with a suffix, **König**tum, **Ewig**keit) except before -**lich** (e.g. **königlich**) and in **Königreich**, where -**ig**- is pronounced [-ɪk-]; before a vowel -**ig**- = [-ɪg-], e.g. **Könige**, **Zwanziger**
			-**igst**, -**igt(e)** in verbs ending in -**igen** also have [ç]: [-ɪçst, -ɪçt(ə)]
h 1	[h]	*H*erz	as in English
2 silent	—	ne*h*men; T*h*eater	see (*a*) **ah**, **eh**, etc., in which **h** is used to show that the preceding vowel is long, (*b*) **th**
i 1 long	[iː]	B*i*bel, Mus*i*k	like *i* in *machine*, only closer
2 short	[i]	Z*i*trone	(in words of foreign origin in unstressed syllables) as **i** 1 but shortened
3 short	[ɪ]	*i*ch, Log*i*k	like *i* in *sick*
4 non-syllabic	[i̯]	as*i*atisch, Pat*i*ent, Mil*i*eu, Stat*i*on, ser*i*ös; (before unstressed vowel) Lin*i*e [-i̯ə], Span*i*en, Cäs*i*um	(in words of foreign origin before a stressed or unstressed vowel— except after certain consonantal combinations difficult to unite with [i̯], e.g. **Bibliothek**, **Adria**; here *i* = [i]) like *y* in *young*
ie, ieh, ih	[iː]	D*ie*sel, V*ieh*, *ih*n	= **i** 1; exceptions are v*ie*rzehn, v*ie*rzig, V*ie*rtel (ie = [ɪ]) and v*ie*lleicht (ie = [i])
j	[j]	*j*ung	like *y* in *young*
k	[k]	*k*alt	as in English, but with more aspiration before a stressed vowel

SPELLING	SYMBOL	EXAMPLES	REMARKS
l	[l]	Sa*lz*	'clear' *l* (formed with the tip of the tongue against the teeth-ridge or the upper front teeth)
m	[m]	*Mann*	as in English
n	[n]	*Name*	as in English
ng 1, n	[ŋ]	bri*ng*en, I*ng*wer, E*ng*land, la*ng*, Ba*nk*, Sphi*nx*	like *ng* in *singer* (NOTE the pronunciation of **Eng-land** and **Eng-länder**)
2	[ŋg]	Li*ng*uist, Ma*ng*an, Ta*ng*o, U*ng*arn, Ko*ng*o	(in words of foreign origin, medially before a full vowel—i.e. any other vowel than [ə]—or r) like *ng* in *finger*
o 1 long	[o:]	*Z*one	like *o* in Scots *no*
2 short	[o]	m*o*ralisch, anthrop*o*id	(in words of foreign origin in unstressed syllables) as **o** 1 but shortened
3 short	[ɔ]	*O*sten, gew*o*rden	like *o* in *got*, but with lip-rounding
oh, oo	[o:]	S*oh*n, M*oo*s	= **o** 1
ö 1 long	[ø:]	sch*ö*n	lips protruded and rounded with tongue in position for **e** 1
2 short	[ø]	*ö*konomisch	(in words of foreign origin in unstressed syllables) as **ö** 1 but shortened
3 short	[œ]	K*ö*ln	lips protruded and rounded with tongue in position for **e** 3
öh	[ø:]	H*öh*le	= **ö** 1
p	[p]	*P*ost, *P*sychologie	as in English, but with more aspiration before a stressed vowel
ph	[f]	*Ph*onetik	as in English
qu	[kv]	be*qu*em	like *kv*
r 1	[r]	*r*ot, ha*r*t, g*r*oß, stö*r*en	entirely different from the *r* (as in *run*) of most English speakers; produced either by vibrating the uvula (the sound is similar to French *r* as in *rue*) or—chiefly in Southern German—by lightly trilling with the tip of the tongue[6]
2 vocalic	[ɐ]	Oh*r*, we*r*den	following a long vowel r, in final position or before a consonant, is

[6] The latter pronunciation is the one used in the singing of classical music.

SPELLING	SYMBOL	EXAMPLES	REMARKS
			regularly realized as [ɐ], a (short) *a*-like sound close to the *u* in *fun*
3 -er	[-ɐ]	*guter*, **Lehr***er*	see note at **e** 4
rh	[r]	*Rh*abarber	= **r** 1
s 1 voiced	[z]	*s*o, *s*ouverän, *S*chick-*s*al, lang-*s*am; ro*s*ig; Am*s*el, impul*s*iv	like English *z*: initially before a vowel, and in the suffixes -**sal**, -**sam**; between vowels; and in -**ls**-, -**ms**-, -**ns**-, -**rs**-; in the South **s** is unvoiced in all these positions
2 unvoiced	[s]	Ei*s*, hoffnung*s*-lo*s*, bö*s*-artig, lö*s*-lich; *S*zene, Fen*s*ter, Pri*s*ma; Erb*s*e, Rät*s*el; *S*ujet	like *s* in *sit*: finally, at the end of an element in a compound, or before a suffix; before a consonant (but see **sp**-, **st**- at 3); after a consonant (except in -**ls**-, -**ms**-, -**ns**-, -**rs**-); and initially before a vowel in some words of foreign origin
3 in **sp**-, **st**-	[ʃ]	*s*prechen, Ge-*s*präch, *S*pirale; *s*tehen, er-*s*taunen, *S*tudent	= **sch**: initially or following a prefix —except in a few words of foreign origin in which [s] is retained, e.g. **Stewardess** (in some both [s] and [ʃ] occur, e.g. **Spektrum, steril**)
sch	[ʃ]	Fi*sch*	like *sh* in *ship*, but with the lips strongly protruded; where -**chen** follows **s**, **s** and **ch** are pronounced separately, e.g. **Häu*s*-*ch*en**
ss, ß	[s]	la*ss*en, So*ß*e	like *ss* in *miss*
t 1	[t]	**Z**ei**t**	as in English, but with more aspiration before a stressed vowel
2 in -**ti**-	[ts]	Ter**ti**a, par**ti**ell, Pa**ti**ent, Na**ti**on, sta**ti**onär, ra**ti**onieren	(in words of foreign origin, when -**ti**- is followed by a vowel) like *ts* in *nuts* (NOTE: before a stressed [iː] as in **Demokra***ti*e **t** is pronounced as in English)
th	[t]	**Th**eater, Timo**th**eus	= **t** 1
tz	[ts]	Ka**tz**e	like *ts* in *nuts*
u 1 long	[uː]	r*u*fen	like the second element in the diphthongized pronunciation [ʊu] of *oo* as in *zoo*; lips strongly rounded and protruded
2 short	[u]	M*u*sik, *zu*sammen	(in words of foreign origin and **zu**-compounds, in unstressed syllables) as **u** 1 but shortened

SPELLING	SYMBOL	EXAMPLES	REMARKS
3 short	[ʊ]	M*u*tter, *U*rteil	like *u* in *put*, but with more lip-rounding
4 non-syllabic	[ŭ]	S*u*ada, akt*u*ell, Stat*u*e	(in words of foreign origin) like *w* in *well*
uh	[uː]	Sch*uh*	= **u** 1
ü 1 long	[yː]	dr*ü*ben	lips positioned for pronouncing **u** 1 (long u), with tongue in position for **i** 1 (long i); like French *u* as in *rue*
2 short	[y]	B*ü*ro	(in words of foreign origin in unstressed syllables) as **ü** 1 but shortened
3 short	[ʏ]	h*ü*bsch	lips rounded with tongue in position for **i** 3 (short i)
üh	[yː]	k*üh*l	= **ü** 1
v 1	[f]	*v*on, *V*ers, akti*v*	like *f* in *fire*; final -**v** in words of foreign origin is always pronounced [f]
2	[v]	*V*ase, Kla*v*ier, ner*v*ös	like *v* in *very*: the usual pronunciation of initial and medial **v** in words of foreign origin
w, wh	[v]	*W*asser, *Wh*isky	like *v* in *very*
x	[ks]	*X*ylophon, Se*x*	like *x* in *six*
y 1 long	[yː]	L*y*rik	= **ü** 1
2 short	[y]	Z*y*presse	(in words of foreign origin in unstressed syllables) as **y** 1 but shortened; in **Z*y*linder** it is pronounced [i]
3 short	[ʏ]	Rh*y*thmus	= **ü** 3
z	[ts]	*z*u, Her*z*	like *ts* in *nuts*

ADDITIONAL PRONUNCIATIONS OCCURRING IN WORDS OF FOREIGN ORIGIN. In words of foreign origin, the letters of the German alphabet (and their combinations) may have different values—normally approximating to their pronunciation(s) in the language of origin—from those listed above. Thus **ai** in words of French origin is pronounced [ɛː] e.g. B*ai*sse, [ɛ] e.g. B*ai*ser, [ae̯] e.g. Det*ai*l, while **au** is realized as [oː] e.g. H*au*sse, [o] e.g. F*au*xpas, [ɔ] e.g. Ch*au*ffeur; **oi** and **oy** are pronounced [ŏa(ː)] e.g. Mem*oi*ren; and the French nasal vowels are similarly nasalized in German, e.g. El*an* with [ãː], Parf*um* with [œ̃ː] (sometimes a denasalized pronunciation is used instead, as in Ball*on* [-ˈlɔŋ]). Similarly, vowels in words from English are pronounced in an approximately English fashion: **a** is reproduced either as [ɛ] e.g. tr*a*mpen or as [eː] e.g. C*a*pe, long **i** as [ae̯] e.g. l*i*ve [laͤf], long **o** (variously spelt) as [oː] e.g. T*oa*st, Sh*ow*, **u** as [a] e.g. R*u*n, **y** as [ae̯] e.g. N*y*lon or as [i] e.g. Part*y*, and so on.

A number of consonants may have values not found in native German words: **c** is pronounced [s] in e.g. **C**ity, A**k**tri**c**e [-sə], **ch** is [tʃ] in English words, e.g. **Ch**ip, but [ʃ] in Gallicisms, e.g. **Ch**ef; **g** and **j** are both [dʒ] e.g. **G**in, **J**et and [ʒ] e.g. **G**enie, **J**ournal; **gn** is [nj] in French and Italian words, e.g. Champa**gn**er; **ll** is [lj] in Bi**ll**ard, Medai**ll**e [-ˈdaljə], Tai**ll**e [ˈtaljə]; **z** is realized as [z] in **G**a**z**e, as [s] in Bron**z**e [ˈbrɔ̃:sə]. Certain consonants are silent in final position as in the source-language French, e.g. **Premier, Etat, Palais**. Finally, the combination **dsch**, used to render English *j* in words of Oriental origin, is pronounced [dʒ] e.g. **Dsch**ungel.

PROPER NAMES: A SELECTION

The list that follows contains a selection of well-known personal and place names from the German-speaking countries and outside whose pronunciation is in some way worthy of note.

Several spellings are peculiar to proper names; others may have values found only in proper names:

ae	[ɛ:]	B**ae**r	**oey**	[ø:]	Bad O**ey**nhausen
ay	[aɛ]	B**ay**ern, M**ay**	**-ow**	[-o]	Trept**ow** (but [-ɔf] in
ey	[aɛ]	M**ey**er, Lorel**ey**			Russian names)
oe	[ø:]	Schr**oe**der	**ue**	[u:]	K**ue**s
	[œ]	**Oe**tker		[ʏ]	M**ue**ller
oe, oi	[o:]	Itzeh**oe**, Tr**oi**sdorf,	**ui**	[y:]	D**ui**sburg
		V**oi**gt [fo:kt]	**y**	[i:]	Schw**y**z

Bach [bax]
Baedeker [ˈbɛ:dəkɐ]
Bayreuth [baɛˈrɔøt]
Beethoven, van [ˈbe:tho:fn̩ (fan)]
Berchtesgaden [bɛrçtəsˈga:dn̩]
Berlin [bɛrˈli:n]
Bethmann Hollweg [ˈbe:tman ˈhɔlve:k]
Beuys [bɔøs]
Bismarck [ˈbɪsmark]
Blücher [ˈblʏçɐ]
Bochum [ˈbo:xʊm]
Bremerhaven [bre:mɐˈha:fn̩]
Breughel [ˈbrɔøgl̩]
Büchner [ˈby:çnɐ]
Buxtehude [bʊkstəˈhu:də]
Calvin [kalˈvi:n]
Cambridge [ˈke:mbrɪtʃ]
Cervantes [sɛrˈvantɛs]
Chemnitz [ˈkɛmnɪts]
Chiemsee [ˈki:mze:]
Chur [ku:ɐ]
Cuxhaven [kʊksˈha:fn̩]
Dante [ˈdantə]
Darwin [ˈdarvi:n]

Dresden [ˈdre:sdn̩]
Duisburg [ˈdy:sbʊrk]
Erfurt [ˈɛrfʊrt]
Erlangen [ˈɛrlaŋən]
Freud [frɔøt]
Gelsenkirchen [gɛlznˈkɪrçn̩]
Goes [gø:s]
Goethe [ˈgø:tə]
Gogh, van [gɔx (fan)]
Goya [ˈgo:ja]
Grosz [grɔs]
Gstaad [kʃta:t]
Haydn [ˈhaɛdn̩]
Heilbronn [haɛlˈbrɔn]
Hohenstaufen [ho:ənˈʃtaɔfn̩]
Hohenzollern [ho:ənˈtsɔlen]
Horváth [ˈhɔrva:t]
Ibsen [ˈɪpsn̩]
Johannesburg [joˈhanəsbʊrk]
Johnson [ˈjo:nzɔn]
Kaiserslautern [kaɛzɐsˈlaɔten]
Koblenz [ˈko:blɛnts]
Lenin [ˈle:ni:n]
Liverpool [ˈlɪvɐpu:l]

London ['lɔndɔn],
  commonly ['lɔndn̩]
  with unvoiced d
Los Angeles [lɔs 'ɛndʒələs]
Luther ['lʊtɐ]
Magdeburg ['makdəbʊrk]
Manchester ['mɛntʃɛstɐ]
Melbourne ['mɛlbɐn]
Mercedes [mɛr'tse:dəs]
Montreal [mɔntre'a:l]
Musil ['mu:zɪl]
Napoleon [na'po:leɔn]
Osnabrück [ɔsna'brʏk]
Ottawa ['ɔtava]
Oxford ['ɔksfɔrt]
Pachelbel ['paxɛlbl̩]
Paderborn [pa:dɐ'bɔrn]
Potsdam ['pɔtsdam]

Recklinghausen [rɛklɪŋ'haɒzn̩]
Reclam ['rɛklam, 're:-]
Roosevelt ['ro:zəvɛlt]
Roth [ro:t]
Saarbrücken [za:ɐ'brʏkn̩]
San Francisco [sanfran'tsɪsko]
Schleswig ['ʃle:svɪç]
Seghers ['ze:gɐs]
Soest [zo:st]
Southampton [saɒ'θɛmptn̩]
Stalin ['sta:li:n, ʃt-]
Telemann ['te:ləman]
Vancouver [vɛn'ku:vɐ]
Velazquez [ve'laskɛs]
Virchow ['fɪrço, 'vɪr-]
Washington ['wɔʃɪŋtn̩]
Wilhelmshaven [vɪlhɛlms'ha:fn̩]
Zermatt [tsɛr'mat]

German Spelling

HISTORICAL NOTE

German spelling was standardized as recently as the beginning of the 20th century, a strong impetus towards orthographical unity having been provided by the political union of 1871. It was in 1902 that the Prussian spelling rules—prescribed for use in that state's schools and widely propagated within and beyond Prussia's boundaries by Konrad Duden's *Vollständiges orthographisches Wörterbuch der deutschen Sprache*, published in 1880—were finally given the blessing of the Reich following a special conference held in Berlin. (Austria and Switzerland followed suit.) At that conference changes in the spelling of certain words were decided on, as a result of which books and articles published before 1902 contain words with spellings no longer given in dictionaries. The changes included the replacement of the **c** that remained in some words of foreign origin, which meant that **Citrone** *lemon* became **Zitrone** and **Accusativ** *accusative* **Akkusativ**, and the substitution of **t** for **th** (except in words of foreign origin), whereby for example **Thal** *valley* and **thun** *to do* became **Tal** and **tun** respectively.

1998 saw the adoption—amid considerable controversy—of a further spelling reform (agreed between the German-speaking countries). Among the changes made were: the substitution of **ss** for **ß** after a short vowel, e.g. **daß** > **dass**; the capitalization of the noun in e.g. **recht haben** > **Recht haben**, **außer acht lassen** > **außer Acht lassen**, **auf deutsch** > **auf Deutsch**, **heute morgen** > **heute Morgen**, **im allgemeinen** > **im Allgemeinen**; the writing of verb + verb compounds as two words instead of one, e.g. **kennenlernen** > **kennen lernen**, **stehenbleiben** > **stehen bleiben**; and the respelling, on etymological grounds, not only of words such as **behende** > **behände**, **Gemse** > **Gämse** (cf. **Hand**, **Gams**), but also—quite improperly —of **Quentchen** > **Quäntchen**, **verbleuen** > **verbläuen**, **belemmert** > **belämmert** (as if they were related to **Quantum**, **blau**, **Lamm**). A great many alternative spellings were created: thus, instead of e.g. **Alptraum**, **Au-pair-Mädchen**, **Countdown**, **Facette**, **Necessaire**, **passé**, **so dass** one may now write **Albtraum**, **Aupairmädchen**, **Count-down**, **Fassette**, **Nessessär**, **passee**, **sodass**. In addition, the rules governing the use of commas were revised.

SPECIAL POINTS

HYPHENATION

The hyphen is used especially (*a*) when part of a compound word is omitted to avoid repetition, e.g. **Buch- und Zeitungstitel** *titles of books and newspapers* (**Buch-** standing for **Buchtitel**), **ein- und ausatmen** *to breathe in and out* (**ein-** for **einatmen**), **bergauf und -ab** *uphill and downhill* (**-ab** for **bergab**); (*b*) to break up compounds felt to be unwieldy, e.g. **das Arbeiter-Unfallversicherungsgesetz** *workers' accident insurance law*; and to avoid a sequence of three identical vowels in a compound, e.g. **die Hawaii-Inseln** *the Hawaiian Islands*; (*c*) in compounds of which one element is a letter, abbreviation, or numeral, e.g. **o-beinig** *bow-legged*, **die U-Bahn** *underground (railway)*, **die CDU-Führung** *the C.D.U. leadership*, **die US-Flotte** *the U.S. fleet*, **der Kfz-Fahrer** *driver of a motor vehicle*, **die 10-Pfennig-Marke** *10 pfennig stamp*; (*d*) in many compounds incorporating proper names, especially if more than one of the components is a name, e.g. **die Max-Planck-Gesellschaft** *the Max Planck Society*, **der Dortmund-Ems-Kanal** *the Dortmund-Ems Canal*, **der Sankt-Gotthard-Pass** *the St. Gotthard Pass*, **der Konrad-Adenauer-Platz**, **die Friedrich-Schiller-Allee** (but cf.—with a single name component—**der Adenauerplatz**, **die Schillerallee**), **die James-Bond-Filme** *the James Bond films*; in the case of geographical names beginning with an adjectival element or one denoting a point of the compass, such as **Neu-**, **Groß-**, **Nord-**, etc., the compound is formed without hyphenation, e.g. **Kleinasien** *Asia Minor*, **Südafrika** *South Africa*, unless the second component is the name of a city, in which case the hyphen is widely used, e.g. **Groß-London** *Greater London*, **Neu-Delhi** *New Delhi*; geographical names of which the first element ends in an uninflected **-(i)sch** also have a hyphen, e.g. **Britisch-Kolumbien** *British Columbia* (more prevalent, of course, in colonial times: **Belgisch-Kongo** *the Belgian Congo*, **Deutsch-Ostafrika** *German East Africa*, etc.); (*e*) in compounds such as **die Lohn-Preis-Spirale** *wage-price spiral*, **der Hals-Nasen-Ohren-Arzt** *ear, throat, and nose specialist*; (*f*) to link two adjectives (see concluding paragraph of *Compound adjectives*, p. 116).

THE SYMBOL ß

ß (known as **Eszett**, which indicates its origin as (long) **s** + **z**) is a ligature peculiar to the German language. It is replaced by **SS** when capital letters are used. Except in Switzerland, where **ss** is regularly used in its place, it is considered incorrect to use **ss** instead of ß where it is prescribed (namely, after long vowels and diphthongs).

Note that the following surnames are spelt with final **-ss** in spite of the rules: **(Richard) Strauss** (but the Austrian composers, father and son, are spelt **Johann Strauß**), **(Peter) Weiss**, **(Carl) Zeiss**.

CAPITAL LETTERS

All nouns are written with an initial capital letter.

Initial capitals are also used in the following instances:

(i) 2ND PERSON PERSONAL PRONOUN **Sie** *you* (and the corresponding adjective **Ihr** *your*). (The pronouns **du** and **ihr** are no longer capitalized in letter-writing under the new spelling.)

(ii) ADJECTIVES following **alles, etwas, nichts**, etc., e.g. **alles Schöne, nichts Gutes** (see p. 53); for *adjectives used as nouns* see p. 55.

(iii) Certain ADJECTIVES CONNECTED WITH NAMES, TITLES when part of a geographical, historical, or institutional name, e.g. **das Tote Meer** *the Dead Sea*, **die Französische Revolution** *the French Revolution*, **der Zweite Weltkrieg** *the Second World War*, **der Eiserne Vorhang** *the Iron Curtain*, **das Auswärtige Amt** *the (German) Foreign Ministry*, **das Rote Kreuz** *the Red Cross*, **die Dritte Welt** *the Third World*.

Initial capitals are *not* used in the following instances:

(i) The particle **von** in personal names is written with a lower-case initial (but has a capital at the beginning of a sentence, unless it is abbreviated to **v.**).

(ii) ADJECTIVES OF NATIONALITY, e.g. **britisch** *British*, **südafrikanisch** *South African*. (Adjectives in official titles do, however, have a capital letter, e.g. **die Deutsche Bank, die Österreichischen Bundesbahnen**.)

ADJECTIVES IN **-(i)sch** DERIVED FROM A PERSONAL NAME and referring to the achievement of the person concerned may be spelt with either a lower-case letter (e.g. **die darwinsche Evolutionstheorie** *Darwin's theory of evolution*, **die lutherische Bibelübersetzung** *Luther's translation of the Bible*) or a capital letter if an apostrophe is inserted after the name concerned (e.g. **die Darwin'sche Evolutionstheorie, die Luther'sche Bibelübersetzung**). The spelling with a lower-case initial is also used where an adjective signifies *named after, in the manner or spirit of* (e.g. **platonische Liebe** *platonic love*).

A TYPOGRAPHICAL NOTE

In order to emphasize a word or phrase in German, printers use either *italics*, as in English, or *letter-spacing* (**Sperrdruck**), e.g. **im Plural dagegen** . . . *in the **plural**, on the other hand,* . . .

TRANSLITERATION OF RUSSIAN NAMES

The differences between the customary German and English transliterations of Russian characters are shown in the following table. In the examples the German transliteration is given in bold, the English in italics.

RUSSIAN CHARACTER		TRANSLITERATION		EXAMPLES
		GERMAN	ENGLISH	
В	в	**w**	*v*	**Wladimir** *Vladimir*, **Rostow** *Rostov*
Е	е	*initially, after vowel, etc.:*		
		je	*ye, e*	**Jewtuschenko** *Yevtushenko*
Ё	ё	**jo**	*yo*	**Pjotr** *Pyotr*
		after certain consonants:		
		o	*e*	**Gorbatschow** *Gorbachev*
Ж	ж	**sch**	*zh*	**Schukow** *Zhukov*
З	з	**s**	*z*	**Sinowjew** *Zinoviev*, **Kasan** *Kazan*
И	и	*after ь:*		
		ji	*yi*	**Iljitsch** *Ilyich*
Й	й	**i**	*y, i*	**Tolstoi** *Tolstoy* (also representing -ий: **Dostojewski** *Dostoyevsky*)
		initially:		
		j	*y*	**Joschkar-Ola** *Yoshkar-Ola*
С	с	*between vowels:*		
		ss	*s*	**Nekrassow** *Nekrasov*
Х	х	**ch**	*kh*	**Charkow** *Kharkov*
Ц	ц	**z**	*ts*	**Winniza** *Vinnitsa*, **Solschenizyn** *Solzhenitsyn*
Ч	ч	**tsch**	*ch*	**Tschernobyl** *Chernobyl*, **Schostakowitsch** *Shostakovich*
Ш	ш	**sch**	*sh*	**Timoschenko** *Timoshenko*
Щ	щ	**schtsch**	*shch*	**Chruschtschow** *Khrushchev*
Ю	ю	**ju**	*yu*	**Iljuschin** *Ilyushin*
Я	я	**ja**	*ya*	**Jakutsk** *Yakutsk*

Punctuation

German punctuation differs from English punctuation in a number of important points:

THE COMMA. The use of the comma in German is strictly *syntactical*, whereas the English comma is often used as a stylistic device to indicate a pause in the sentence: *he, however, was convinced that* . . . (compare: **er aber war überzeugt, dass . . .**), *luckily, she was in when I rang* (**zum Glück war sie zu Hause, als ich anrief**).

The German comma *separates clauses*:

> **er sagte, er sei zu Fuß gekommen** *he said he came on foot*
> **sie sucht einen Partner, der sie versteht** *she is looking for a partner who understands her*
> **ich konnte ihn schlecht verstehen, weil das Radio so laut war** *I had difficulty in understanding him because the radio was so loud*

When, however, clauses are linked by **und** *and* or **oder** *or* there is normally no comma:

> **sie blieb zu Hause und ihre Mutter ging einkaufen** *she stayed at home and her mother went shopping*

For clarity's sake a comma may be used before **und** or **oder** in e.g. **er fotografierte die Berge(,) und seine Frau lag in der Sonne** *he photographed the mountains and his wife lay in the sun*. Also, if a subordinate clause follows **und** or **oder** a comma may be used to make the structure of the sentence clear, e.g. **ich habe ihn oft besucht(,) und wenn er in guter Stimmung war, saßen wir bis spät in die Nacht zusammen** *I have often visited him, and when he was in a good mood we would sit up together until late into the night.*

A comma is optional before an infinitive phrase with **zu**:

> **sie war bereit(,) an dem Buch mitzuarbeiten** *she was willing to collaborate on the book*
> **er versuchte(,) den Text in seine Muttersprache zu übersetzen** *he attempted to translate the text into his mother tongue*

But sometimes one may be necessary to make the meaning clear: the sentence **Sabine versprach ihrem Vater einen Brief zu schreiben** is unclear, and a comma is called for either before or after **ihrem Vater: Sabine versprach, ihrem Vater einen Brief zu schreiben** *Sabine promised to write her father a letter* or **Sabine versprach ihrem Vater, einen Brief zu schreiben** *Sabine promised her father that she would write a letter.*

An infinitive phrase (unless it consists solely of **zu** + infinitive) is preceded by a comma where it is anticipated by **es** or a **da**-compound:

sein größter Wunsch ist es, eine Familie zu gründen *it is his greatest wish to start a family*
er freute sich darauf, seine Freundin wiederzusehen *he looked forward to seeing his girl-friend again*

A comma is also optional following a participial phrase at the beginning of a sentence:

durch viele Tassen Kaffee gestärkt(,) nahm der Dozent die Korrektur der Klausuren in Angriff *fortified by many cups of coffee, the lecturer set about marking the examination papers*

The German comma is often placed *between main clauses*, where English would have a semi-colon. The following examples from modern narrative prose are given with the corresponding sentences in published translations:

Die Tür war nur mit Draht gesichert, sie bogen ihn auseinander und traten in die Hütte, . . . *The door was secured only by wire; they bent it apart and stepped into the cabin, . . .* (S. Lenz, *Der Verzicht*, transl. S. Spencer).

Wir kletterten hinüber, Großvater blutete an der Hand, ich am Knie *We clambered over; grandfather's hand was bleeding, so was my knee* (G. de Bruyn, *Fedezeen*, transl. P. Anthony).

Another function not shared with the English comma is as an alternative to a dash or bracket, to indicate the beginning or end of a parenthesis, e.g. **Eines Tages, es war mitten im Winter, stand ein Hirsch in unserem Garten** *One day—it was midwinter—there was a stag standing in our garden.*

Two or more adjectives are separated by a comma when they are of equal weight and could be linked by **und**, e.g. **neue, computergestützte Lehrverfahren** *new, computer-assisted teaching methods.* (The rule is, however, often ignored.) No comma is used if the second adjective and the noun are perceived as forming one concept, e.g. **neue computergestützte Lehrverfahren** *new computer-assisted teaching methods* (as opposed to older computer-assisted teaching methods).

In the case of a series of adjectives there is no comma before **und**, e.g. **junge, gut bezahlte und erfolgreiche Lehrer** *young, well-paid, and successful teachers.*

In numerals the comma marks the *decimal point*, e.g. **17,5** (read as **siebzehn Komma fünf**).

THE COLON. The colon is used broadly as in English. (For its use in introducing direct speech see *Quotation marks* below.) It also appears in the score of games, where English has the dash, e.g. **sie haben 3:4 [drei zu vier] verloren** *they lost 3–4*, **es** (or **das Spiel**) **steht 1:0 [eins zu null]** *the score is 1–0.*

A word following a colon is as a rule written with a *capital letter* if the colon introduces an utterance that is effectively a self-contained sentence, e.g. **Wir alle sind einer Meinung: Er ist ein Mensch, dem man voll**

vertrauen kann *We are all of the same opinion: he is a person who can be fully trusted.* Otherwise a small letter is used, as when factors etc. are enumerated or the consequence of some action is stated, e.g. **Das Ende war vorauszusehen: er verlor alles, was er hatte** *The end was foreseeable: he lost everything he had.*

THE FULL STOP (PERIOD). (*a*) *After a numeral,* a full stop indicates that it represents an ordinal number, e.g. **am 10.** [read as **zehnten**] **Mai** *on 10th May,* **Heinrich VIII.** [**der Achte**] *Henry VIII,* **12.** [**zwölfte**] **Auflage** *12th edition.* (*b*) It is used *in abbreviations* when the words abbreviated are spoken in full, e.g. **d.h.** [**das heißt**] *i.e.,* **z.B.** [**zum Beispiel**] *e.g.,* **Frankfurt a.M.** [**am Main**], (after the last letter) **Frl.** [**Fräulein**], **usw.** [**und so weiter**] *etc.* The full stop is *not* used in abbreviations in which the letters are pronounced individually, e.g. **CDU, DNS, EU, LKW** or **Lkw, SPD,** nor in acronyms like **NATO,** nor in the abbreviations of metric weights and measures, e.g. **g** for **Gramm, m** for **Meter.**

THE EXCLAMATION MARK. Unlike the English exclamation mark, the German symbol is also used in public notices: **Zutritt verboten!** *No admittance,* **Abflüge werden nicht ausgerufen!** *Departures will not be announced,* **Vorsicht, Glas!** *Glass—with care.* It is sometimes used in addressing someone at the beginning of a letter: **Sehr geehrter Herr Schmidt!, Liebe Anna!** (Here a comma may be used instead, in which case the first word of the text of the letter does not have an initial capital unless capitalized anyway.) Closing formulas such as **herzliche Grüße** *kind regards* do not have the exclamation mark.

THE DASH. Over and above the functions it shares with its English counterpart, the German dash has one special use, namely to indicate some kind of transition, for instance to a new topic, as in the first example (from a letter) that follows; in the second (from a narrative) the passage of time is evoked:

> . . . **Und ich kann die Arbeiten nachholen, die ich während der Schönwetterperiode vernachlässigt habe.—Da gleich meine Familie nach Hause kommt, muss ich nun schnell mit dem Mittagessenkochen beginnen** . . . *And I can catch up on the jobs I've neglected during this spell of lovely weather. As my family will be coming home in a minute I must get on with cooking lunch*

> . . . **Ich kann sagen, dass es der am härtesten verdiente Penny meines Lebens war.—Der Abend kam, und die Stühle wurden leer** . . . *. . . I may say that it was the hardest-earned penny of my life. Evening came, and the chairs emptied . . .* (A. Spoerl, *Memoiren eines mittelmäßigen Schülers*).

BRACKETS. In German square brackets are used when brackets within brackets are required.

QUOTATION MARKS. The normal quotation marks are „". Officially called **Anführungszeichen**, they are informally known as **Gänsefüßchen**. Quotations are introduced by a colon: **er sagte: „...........";** if the quotation comes first, a comma follows the quotation: **„...........", dachte sie.** In literary texts speech or thoughts are sometimes quoted without quotation marks, e.g. **Er sollte ausspannen, sagte die alte Frau, sorgen Sie doch dafür, ihr habt doch noch keine Ferien gehabt in diesem Jahr** *'He ought to take a rest,' the old lady said. 'Why don't you arrange it? After all, you haven't had a holiday yet this year'* (I. Bachmann, *Das Gebell*, transl. F. Kyle); **Frau Andrew legt ihren Arm um die Tochter, das hätten wir längst tun sollen, denkt sie, einmal heraus aus dem Alltag, und alles wird gut** *Mrs Andrew put her arm round her daughter. 'We should have done this long ago,' she thought. 'Once we get away from the daily routine, everything will be all right again'* (M. L. Kaschnitz, *Jennifers Träume*, transl. H. Taylor). 'Quotes within quotes' have single quotation marks. (For the position of quotation marks in e.g. **als Abonnent des „Spiegels"** see p. 40.)

Glossary Of Grammatical Terms

Terms used in these definitions which are defined in the glossary are asterisked.

ACCUSATIVE. A *case that is used chiefly to identify the *direct object of a *finite verb.

ADJECTIVAL NOUN. An adjective used as a noun. In the sentence *the rich pay higher taxes*, the word *rich* is an adjectival noun (with the *definite article).

ADJECTIVE. A word describing a noun, e.g. *large, exciting*.

ADVERB. A word that modifies a whole sentence (*happily* in *happily, he still had the address*), a verb (*strongly* in *he swam strongly*), an adjective (*extremely* in *an extremely interesting article*), or another adverb (*extraordinarily* in *she sang extraordinarily well*).

AGREEMENT. Having the same *number, *gender, *case, or person.

ANTECEDENT. A word or phrase to which a *relative pronoun refers. In the sentence *people who say that shouldn't*, the word *people* is the antecedent of *who*.

APPOSITION. A construction in which a noun or noun phrase is placed after another noun or noun phrase in order to qualify or explain it. In the sentence *the mayor, the brother of the local MP, is unmarried* the phrase *the brother of the local MP* is in apposition to *the mayor*.

ARTICLE. See *Definite article, *Indefinite article.

AUXILIARY VERB. A verb used to indicate the *tense, voice, or mood of another verb. In the sentences *he will eat* and *he was killed*, *will* and *was* are auxiliary verbs.

CASE. The indication of the role played by a noun or pronoun etc. in the sentence by means of *inflection. In English, case still survives in the pronouns *I/me, he/him, they/them*, etc.

CLAUSE. A distinct part of a sentence, including a *subject and a predicate. The sentence *she often visits Tuscany because she likes the climate* contains two clauses: *she often visits Tuscany* and *because she likes the climate*.

COMPARATIVE. The form produced in English by adding *-er* or prefixing *more* to an adjective or adverb: *larger* and *more interesting* are comparatives.

COMPLEMENT. An adjective or noun used after verbs such as *to be* or *to become*, and describing the *subject of the verb. In the sentences *I was delighted* and *I was a soldier* the words *delighted* and *a soldier* are complements.

COMPOUND. A word formed by joining two (or more) existing words together, e.g. *teapot, machine-readable, test-drive*.

CONCESSIVE CLAUSE. A *clause describing a state of affairs that might have been expected to rule out what is described in the main clause but in fact does not, e.g. *although he had no money* in the sentence *although he had no money, he did not consider himself poor*.

CONJUGATION. The complete set of the *inflections of a verb.

CONJUNCTION. A word that connects *clauses, sentences, or words in the same clause, e.g. *and, or, when*.

DATIVE. A *case used chiefly to express the *indirect object of a verb.

DECLENSION. The *inflection of nouns, pronouns, or adjectives for *case, *number, and *gender.

DEFINITE ARTICLE. *The* in English, **der, die, das** in German.

DEMONSTRATIVE. A word used to point out a particular person or thing, e.g. *this, that*. Demonstratives may be adjectives or pronouns.

DEPENDENT CLAUSE. See *Subordinate clause.

DIRECT OBJECT. The person or thing that is directly affected by the action of the verb. In the sentence *Mahler composed symphonies*, the word *symphonies* is the direct object.

FINITE VERB. A verb form that agrees with its *subject in person and *number. *Am, is, are, was,* and *were* are the finite forms of *to be*; the non-finite forms are *be, being,* and *been*.

GENDER. The classification of a noun or pronoun as (in German) masculine, feminine, or neuter. In English gender is only found in pronouns (*he, she, it,* etc.).

GENITIVE. A *case that is used to indicate possession.

HISTORIC PRESENT. The present *tense used to recount past events, with the intention of making the narrative more vivid.

IMPERATIVE. The form of the verb used to express commands.

IMPERSONAL VERB. A verb used only with a formal *subject (*it*) and expressing an action not attributable to a definite subject, e.g. *it is raining*.

INDEFINITE ARTICLE. *A, an* in English, **ein** in German.

INDICATIVE. The form of the verb used to make statements or ask questions.

INDIRECT OBJECT. The person or thing that is indirectly affected by the action of the verb. In English the indirect object either precedes the *direct object (e.g. *the postman gave my father the parcel*) or follows it in a phrase introduced by *to* (e.g. *the postman gave the parcel to my father*).

INDIRECT QUESTION. A question reported in *indirect speech, e.g. *he asked what they were doing*.

INDIRECT (OR REPORTED) SPEECH. The reporting of something said by conveying what was meant rather than quoting the exact words, e.g. *They told me their name was Smith* as opposed to *They told me, 'Our name is Smith'*.

INFINITIVE. The basic form of a verb. In English, it is usually preceded by *to*, e.g. *to think*.

INFLECTION. (*a*) Changing the form of a word to show its grammatical function in a sentence. (*b*) A suffix used to inflect a word.

INTERJECTION. A word or phrase used as an exclamation.

INTERROGATIVE. Interrogative words are used to ask a question, e.g. the interrogative adverb *when?*, the interrogative pronoun *who?*

INTRANSITIVE VERB. A verb which does not take a *direct object.

MODAL AUXILIARY. A verb that is used with another verb (not a modal auxiliary) to express possibility, permission, or obligation, e.g. *can, may, must.*

MODAL PARTICLE. A word used to express the speaker's attitude to what is being said, e.g. *just* in the sentence *we just have to soldier on.*

NOMINATIVE. A *case expressing the *subject or *complement of a verb.

NOUN. A word that names a person or thing, e.g. *man, Tutankhamun, house, mouse, grammar.*

NUMBER. The classification of words by their singular or plural forms.

OBJECT. see *Direct object, *Indirect object.

PASSIVE. Form of the verb used when the grammatical *subject is affected by the action of the verb, e.g. *they were injured by a passing bus.*

PAST PARTICIPLE. A verb form used with an *auxiliary to form compound past tenses and the *passive, e.g. *eaten*/**gegessen**.

PAST TENSE. A *tense formed in English by adding *-ed* to the verb and in German by adding **-te** to the verb stem, or (in both languages) by changing the stem vowel, e.g. *played*/**spielte**, *gave*/**gab**.

PERFECT TENSE. A *tense formed in English with the present tense of the *auxiliary *have* and the *past participle, e.g. *I have played*; and in German with the present tense of either the auxiliary **haben** or the auxiliary **sein** and the past participle, e.g. **ich habe gespielt, ich bin gegangen**.

PLUPERFECT TENSE. A *tense formed in English with the past tense of the *auxiliary *have* and the *past participle, e.g. *I had played*; and in German with the past tense of either the auxiliary **haben** or the auxiliary **sein** and the past participle, e.g. **ich hatte gespielt, ich war gegangen**.

PREFIX. An element added to the beginning of a word, e.g. *anti-, dis-, un-*.

PREPOSITION. A word such as *at, on, by, with* used before a noun or pronoun to show place, time, method, etc.

PRESENT PARTICIPLE. The verb form made in English by adding *-ing* to the verb, in German by adding **-d** to the infinitive.

PRONOUN. A word such as *he, we, mine, which* that is used instead of a noun usually already mentioned.

REFLEXIVE VERB. A verb used *transitively with the reflexive pronoun (e.g. *himself, ourselves*) as its *direct object.

RELATIVE PRONOUN. A pronoun that refers to an *antecedent and attaches a *subordinate clause to it, e.g. *which* in the sentence *that is the dog* (antecedent) *which chased the postman.*

REPORTED SPEECH. See *Indirect speech.

STRONG VERB. Verb forming the *past tense and *past participle by internal vowel change, e.g. *sing, sang, sung.*

SUBJECT. The word(s) in a sentence about which something is stated, e.g. *the countryside* in the sentence *the countryside fascinated him.*

SUBJUNCTIVE. A verb form that is used in German chiefly to convey *indirect speech and in conditional sentences.

SUBORDINATE (OR DEPENDENT) CLAUSE. A *clause that is dependent on a main clause and which cannot convey a meaning on its own, e.g. *when she heard the news* in the sentence *she laughed when she heard the news.*

SUFFIX. An element added to the end of a word, e.g. *-able, -ness.*

SUPERLATIVE. The form produced in English by adding *-est* or prefixing *most* to an adjective or adverb: *tallest* and *most exciting* are superlatives.

TENSE. The form of the verb that indicates the time of the action or state expressed by the verb.

TRANSITIVE VERB. A verb taking a *direct object.

VERB. A word expressing an action, an event, or a state, e.g. *take, happen, remain.*

VERBAL NOUN. A noun formed from a verb, e.g. *talking, swimming.*

WEAK MASCULINE. In German, a noun which adds **-en** or **-n** in all cases (singular and plural) except the *nominative singular, e.g. **der Mensch, der Schotte**.

WEAK VERB. A verb forming the *past tense and *past participle by adding (in English) the suffix *-(e)d* (e.g. *grill, grilled, grilled*) and not by changing the vowel.

Case and Gender

CASE

GERMAN AND ENGLISH: A HISTORICAL NOTE. German and English are cousins in the Germanic family of languages, and the similarities between them, resulting from their common origin, are obvious to anyone studying German. With the passage of time, however, they have grown further apart: phonetically, lexically, and, to a very significant degree, grammatically.

The grammar of Old English was much like that of modern German, as illustrated by the word order and use of inflexions in a sentence of King Alfred's: *Ða ongan ic, ongemang oðrum mislicum and manigfealdum bisgum ðisses kynerices, ða boc wendan on Englisc* 'Then I began, among other diverse and manifold affairs of this kingdom, to turn (translate) the book into English'. But in the succeeding centuries English grammar became greatly simplified, shedding most of the inflexional endings whose counterparts German still retains. At the same time English word order grew more fixed and now has the basic pattern Subject-Verb(-Object): whether we say *the man fleas the dog, the fleas dog the man*, or even *the fleas man the dog* it is always clear who is doing what to whom—because of the word-order.

German has not undergone these sweeping grammatical changes—a fact which is of major consequence for the study of German by English speakers. To return to our first example: a German would most likely say **der Mann flöht den Hund** with the subject first, but it is also possible to say **den Hund flöht der Mann**; the sense is the same, only the emphasis is different. That it is the dog that is the object of the action is clear not from the word order but from the fact that the word for *the* in front of **Hund** is in the accusative case and that in front of **Mann** is in the nominative.

German case endings are therefore important, often being the means whereby the relationship between words is shown; and any learner aiming to communicate in German (whether spoken or written) with competence and confidence needs to learn and be able to produce the various inflexional endings accurately.

German has four cases: the NOMINATIVE, ACCUSATIVE, GENITIVE, and DATIVE.

The NOMINATIVE is used:

(i) for the SUBJECT[7] of a sentence or clause:

  der Lehrer fährt einen Mercedes *the teacher drives a Mercedes*
  die Geschäftsfrau ist Französin *the businesswoman is French*
  das Videospiel interessiert mich nicht *the video game doesn't interest me*

(ii) for the COMPLEMENT of **sein** *to be*, **werden** *to become*, **bleiben** *to remain*, **heißen** *to be called*:

  Herr Stumpf ist *ein begabter Lehrer* Herr Stumpf is a gifted teacher
  das Buch wurde *ein großer Erfolg* the book was a great success
  er blieb *ihr guter Freund* he remained her good friend

[7] Grammatical terms are explained in a special glossary, pp. 21–4.

The ACCUSATIVE is used:

(i) for the DIRECT OBJECT of a verb:

kennen Sie *den Lehrer?* *do you know the teacher?*
wir haben *die Französin* **wiedererkannt** *we recognized the Frenchwoman*
das Museum enthält *viele Kostbarkeiten* *the museum contains many precious objects*

(ii) after certain PREPOSITIONS (see p. 66):

ich habe einen Aufsatz für *unseren Lehrer* **geschrieben** *I've written an essay for our teacher*
wir sind ohne *unsere Mutter* **nach Athen gestartet** *we set off for Athens without our mother*

(iii) with a handful of adjectives in constructions with **sein** or **werden**: **gewohnt** *used to* (with **sein**), **satt** *fed up with* (with **sein, werden**), **wert** *worth* (with **sein**), and **schuldig** in **jemandem etwas schuldig sein** *to owe someone something*:

ich bin solche Temperamentsausbrüche nicht gewohnt *I'm not used to such temperamental outbursts*
du bist mir eine Erklärung schuldig *you owe me an explanation*
der Teppich ist das Geld nicht wert *the carpet isn't worth the money*

(iv) in expressions of DEFINITE TIME:

sie fahren *jeden Morgen* **mit der Straßenbahn** *they go by tram every morning*
wir haben *den ganzen Nachmittag* **gesucht** *we've been looking the whole afternoon*
dieses Jahr **gab es eine gute Ernte** *there was a good crop this year*

(v) to indicate (*a*) DURATION OF TIME (the phrase often being reinforced by **lang**), (*b*) DISTANCE COVERED:

es hat *den ganzen Morgen* **(lang) geschneit** *it's been snowing/it snowed all morning*
er ist mit dem Auto *den Berg* **hinuntergefahren** *he drove down the hill/mountain in the car*

The GENITIVE is used:

(i) to indicate POSSESSION:[8]

das Haus *unseres Lehrers* *our teacher's house*
die Hoffnungen *der jungen Frau* *the young woman's hopes*

---

[8] Note that the thing or person possessed precedes the possessor in German. With personal names, however, the possessor is named first (without an apostrophe), e.g. **Friedrichs Auto** *Friedrich's car*, **Tschechows Dramen** *Chekhov's dramas*.

(ii) after certain PREPOSITIONS (see p. 66):

> sie hat *trotz ihres Akzents* den Job bekommen *she got the job in spite of her accent*
> sie haben *während der Pause* Eis gegessen *during the interval they ate ice cream*

(iii) (chiefly in literary usage) with a few verbs taking a GENITIVE OBJECT, including:

> **sich bedienen** *to use, make use of*
> **bedürfen** *to need, require*
> **sich enthalten** *to refrain/abstain from*
> **sich entsinnen** *to recall*
> **sich erfreuen** *to enjoy (good health, privilege, etc.)*
> **sich erinnern** *to recall* (usually **sich erinnern an** + ACC.)
> **gedenken** *to think of, remember*
> **harren** *to await*
> **sich rühmen** *to boast of*
> **sich schämen** *to be ashamed of*
> **sich vergewissern** *to make sure of*

Thus:

> **diese Tatsachen bedürfen** *keiner Erklärung* *these facts need no explanation*
> **er konnte sich** *eines Lächelns* **nicht enthalten** *he could not refrain from smiling*

(iv) with certain ADJECTIVES (the genitive noun or pronoun precedes the adjective):

> **ich bin mir** *seiner Macht* **bewusst** *I'm conscious of his power*
> **sie fühlte sich** *seiner* **nicht würdig** *she did not feel worthy of him*

(v) in expressions of INDEFINITE TIME:

> *eines Tages* **werde ich einen Volvo kaufen** *one day I'm going to buy a Volvo*
> **er ist** *eines Morgens* **tot aufgefunden worden** *he was found dead one morning*

(vi) in set phrases EXPRESSING MANNER, including:

> **allen Ernstes** *in all seriousness*
> **schweren Herzens** *with a heavy heart*
> **gemessenen Schrittes** *with measured tread*
> **erster/zweiter Klasse (fahren)** *(to travel) first/second class*

Where the genitive case cannot be shown, it is replaced by von, e.g. **der Export von Kohle** *the export of coal*, **als Übersetzer von Storms Gedichten** *as a translator of Storm's poems*, **die Lösung von Problemen** *the solving of* *problems* (as opposed to **die Lösung schwieriger Probleme** *the solving of difficult problems*, where the **-er** ending indicates the genitive plural).

In spoken German the genitive is commonly replaced by **von** + the dative.

The DATIVE is used:

(i) for the INDIRECT OBJECT of a verb:

sein Vater hat *ihm* **ein neues Wörterbuch gekauft** *his father has bought him a new dictionary*
wer hat *unserem Lehrer* **den Mercedes gestohlen?** *who stole the Mercedes from our teacher?*

(ii) with a number of common verbs taking a DATIVE OBJECT, including:

antworten *to answer*
begegnen *to meet (by chance)*
bekommen *to agree with* (of food)
danken *to thank*
dienen *to serve*
entsprechen *to correspond to*
folgen *to follow*
gefallen *to please*
gehorchen *to obey*
gehören *to belong to*
helfen *to help*
nützen *to be of use to*
passen *to fit*
raten *to advise*
schaden *to harm, damage*
stehen *to suit*
trauen *to trust*
widerstehen *to resist*

Thus:

der Polizist hat *mir* **sehr unfreundlich geantwortet** *the policeman answered me in a very unfriendly manner*
das Mädchen ist *ihrem Vater* **gefolgt** *the girl followed her father*
der Patient hilft *der Krankenschwester* *the patient is helping the nurse*
der Hut steht *dir* **nicht** *that hat doesn't suit you*

(iii) after certain PREPOSITIONS (see p. 66):

der Chef hat das Projekt *aus verschiedenen Gründen* **abgelehnt** *the boss turned down the project for various reasons*
sie besucht das Museum *mit ihrem Bruder* *she is visiting the museum with her brother*

(iv) with certain ADJECTIVES and NOUNS (where English uses *to*; the dative noun or pronoun precedes the adjective):

seine Haltung war *mir* **unbegreiflich** *his attitude was incomprehensible*
  to me
sie war *ihrem Sohn* **eine gute Mutter** *she was a good mother to her son*

APPOSITION. Nouns in apposition (i.e. positioned after another noun or a pronoun and used—in G. N. Garmonsway's definition—to 'amplify and parallel'
it) take the same case as the noun or pronoun they refer to, e.g. **sie hat**
ihrem Onkel, dem Zollbeamten, **lange nicht geschrieben** *she hasn't written
to her uncle, the customs officer, for a long time.* Here the two nouns concerned are both in the dative. Other examples:

  (with accusative) **sein Krieg gegen** *die Sowjetunion, den letzten
  Verbündeten* **Großbritanniens auf dem Kontinent** *his war against the
  Soviet Union, Great Britain's last ally on the Continent*
  (with genitive) **eine Beschreibung** *seines Geburtsortes, eines Dorfes* **in der
  Normandie** *a description of his birthplace, a village in Normandy*
  (with dative) *am Sonntag, dem 1. Februar* *on Sunday, February 1st*
  (with dative) **das Bild stammt von** *dem Maler* **Hans Holbein** *dem Jüngeren*
  the picture is by the painter Hans Holbein the Younger[9]

GENDER

German has three genders: MASCULINE, FEMININE, and NEUTER; in the plural no
distinction of gender is made. Compound nouns, e.g. **der Apfelbaum** *apple
tree,* take the gender of their last component (in this instance **der Baum**).[10]

The gender of nouns is often indicated by the preceding word, especially
the definite article (**der** masculine, **die** feminine, **das** neuter). Unlike gender
in English, which is based on sex (*he, she, it*), gender in German is arbitrary
(although usually male beings are masculine and female beings feminine).

Often the ending of a noun shows its gender:

ENDING	GENDER	EXAMPLES
–ade (*pl.* **-n**)	F	**die Brigade** *brigade,* **die Limonade** *fizzy drink,* **die Olympiade** *Olympics*
–age (*pl.* **-n**)	F	**die Sabotage** *sabotage,* **die Persiflage** *spoof,* **die Etage** *floor, storey*
–ant (*weak*)	M	**der Demonstrant** *demonstrator,* **der Elefant** *elephant,* **der Konsonant** *consonant,* **der Diamant** *diamond*

[9] Note also appositional phrases introduced by **als** or **wie**, e.g. **sie feierten** *ihn* **als** *Helden*
they acclaimed him as a hero, **in** *einer slawischen Sprache* **wie** *dem Russischen* *in a Slavonic
language like Russian.* (The nominative is, however, used when an **als**-phrase *without article*
follows the genitive, e.g. **der Ruf Josef Stalins als Staatsmann** *Joseph Stalin's reputation as
a statesman*; with **wie**, case agreement is sometimes dropped in favour of the nominative,
e.g. **für einen Menschen wie du (dich)** *for a person like you.*)
[10] Note, however, that while **der Teil** *part* is masculine several of its compounds are neuter: **das
Abteil** *compartment (of train),* **das Gegenteil** *opposite,* **das Urteil** *judgment; verdict.*

ENDING	GENDER	EXAMPLES
–anz (*pl.* -en)	F	die **Arroganz** *arrogance*, die **Diskrepanz** *discrepancy*, die **Resonanz** *resonance; response*
–ar (= *person*) (*pl.* -e)	M	der **Bibliothekar** *librarian*, der **Missionar** *missionary*, der **Kommentar** *comment; commentary*[11]
–är (= *person*) (*pl.* -e)	M	der **Legionär** *legionnaire; legionary*, der **Millionär** *millionaire*[12]
–at (= *person*) (*weak*)	M	der **Demokrat** *democrat*, der **Kandidat** *candidate*, der **Soldat** *soldier*, der **Adressat** *addressee*[13]
–chen (*pl. same*)	N	das **Kaninchen** *rabbit*, das **Kätzchen** *kitten; catkin*
–ei (–elei, –erei) (*pl.* -en)	F	die **Kartei** *card index*, die **Nörgelei** *grumbling*, die **Kellerei** *wine cellars*, die **Meuterei** *mutiny*
–ent (*weak*)	M	der **Student** (*university etc.*) *student*, der **Dirigent** *conductor (of orchestra)*[14]
–enz (*pl.* -en)	F	die **Tendenz** *tendency, trend*, die **Frequenz** *frequency* (physics); *numbers attending; volume of traffic*
–er (*from verb*) (*pl. same*)	M	der **Schneider** *tailor*, der **Angeber** *boaster, show-off*, der **Rechner** *calculator*
–heit (*pl.* -en)	F	die **Schönheit** *beauty*, die **Menschheit** *humanity, humankind*
–ie (*pl.* -n)	F	die **Chemie** *chemistry*, die **Phobie** *phobia*
–ik (*pl.* -en)	F	die **Informatik** *computer science*, die **Technik** *technology; technique*, die **Romantik** *Romanticism*[15]
–in (*pl.* -nen)	F	die **Journalistin** (*woman*) *journalist*, die **Füchsin** *vixen*

[11] Other masculines in -ar include der **Jaguar**, der **Januar** *January*, der **Februar** *February*. Neuter are e.g. das **Inventar** *inventory*, das **Mobiliar** *furnishings*, das **Glossar** *glossary*, das **Formular** *form*.
[12] Note das **Militär** *armed forces, army*.
[13] The inanimate der **Automat** *slot-* or *vending-machine; automaton* is also declined as a weak noun. Other masculines in -at (not, however, declined weak) include der **Apparat** *apparatus; set; camera*, der **Salat** *salad; lettuce*, der **Spinat** *spinach*, der **Muskat** *nutmeg*, der **Passat** *trade wind*, der **Senat** *senate* (plurals add -e). The many neuters in -at include das **Internat** *boarding school*, das **Konsulat** *consulate*, das **Transplantat** *transplant (= organ)*, das **Telefonat** *telephone call*, das **Quadrat** *square*, das **Resultat** *result*, das **Format** *size; format; calibre*, das **Attentat** *attempted assassination* (plurals likewise add -e).
[14] Also masculine (but not declined weak) are der **Akzent** *accent*, der **Orient** *the Middle East*; neuters include das **Transparent** *banner*, das **Kontingent** *quota; contingent*, das **Äquivalent** *equivalent* (Plurals add -e).
[15] Exceptions: the oceans der **Atlantik** and der **Pazifik**, der **Katholik** *Catholic*.

ENDING	GENDER	EXAMPLES
–ion (*pl.* -en)	F	die Nation *nation,* die Kommission *commission*[16]
–ismus (*pl.* –ismen)	M	der Sozialismus *socialism,* der Sadismus *sadism*
–ist (*weak*)	M	der Journalist *journalist,* der Spezialist *specialist*
–ität (*pl.* -en)	F	die Aggressivität *aggressiveness,* die Universität *university*
–keit (*pl.* -en)	F	die Einigkeit *unity,* die Dankbarkeit *gratitude*
–ling (*pl.* -e)	M	der Lehrling *apprentice,* der Prüfling *examinee*
–ma (*pl.* –men)	N	das Thema *topic; subject; theme,* das Prisma *prism*
–ment (*pl.* -e)	N	das Dokument *document,* das Moment *factor*[17]
–or (*pl.* -en)	M	der Professor *professor,* der Sektor *sector*[18]
–schaft (*pl.* -en)	F	die Gewerkschaft *trade union,* die Leidenschaft *passion*
–tum	N	das Heldentum *heroism,* das Unternehmertum *employers* (collectively)[19]
–um (*pl. varies*)	N	das Zentrum *centre,* das Maximum *maximum*
–ung (*pl.* -en)	F	die Hoffnung *hope,* die Regierung *government*
–ur (*pl.* -en)	F	die Natur *nature,* die Fraktur *Gothic type; fracture* (medicine)[20]
–us (*pl. varies*)	M	der Rhythmus *rhythm,* der Zirkus *circus*

Most nouns in **Ge-** are neuter, e.g. **das Gebäude** *building,* **das Gesicht** *face,* **das Gerippe** *skeleton,* **das Gehalt** *salary,* as are all nouns with **Ge-** prefixed to verb-stems and denoting a continual activity or repeated occurrence, e.g. **das Gebrüll** *roaring.* Note, however, the masculines **der Gebrauch** *use,* **der Gedanke** *thought, idea,* **der Gefallen** *favour,* **der Gehalt** (*intellectual*) *content* (in Austrian German also *salary*), **der Gehorsam** *obedience,* **der Genosse** *comrade,* **der Genuss** *pleasure; consumption,* **der Geruch** *smell,* **der Gesang** *song; singing; canto,* **der Geschmack** *taste, flavour,* **der Gestank** *stink,* **der Gewinn** *profit; winnings;* and the feminines **die Gebühr** *fee; charge,* **die Geburt** *birth,* **die Geduld** *patience,* **die Gefahr** *danger,* **die Gemeinde** *community; municipality; parish,* **die Geschichte** *history; story,* **die Gestalt** *shape, form; build,* **die Gewalt** *force; authority,* **die Gewähr** *guarantee.*

---

[16] Not to be confused with the unstressed neuter ending –ion (plural –ien) in words of Greek origin, e.g. **das Stadion** *stadium,* **das Symposion** *symposium.*
[17] Exceptions: **der Moment** *moment,* **der Zement** *cement.*
[18] Exception: **das Labor** *laboratory.*
[19] Exceptions: **der Irrtum** *error,* **der Reichtum** *wealth.*
[20] Exception: **das Abitur** *Abitur* (school-leaving examination at the Gymnasium).

Articles

DEFINITE ARTICLE

der, die, das *the*

	SINGULAR			PLURAL
	MASC.	FEM.	NEUT.	ALL GENDERS
NOM.	der	die	das	die
ACC.	den	die	das	die
GEN.	des	der	des	der
DAT.	dem	der	dem	den

Certain other words take the same endings as the definite article, namely **dieser, diese, dieses** *this, that,* **jeder, jede, jedes** *each, every,* **jener, jene, jenes** *that,* **mancher, manche, manches** *many a,* **solcher, solche, solches** *such a,* **welcher, welche, welches** *which*—with the exception that where the definite article takes the form **die** they have the ending **-e** (e.g. **diese**), and in the nominative and accusative neuter they have the ending **-es** (e.g. **dieses**).

The use of the definite article in German broadly corresponds to that of English *the*. There are, however, certain differences in usage:

(i) = no article in English:

(*a*) ABSTRACT NOUNS (e.g. **die Natur** *nature,* **das Leben** *life,* **das Schicksal** *fate,* **die Liebe** *love,* **die Jugend** *youth,* **die Zeit** *time,* **die Wissenschaft** *scholarship, science,* **das Bankwesen** *banking,* **die Gesellschaft** *society,* **die Klassik** *classicism,* **der Kommunismus** *Communism,* **das Christentum** *Christianity*); sometimes, however, the article is omitted, its use (or non-use) often being as much a question of style and usage as of grammar;

(*b*) CONCEPTS such as **der Himmel** *heaven,* **die Hölle** *hell,* **das Paradies** *paradise,* and the INSTITUTIONS **das Parlament** *Parliament,* **die Schule** *school,* **das Gefängnis** *prison,* **das Krankenhaus** *hospital,* **die Kirche** *church;*

(*c*) **der Mensch** *man,* **die Leute** *people;*

(*d*) THE NAMES OF THE SEASONS, MONTHS, and also MEALS (e.g. **der Frühling** *spring,* **der Juni** *June,* **das Frühstück** *breakfast*), although in certain contexts—e.g. **es war Frühling/Juni** *it was spring/June*—the article is dropped; in the case of the DAYS OF THE WEEK the article is sometimes used (e.g. **(der) Montag** *Monday; on Monday* etc. is **am Montag** etc.);

(*e*) masculine and feminine GEOGRAPHICAL NAMES (e.g. **die Schweiz** *Switzerland,* **die Provence** *Provence,* **die Schellingstraße** *Schellingstrasse,* **der Petersplatz** *St Peter's*

Square, der **Hydepark** *Hyde Park,* der **Kilimandscharo** *Kilimanjaro,* der **Vesuv** *Vesuvius,* der **Titicacasee** *Lake Titicaca*), also das **Elsass** ['ɛlzas] *Alsace;*

(*f*) PROPER NAMES PRECEDED BY AN ADJECTIVE (e.g. die **kleine Susi** *little Susi,* das **heutige Frankreich** *present-day France*);

(*g*) IN CERTAIN PHRASES, e.g. **im/ins Ausland** *abroad,* **im Bett** *in bed,* **in der Stadt** *in town,* **mit der Bahn, dem Schiff,** etc. *by rail, ship,* etc., **mit der Post** *by post.*

(ii) = possessive adjective in English—referring to PARTS OF THE BODY OR ARTICLES OF CLOTHING:

er steckte die Hände in die Taschen *he put his hands in his pockets*
er zog die Jacke aus *he took off his jacket*
ich schüttelte ihr die Hand *I shook her hand*
sie wusch sich (DAT.) die Haare *she washed her hair*
das Blut schoss ihr ins Gesicht *blood rushed to her face*

The possessive adjective is, however, used for the subject, e.g. **seine Augen sind blau** *his eyes are blue.*

(iii) = *a*—used distributively, e.g. **fünf Mark das Pfund** *five marks a pound.*

INDEFINITE ARTICLE

ein *a*

	MASC.	FEM.	NEUT.
NOM.	**ein**	**eine**	**ein**
ACC.	**einen**	**eine**	**ein**
GEN.	**eines**	**einer**	**eines**
DAT.	**einem**	**einer**	**einem**

The negative **kein** *not a/any, no* takes the same endings in the singular as **ein**; the plural forms are (NOM., ACC.) **keine,** (GEN.) **keiner,** (DAT.) **keinen.**

The use of the indefinite article broadly corresponds to that of English *a.* There are, however, certain differences in usage:

(i) no article in German = *a*—with nouns indicating PROFESSION or NATIONALITY (or other geographical identification) used as the complement of **sein, werden,** or **bleiben:**

er war Architekt *he was an architect*
sie ist Neuseeländerin *she's a New Zealander*
er ist Bayer/Berliner *he's a Bavarian/Berliner*

The article is also as a rule omitted with other nouns referring to an individual belonging to a category of persons, although in some cases usage vacillates between using and omitting the article:

sie ist Witwe *she's a widow*
er wollte Junggeselle bleiben *he wanted to stay a bachelor*
er ist (ein) Katholik *he's a Catholic*
er war schon immer (ein) Optimist *he was always an optimist*

Where the noun is preceded by an adjective the article is always used:

er war ein hervorragender Architekt *he was an outstanding architect*
ich bin ein unverbesserlicher Optimist *I'm an incurable optimist*

(ii) **als** without article = *as a* (or, in appropriate contexts, *as the*), e.g. **als Mensch** *as a human being,* **als Warnung** *as a warning*; in a case like **er starb als Christ** *he died a Christian,* a alone is used.

(iii) **ein** = *a pair of . . . s,* e.g. **eine Brille** *a pair of glasses,* **eine Schere** *a pair of scissors,* **eine Zange** *a pair of tongs,* **eine Hose** *a pair of trousers.*

(iv) **ein** = *a piece of . . .* or is rendered by the English noun alone, e.g. **eine Information** *(a piece of) information,* **eine Nachricht** *(a piece of) news,* **ein Rat** *(a piece of) advice.*

(v) *not a* is expressed by **kein**:

kein Laut war zu hören *not a sound was to be heard*
ich hatte kein Auto *I didn't have a car*

(vi) The indefinite article is omitted in many descriptive phrases of the type PREPOSITION + ADJECTIVE + NOUN where English has *a,* e.g. **ein Haus mit flachem Dach** *a house with a flat roof,* **auf geheimnisvolle Weise** *in a mysterious manner,* **in hohem Alter** *at an advanced age,* **mit lauter/leiser Stimme** *in a loud/low voice,* **mit großer Mehrheit** *by a large majority.*

OMISSION OF ARTICLE WITH NOUNS USED IN PAIRS. The definite article is frequently omitted where nouns are used in pairs:

der Einfluss von Sonne und Mond auf Ebbe und Flut *the influence of the sun and moon on the tides*
das einzige dicht besiedelte Gebiet zwischen Tweed und Forth *the only densely populated area between the Tweed and the Forth*

Nouns

SINGULAR

German nouns, which are written with a capital initial letter, may be divided into three main groups in the singular:

(i) MASCULINES (except weak masculines) and NEUTERS. These form the genitive by adding -s (e.g. **der Deckel** *lid* / **des Deckels**, **das Fenster** *window* / **des Fensters**) or, in the case of native (but not 'foreign') *monosyllables*, -es (e.g. **der Tag** *day* / **des Tages**, **das Schiff** *ship* / **des Schiffes**: contrast **das Gen** *gene* / **des Gens**).[21] (Exception: monosyllables ending in a vowel or vowel + h, e.g. **der Schuh** *shoe* / **des Schuhs**.)

Nouns ending in **s, ss, ß, tz, x**, or **z** also add **-es** (e.g. **der Komplex** *complex* / **des Komplexes**, **das Walross** *walrus* / **des Walrosses**),[22] with the exception of those in **-as, -os, -us**, which have *no* genitive ending (e.g. **der Kubismus** *cubism* / **des Kubismus**, **das Epos** *epic* / **des Epos**) (note, however, **der Bus** *bus* / **des Busses**).[23] In the case of *abbreviations* the ending **-s** is optional.

The optional dative ending -e (after monosyllables)—so common in the writings of, for example, Thomas Mann or Hermann Broch—has fallen largely into disuse; it survives chiefly in set phrases such as **auf dem Lande** *in the country*, **in hohem Maße** *to a high degree*, **zu Hause** *at home*.

(ii) WEAK MASCULINES. These take the ending **-en** or (when **e** is already present) **-n** in all cases of the singular except the nominative (also throughout the plural):

NOM.	**der Mensch** (*man*,[24] *person*)	**der Hase** (*hare*)
ACC.	**den Menschen**	**den Hasen**
GEN.	**des Menschen**	**des Hasen**
DAT.	**dem Menschen**	**dem Hasen**

This category includes (*a*) nouns (designating chiefly persons) that end in **-ant, -ent, -ist, -graph, -loge**, e.g. **der Demonstrant** *demonstrator*, **der Student** *student*, **der Realist** *realist*, **der Geograph** *geographer*, **der Theologe** *theologian*; and (*b*) nouns in **-e** denoting nationalities, e.g. **der Chinese**

---

[21] Native monosyllabic nouns sometimes, especially in less formal usage, have the ending -s instead.

[22] Neuter nouns in -nis double the s, e.g. **das Ereignis** *event* / **des Ereignisses**.

[23] In some disyllabic nouns with unstressed prefixes (e.g. **der Vertrag** *contract, treaty*) and, especially for reasons of euphony, certain 'foreign' nouns of more than one syllable (e.g. **das Produkt** *product*) the ending **-es** may occur as an alternative to **-s**.

[24] *Man* in the sense of *homo sapiens*.

Chinese, **der Franzose** *Frenchman*, **der Schwede** *Swede*. (Not, however, **der Deutsche** *German*, which is declined like an adjective: see p. 55.)

Der Herr *gentleman*, *master* has the ending **-n** in the accusative, genitive, and dative singular (but **-en** in the plural).

A small group of nouns—sometimes known as 'mixed' nouns—are declined like weak masculines except in the genitive singular, which has the ending -ns. They are: **der Buchstabe** *letter (of the alphabet)*, **der Gedanke** *thought; idea*, **der Glaube** *belief*, **der Name** *name*, **der Wille** *will*. One neuter noun, **das Herz** *heart*, follows a similar pattern: **Herz, Herz, Herzens, Herzen**.

(iii) FEMININES. These remain unchanged throughout the singular.

PLURAL

The nominative, accusative, and genitive plural forms are identical; the dative plural adds -n (e.g. **die Häuser** *the houses*, dative **den Häusern**) where **n** is not already present, except in the case of nouns that add -s to form the plural.

Plurals are formed in various ways in German: by adding **-e** with or without umlaut (¨), **-en** or **-n**, **-er** with or without umlaut, **-s** (chiefly added to words of foreign origin), or—in the case of nouns ending in **-el**, **-en**, **-er**—by retaining the singular form unchanged or with umlaut.

(i) **-e** or **-̈e**:

(*a*) most MASCULINES; of those which can mutate the vowel, some do while others do not—e.g. **der Arm** *arm* / **Arme**, **der Arzt** *doctor* / **Ärzte**, **der Baum** *tree* / **Bäume**, **der Fisch** *fish* / **Fische**.

(*b*) a number of major FEMININE monosyllables, always with umlaut—e.g. **die Angst** *fear; anxiety* / **Ängste**, **die Frucht** *fruit* / **Früchte**, **die Gans** *goose* / **Gänse**, **die Nacht** *night* / **Nächte**.

(*c*) some NEUTER monosyllables, without umlaut (except **das Floß** *raft* / **Flöße**)—e.g. **das Boot** *boat* / **Boote**, **das Jahr** *year* / **Jahre**, **das Pferd** *horse* / **Pferde**, **das Spiel** *game* / **Spiele**.

(ii) **-en** or **-n**:

(*a*) most FEMININES: 1. the vast majority of those ending in a consonant take **-en**—e.g. **die Schlacht** *battle* / **Schlachten**, **die Tat** *deed* / **Taten**, **die Uhr** *clock; watch* / **Uhren**, **die Zeit** *time* / **Zeiten**; likewise nouns in **-ei**, **-heit**, **-in** (with doubling of **n** in the plural), **-keit**, **-schaft**, **-ung**—e.g. **die Bäckerei** *bakery* / **Bäckereien**, **die Füchsin** *vixen* / **Füchsinnen**, **die Bemerkung** *remark* / **Bemerkungen**; 2. all feminines ending in -e take **-n** in the plural—e.g. **die Blume** *flower* / **Blumen**, **die Farbe** *colour; paint* / **Farben**, **die Minute** *minute* / **Minuten**, **die Schwalbe** *swallow* / **Schwalben**.

(*b*) a number of MASCULINES and a few NEUTERS—e.g. **der Schmerz** *pain* / **Schmerzen**, **der See** *lake* / **Seen**, **der Staat** *state* / **Staaten**, **der Strahl** *ray* / **Strahlen**; **das Auge** *eye* / **Augen**, **das Ohr** *ear* / **Ohren**, **das Bett** *bed* / **Betten**, **das Ende** *end* / **Enden**.

(*c*) all WEAK MASCULINES—e.g. **der Hase** *hare* / **Hasen**, **der Prinz** *prince* / **Prinzen**, **der Student** *student* / **Studenten**.

(d) nouns in **-or** (which shift the stress in the plural)—e.g. **der Organisátor** *organizer* / **Organisatóren, der Proféssor** *professor* / **Professóren.**

(e) nouns of foreign origin in which **-en** replaces the singular ending to form the plural—e.g. **das Drama** *drama* / **Dramen, das Epos** *epic* / **Epen, das Konto** *(bank) account* / **Konten, das Album** *album* / **Alben, das Individuum** *individual* / **Individuen, der Rhythmus** *rhythm* / **Rhythmen, der Organismus** *organism* / **Organismen.**

(iii) **-er** or **⁻er:**

most NEUTERS and a few MASCULINES, with umlaut where possible—e.g. **das Dorf** *village* / **Dörfer, das Ei** *egg* / **Eier, das Kind** *child* / **Kinder, das Land** *country* / **Länder; der Geist** *mind; spirit; ghost* / **Geister, der Gott** *god* / **Götter, der Mann** *man; husband* / **Männer, der Wald** *forest* / **Wälder.**

(iv) **-s:**

(a) some nouns of foreign origin—e.g. **der Bikini** *bikini* / **Bikinis, der Store** *net curtain* / **Stores, der Laptop** *laptop* / **Laptops, der Streik** *strike* / **Streiks; die City** *city centre* / **Citys, die Hazienda** *hacienda* / **Haziendas, die Sauna** *sauna* / **Saunas; das Büro** *office* / **Büros, das Ensemble** *ensemble* / **Ensembles, das Kino** *cinema* / **Kinos.**

(b) the nautical terms **das Deck** *deck* / **Decks, das Dock** *dock* / **Docks, das Wrack** *wreck* / **Wracks.**

(c) a few words which form a colloquial plural in **-s** in addition to the standard form—e.g. **der Kerl** *fellow* / **Kerle,** coll. **Kerls, das Fräulein** *young lady* / **Fräulein,** coll. **Fräuleins.**

(v) **-** or **⁻e:** nouns in **-el, -en, -er:**

(a) MASCULINES, usually with umlaut where possible—e.g. **der Engel** *angel* / **Engel, der Vogel** *bird* / **Vögel, der Garten** *garden* / **Gärten, der Vater** *father* / **Väter.**

(b) NEUTERS, without umlaut (except **das Kloster** *monastery; convent* / **Klöster**)—e.g. **das Segel** *sail* / **Segel, das Zeichen** *sign* / **Zeichen, das Ufer** *shore* / **Ufer, das Zimmer** *room* / **Zimmer.**

(c) two FEMININES: **die Mutter** *mother* / **Mütter, die Tochter** *daughter* / **Töchter.**

(vi) other endings used with words of foreign origin:

e.g. **das Adverb** *adverb* / **Adverbien, das Prinzip** *principle* / **Prinzipien; der Atlas** *atlas* / **Atlanten; das Paradoxon** [pa'raːdɔksɔn] *paradox* / **Paradoxa;** grammatical terms such as **das Nomen** *noun* / **Nomina, das Tempus** *tense* / **Tempora, der Kasus** *case* / **Kasus** [-uːs]**, der Modus** *mood* / **Modi.**

Some nouns have different plural forms corresponding to different meanings of the singular: e.g. **der Bau** *building* / **Bauten,** *burrow, earth* / **Baue; der Faden** *thread* / **Fäden,** *fathom* / **Faden; das Wort** *word* / **Worte** *(connected) words,* **Wörter** *(single) words* as in a **Wörterbuch.**

Other nouns do not have a plural form as such, the place of the 'missing' plural being taken by a compound in the plural, e.g. **der Tod** *death*— **Todesfälle** *deaths* (literally *cases of death*), **der Sport** *sport*—**Sportarten** *sports* (literally *types of sport*), **der Käse** *cheese*—**Käsesorten** *cheeses* (literally *kinds of cheese*).

POINTS REGARDING NUMBER (INCLUDING AGREEMENT IN NUMBER) WHERE GERMAN USAGE DIFFERS FROM ENGLISH

(i) Some German nouns in the singular correspond to an English plural, and vice versa:

(*a*) German singular = English plural, e.g. **der Hafer** *oats,* **das Gemüse** *vegetables,* **das Geweih** *antlers,* **die Treppe** *stairs,* **die Kaserne** *barracks,* **das Feuerwerk** *fireworks,* **das Uhrwerk** *works (of a clock or watch),* **der Erlös** *proceeds,* **der Lohn** *wages,* **der Schadenersatz** *damages,* **der Dank** *thanks,* **der Inhalt** *contents,* **das Mittel** *means,* **die Umgebung** *surroundings,* **die Mathematik** *mathematics,* **die Physik** *physics,* the names of the suits in cards (**Herz** *hearts,* **Karo** *diamonds,* **Pik** *spades,* **Kreuz** *clubs*), **das Mittelalter** *the Middle Ages,* **Westindien** *the West Indies.*

(*b*) German plural = English singular, e.g. **die Haare** (also **das Haar**) *hair* (in collective sense), **die Möbel** *furniture,* **die Lebensmittel** *food,* **die Flitterwochen** *honeymoon,* **die Zinsen** *interest (on money lent),* **die Fortschritte** *progress* (as in **Fortschritte machen** *to make progress*), **die Kenntnisse** *knowledge* (of a subject etc.).

(ii) In the case of masculine and neuter nouns indicating a weight or measure, as well as the feminine **Mark**, the singular form is used after numerals (or expressions such as **ein paar** *a few,* **mehrere** *several*) instead of the plural, e.g. **zwei Glas Bier** *two glasses of beer,* **drei Pfund Tee** *three pounds of tea,* **vier Dutzend Eier** *four dozen eggs,* **zehn Grad (Celsius)** *ten degrees (Celsius),* **vier Paar Schuhe** *four pairs of shoes,* **fünf Stück (Apfelsinen** etc.) *five (oranges* etc.), **50 000 Mann** *50,000 men* (if viewed as a single unit, as when constituting a fighting force: **eine Armee von 50 000 Mann** *an army of 50,000 men*), **100 Schritt** *100 paces,* **20 Pfennig** *20 pfennigs,* **30 Mark** *30 marks,* **50 englische Pfund** *50 pounds sterling,* **100 Dollar** *100 dollars.* (Feminine nouns of this type—except **Mark**—form the plural in the usual way, e.g. **drei Tassen Tee** *three cups of tea,* **100 Drachmen** *100 drachmas.*) On the other hand, where the items referred to are conceived of essentially as individual objects, the plural form is used, e.g. **zwei Fässer Bier** *two (individual) barrels of beer* (to be compared with **zwei Fass Bier** *two barrels of beer* as a quantity ordered etc.).

(iii) If two or more attributes refer to identical nouns, only the last noun is given—in the singular (whereas English has the plural), e.g. **das Alte (Testament** understood) **und Neue Testament** *the Old and New Testaments,* **im 17., 18. und 19. Jahrhundert** *in the 17th, 18th, and 19th centuries.* (This also applies when two compounds share the same last element, e.g. **in der Morgen- und Abendausgabe** *in the morning and evening editions.*)

(iv) In German the singular is used in a distributive sense (where English has the plural) with reference to something concrete or abstract that applies to a number of persons:

wir nahmen den Hut ab *we took off our hats*
alle hoben die rechte Hand *all raised their right hands*
sie redete die Leute nie mit dem Namen an *she never addressed people by their names*
manche Leute haben ein sehr leichtes Leben *some people have very easy lives*

(v) Where a noun denoting a quantity (such as **eine Anzahl** *a number*, **eine Menge** *a quantity*, **eine Herde** *a herd*) is followed by a plural noun, it may take a singular or plural verb according to whether the emphasis is more on the noun of quantity or on the following plural noun respectively, e.g. **ein Dutzend Eier kostet 5 Mark** *a dozen eggs cost 5 marks*, **eine riesige Menge Menschen war(en) versammelt** *a huge crowd of people was gathered* (**war** stresses the collective presence of the crowd, **waren** emphasizes the people concerned).

(vi) **Die USA** *the USA*, like **die Vereinigten Staaten** *the United States*, is treated as plural, e.g. **die USA haben den Vertrag ratifiziert** *the USA has ratified the treaty*; the corresponding personal pronoun is therefore **sie** (plural), translated by *it, she*.

(vii) Even if the complement precedes the verb and subject, the verb agrees in number with the subject, e.g. **seine große Leidenschaft sind Schmetterlinge** *his great passion is butterflies*.

(viii) The English plural form in phrases of the type *in . . . respects/ways* corresponds to a German singular:

in mancher Beziehung/Hinsicht *in some respects*
auf verschiedene Weise *in various ways*
auf tausenderlei Art *in a thousand ways*

PROPER NAMES

FORENAMES and SURNAMES, whether masculine or feminine, take **-s** in the genitive singular, e.g. **Juttas Fahrrad** *Jutta's bicycle*, **(Richard) Wagners Opern** or **die Opern (Richard) Wagners** *(Richard) Wagner's operas*, **die Ermordung Kennedys** *Kennedy's assassination*. (After **s, ss, ß, tz, x**, or **z** an apostrophe is used, e.g. **Agnes' Hut** *Agnes's hat*, **Strauß' Walzer** *Strauss's waltzes*, **Marx' Ideen** *Marx's ideas*; however, **von** is sometimes used instead, e.g. **die Walzer von Strauß**; especially with classical names the definite article is often used to indicate genitive case, e.g. **der Tod des Sokrates** *the death of Socrates*; **Jesus Christus** has the genitive **Jesu Christi**.) Surnames usually add **-s** in the plural, those ending in a sibilant add **-ens**, e.g. **(die) Schulzens** *the Schulzes*.

GEOGRAPHICAL NAMES also take the genitive **-s** (unless feminine like **die Schweiz** *Switzerland*), e.g. **die Bevölkerung Dänemarks** *the population of Denmark*,

die Geschichte Roms *the history of Rome,* **außerhalb Moskaus** *outside Moscow.* (After **s**, **ss**, **ß**, **tz**, **x**, or **z** it is customary to use **von**, e.g. **das Erbe von Byzanz** *the heritage of Byzantium,* **die Theater von Paris** *the theatres of Paris.*)²⁵

The names of continents (other than **die Antarktis** *Antarctica*), countries and regions (with certain exceptions, e.g. **der Sudan** *the Sudan,* **der Balkan** *the Balkans,* **die Schweiz, die Türkei** *Turkey,* **die Provence** *Provence,* **die Normandie** *Normandy,* **die Bretagne** *Britanny,* **die Toskana** *Tuscany,* (plural) **die USA** *the USA*)²⁶ and cities are all used without an article, and are neuter—as becomes apparent when, exceptionally, the definite article is required, namely when an adjective precedes the name or a genitive phrase follows, e.g. **das südliche Spanien** *southern Spain,* **das Frankreich Ludwigs XIV.** (= **des Vierzehnten**) *the France of Louis XIV,* **das Warschau von heute** *present-day Warsaw.*

Mountains (and mountain ranges) have the definite article, and are usually masculine, e.g. **der Brocken** *the Brocken,* **der Montblanc** *Mont Blanc,* **der Fudschijama** *Fujiyama,* **der Mount Everest** *Mount Everest,* **der Ural** *the Urals* (but **die Eifel**). Some occur as plurals, e.g. **die Alpen** *the Alps,* **die Vogesen** *the Vosges,* **die Pyrenäen** *the Pyrenees,* **die Kordilleren** *the Cordilleras.*

Rivers in Germany are mostly feminine (e.g. **die Mosel** *the Moselle,* **die Donau** *the Danube*), as are foreign rivers in -a and -e (e.g. **die Wolga** *the Volga,* **die Themse** *the Thames,* **die Seine**); but several major German rivers (e.g. **der Rhein, der Main, der Neckar, der Inn**) and most foreign ones (e.g. **der Amazonas** *the Amazon,* **der Jangtse(kiang)** *the Yangtze (Kiang),* **der Limpopo, der Mississippi, der Tweed**) have masculine gender.

The planets also have the definite article, and are mostly masculine: **der Merkur** *Mercury,* **der Mars** *Mars,* **der Jupiter** *Jupiter,* **der Saturn** *Saturn,* **der Uranus** *Uranus,* **der Neptun** *Neptune,* **der Pluto** *Pluto*; two are feminines: **die Venus** *Venus,* **die Erde** *Earth.*

CARS are generally masculine, e.g. **der Mercedes, der Renault, der Rolls-Royce, der Volvo.** SHIPS are usually feminine, e.g. **die „Graf Spee", die „Titanic"** [ti'taːnɪk]; so too are AIRCRAFT, e.g. **die Boeing, die DC-8, die Messerschmitt** (but **der Airbus, der Jumbo**).

The titles of WORKS OF ART, NEWSPAPERS, ETC. are inflected, e.g. **hast du „Iwan den Schrecklichen" gesehen?** *have you seen 'Ivan the Terrible'?* Where a title beginning with a definite article is in an oblique case the article is placed outside the quotation marks, e.g. **als Abonnent des „Spiegels"** *as a subscriber to 'Der Spiegel',* **im „Kapital" heißt es . . .** *it says in 'Das Kapital' . . .*; the article is dropped following an artist's name in the genitive, e.g. **die**

---

²⁵ **Von** is also usual in e.g. **der König/Präsident von . . .** *the King/President of . . .* (but **der Präsident der Vereinigten Staaten**).
²⁶ The article is optional in **(der) Irak** *Iraq,* **(der) Iran** *Iran,* **(der) Jemen** *Yemen.*

Ouvertüre zu Wagners „Fliegendem Holländer" *the overture to Wagner's 'Flying Dutchman'.*

LANGUAGES

Languages with names in **-isch** (**-sch**) have two forms: the *uninflected* form (e.g. **Englisch, Deutsch**), which is neuter, although the gender is not always apparent, and the—likewise neuter—*inflected* form, consisting of the corresponding adjectival noun with definite article (e.g. **das Englische/ Deutsche**); other languages such as **(das) Hindi** *Hindi,* **(das) Suaheli** *Swahili,* **(das) Haussa** *Hausa,* also **(das) Esperanto** *Esperanto* have a single name only.

The uninflected form is used to refer either to a language in a general sense (without an article)—e.g. **Deutsch sprechen** *to speak German,* **gut/ fließend Deutsch sprechen** *to speak German well/fluently,* **Serbokroatisch ist nicht mein Fall** *Serbo-Croat is not my cup of tea*—or to a particular *type* of the language concerned, e.g. **gutes Deutsch** *good German,* **das amerikanische Englisch** *American English,* **Luthers Deutsch** *Luther's German,* **das Kaufmannsdeutsch** *commercial German,* **im heutigen Deutsch** *in present-day German.* The adjectival noun, on the other hand, can only refer to a language in a general sense, *the . . . language,* e.g. **das Englische ist eine indogermanische Sprache** *English is an Indo-European language,* **die Aussprache des Russischen** *the pronunciation of Russian,* also **etwas aus dem (Deutschen etc.) ins (Englische etc.) übersetzen** *to translate something from (German etc.) into (English etc.).*

In German, English, etc. is **auf Deutsch, Englisch,** etc.; where an adjective precedes the noun **in** is used, e.g. **in fließendem/gebrochenem Deutsch** *in fluent/broken German. In Hindi, Hausa,* etc. = **auf Hindi, Haussa,** etc.

ADVERBIAL USE OF **deutsch** ETC.: e.g. **deutsch denken/sprechen** *to think in German/speak (in) German,* **der Brief ist deutsch geschrieben** *the letter is (written) in German* (also **in Deutsch**).

Pronouns

PERSONAL PRONOUNS

SINGULAR

| | 1ST PERS. *I* | 2ND PERS. *YOU* (FAMILIAR FORM) | 3RD PERS. *HE/SHE/IT* | | |
			MASC.	FEM.	NEUT.
NOM.	ich	du	er	sie	es
ACC.	mich	dich	ihn	sie	es
GEN.	meiner	deiner	seiner	ihrer	seiner
DAT.	mir	dir	ihm	ihr	ihm

SINGULAR AND PLURAL

Sie *you*

NOM.	Sie
ACC.	Sie
GEN.	Ihrer
DAT.	Ihnen

PLURAL

	1ST PERS. *WE*	2ND PERS. *YOU* (FAMILIAR FORM)	3RD PERS. *THEY*
NOM.	wir	ihr	sie
ACC.	uns	euch	sie
GEN.	unser	euer	ihrer
DAT.	uns	euch	ihnen

NOTE: The genitive forms are relatively rare, occurring chiefly with verbs and adjectives that govern the genitive.

The familiar 2nd person pronouns **du** and **ihr** are used when addressing relatives, close friends, one's peers (among certain groups such as workmen), children, animals, God (**Du**), and (in poetry) personified inanimate objects;

the reader of a book, advertisement, etc. is also addressed in the familiar form, e.g. **siehe** ... *see* ... , **trink Coca-Cola** *drink Coca-Cola*, and in the plural **schützt unsere Wälder!** *protect our forests*. Otherwise **Sie** is used.

The personal pronouns of the 3rd person singular agree in gender with the noun they refer to, thus *it* may be expressed by **er** (referring to a masculine), **sie** (referring to a feminine) or **es** (referring to a neuter), e.g. **ich liebe diesen Garten—er ist so groß** *I love this garden—it's so large*. (The use in English of *she* to refer to countries necessarily differs from German usage: the great majority of countries being neuter in German, they are referred to by **es**.)

Although in accordance with the rules of congruence one would expect the neuter pronoun to be used in connection with the neuter nouns **Mädchen** and **Fräulein**, in practice 'natural gender' tends to assert itself, and the feminine pronoun is widely used instead, e.g. **was hat das Mädchen?—ist sie immer so?** *what's wrong with the girl?— is she always like that?* (Likewise, the feminine possessive adjective **ihr** is widely used instead of neuter **sein**, e.g. **das Mädchen von nebenan hat ihren Pass verloren** *the girl next door has lost her passport*.) In the case of the relative pronoun, however, congruence is always observed, e.g. **das Fräulein, das** (neuter relative pronoun) **uns bediente** *the young lady who served us*.

After the commoner prepositions (**an, auf, aus, bei, durch, für, gegen, hinter, in, mit, nach, neben, über, unter, um, von, vor, zu, zwischen**) the personal pronouns of the 3rd person are normally used with reference to persons, e.g. **mit ihm** *with him*. If things are referred to, an adverbial compound consisting of **da-** (before a vowel **dar-**) + preposition is generally used instead, e.g. **damit** *with it/them*, **darauf** *on it/them*; not infrequently, however, the construction preposition + pronoun is preferred, e.g. **mehrere Jungen stehen um einen Fußball—und wissen nicht, was sie mit ihm (= damit) anfangen sollen** (newspaper report) *several boys are standing round a football, not knowing what to do with it.*

The particle **da-** (**dar-**) is also used to anticipate a following noun clause with **dass, ob**, etc. or a construction with **zu** + infinitive:

(i) (with **dass**-clause) *the fact that* or *—ing*, e.g. **ich machte ihn darauf aufmerksam, dass es regnete** *I drew his attention to the fact that it was raining*, **ihre Enttäuschung darüber, dass sie übergangen wurde** *her disappointment at being passed over.*

(ii) (with **ob, was, wie**, etc.): **da-**element untranslated, e.g. **wir haben noch nicht darüber entschieden, ob** ... *we haven't yet decided on whether* ... , **wir sind uns darin einig, wie** ... *we're in agreement on how.* ...

(iii) (with **zu** + infinitive) *—ing*, with **da-**element untranslated, e.g. **der Kaiser träumte davon, Oberitalien zu erobern** *the emperor dreamed of conquering Northern Italy*; or (**dazu zu** ...) *to* + infinitive, e.g. **sie brachte ihn dazu, seinen Job aufzugeben** *she got him to give up his job.*

In a clause introduced by **wie** *such as*, a 3rd person pronoun is used to refer to the antecedent, e.g. (with pronoun as subject) **der traditionelle Empfang für die Vertreter der Kirche, wie er in der Ära Ulbricht üblich**

war *the traditional reception for the representatives of the Church, such as was customary in the Ulbricht era,* (as object) **Geschichten, wie man sie überall in der Welt lesen kann** *stories such as one may read all over the world*; the pronoun **einer, eine, ein(e)s** *one* may be used in a similar way, e.g. **ein Sonnenaufgang, wie wir noch nie einen gesehen hatten** *a sunrise such as we had never seen before.*

Es has a number of special functions:

(i) It is used with the verb *sein* with DEMONSTRATIVE FORCE, e.g. **es ist der Briefträger** *it's the postman,* (with plural noun determining number of verb) **es sind meine Tanten** *it's my aunts.*

It's me etc.: The personal pronoun is here followed by the verb **sein** (the number and person of which it determines) and **es**, e.g. **ich bin's** (or **bin es**) *it's me,* **er war's** (or **war es**) *it was him* (in questions the verb comes first, e.g. **bist du's** (or **du es)?** *is it you?*). The same word order applies when a relative clause follows, e.g. **ich war es, der/die** . . . *it was I who.* . . .

(ii) It anticipates:

(*a*) a NOUN SUBJECT (which tends to be emphasized by the construction), e.g. **es geschah etwas Merkwürdiges** *something remarkable happened,* **es wurde ein Stück aufgeführt, das** . . . *a play was performed which* . . . , (= *there*) **es scheint keiner zu Hause zu sein** *there doesn't seem to be anybody at home,* also the formulaic **es war einmal** . . . *once upon a time there was* . . . ; where the anticipated subject is in the plural, the verb is also, e.g. **es kamen viele Briefe** *many letters came,* **es sind nicht alle Schlangen giftig** *not all snakes are poisonous,* **es waren zwei Fliegen im Zimmer** *there were two flies in the room* (see p. 95).

(*b*) a NOUN CLAUSE or INFINITIVE PHRASE, e.g. (as subject, = English *it*) **es ist möglich, dass** . . . *it is possible that* . . . , **es ist mir egal, ob** . . . *it makes no difference to me whether* . . . , **es lohnt sich zu** . . . *it pays to* . . . ; (as object—sometimes optional) **(es) verheimlichen, dass** . . . *to conceal the fact that* . . . , **es ablehnen zu** . . . *to decline to* . . . , **(es) vorziehen zu** . . . *to prefer to* . . . , (= English *it*) **es für richtig halten zu** . . . *to think it right to.* . . .

(iii) In sentences such as **er ist gutmütig und wird es immer sein** *he is good-natured and always will be,* **ihre Mutter war eine Dame, sie aber war es nicht** *her mother was a lady, but she was not* it COMPLETES THE PREDICATE, in place of an adjective or a noun already referred to (here **gutmütig, eine Dame**); in English this **es** has no equivalent, the complement being understood. **Es** is also without a corresponding pronoun in English in CLAUSES OF COMPARISON beginning **als/wie es** . . . = English *than/as* + inversion, e.g. **wie es Sitte ist** *as is the custom,* **wie es sich gehört** *as is proper,* **als es der Fall ist** *than is the case.*

(iv) It is used as an INDEFINITE OBJECT in many idioms (cf. English *it* in *to carry it off, to go it alone*), e.g. **es weit bringen** *to go a long way, go far,* **es eilig haben** *to be in a hurry,* **es gut meinen** *to mean well,* **es zu bunt treiben** *to go too far.*

REFLEXIVE PRONOUNS

The reflexive pronouns are identical with the personal pronouns in all instances except the accusative and dative (singular and plural) of the 3rd person (**er, sie, es**; pl. **sie**) and of **Sie**—in these instances the form **sich** is used; thus the conjugation of **sich waschen** to wash (oneself) runs:

ich wasche mich	**wir waschen uns**
du wäschst dich	**ihr wascht euch**
er/sie/es wäscht sich	**sie, Sie waschen sich**

When the reflexive pronoun is in the dative, the conjugation—illustrated by **sich** (DAT.) **schmeicheln** to flatter oneself—goes as follows:

ich schmeichele mir	**wir schmeicheln uns**
du schmeichelst dir	**ihr schmeichelt euch**
er/sie/es schmeichelt sich	**sie, Sie schmeicheln sich**

The perfect and pluperfect tenses are conjugated with **haben**—except where the reflexive pronoun is used as a dative in the reciprocal sense with a verb that takes **sein**, in which case this auxiliary is used, e.g. **sie sind sich neulich vor dem Bahnhof begegnet** they recently met outside the station.

The reflexive pronouns refer back to the subject performing the action concerned, as do the English equivalents myself, yourself, oneself, etc.[27] After a preposition English substitutes a personal pronoun for the reflexive, e.g. I have no money **on me**, thus paralleling German in the 1st and 2nd persons where there is no special reflexive form: **ich habe kein Geld bei mir**; but in the 3rd person, for which German has the reflexive **sich**, the latter must be used, e.g. he closed the door **behind him** **er schloss die Tür hinter sich**.

The reflexive pronouns may be reinforced by **selbst** (colloquially **selber**) when emphasis is called for, e.g. **sie bemitleiden sich selbst** they feel sorry for themselves.

See also p. 92, Reflexive verbs.

POSSESSIVE PRONOUNS

There are two forms of possessive pronoun in German:

(i) (the usual form) **meiner, meine, mein(e)s** mine, **deiner** etc. yours (familiar), **seiner** etc. his, its, **ihrer** etc. hers, its, **uns(e)rer** etc. ours, **eu(e)rer** etc. yours (familiar plural), **ihrer** etc. theirs, **Ihrer** etc. yours; these are declined like the definite article:

---

[27] This reflexive use of the English pronouns formed with -self should be distinguished from their function as emphatic pronouns, for which the German equivalent is **selbst** (colloquially **selber**), e.g. the author himself was present **der Autor selbst war / war selbst anwesend**, she does the cooking herself **sie kocht selbst**, I myself have found that . . . **ich habe selbst die Erfahrung gemacht, dass . . .**

	SINGULAR			PLURAL
	MASC.	FEM.	NEUT.	ALL GENDERS
NOM.	meiner	meine	mein(e)s	meine
ACC.	meinen	meine	mein(e)s	meine
DAT.	meinem	meiner	meinem	meinen

The genitive is not shown, being replaced by **von** + dative, e.g. **von meinem/meiner/meinen** *of mine*. Examples:

> **ihr Hut ist noch da, aber meiner ist verschwunden** *her hat's still there, but mine's disappeared*
>
> **mein Auto ist größer als deins** *my car's bigger than yours*
>
> **Vati hat meinen Pass—wer hat deinen?** *Dad's got my passport—who's got yours?*

(ii) (in literary usage) with the definite article and weak endings, either with or without -**ig**-: **der/die/das** . . .**(ig)e**, e.g. **der/die/das mein(ig)e** *mine*.

There also exists an archaic literary form, namely uninflected **mein, dein, sein, unser, euer** (not, however, **ihr** or **Ihr**), used predicatively as the complement of **sein, werden**, etc. to express possession, e.g. **Dein ist mein Herz** *Thine is my heart* (in Schubert's *Die schöne Müllerin*).

INTERROGATIVE PRONOUNS

	wer? *who?*	**was?** *what?*
NOM.	**wer?**	**was?**
ACC.	**wen?**	**was?**
GEN.	**wessen?**	**wessen?**
DAT.	**wem?**	—

The neuter pronoun **was** is replaced by **wo-** (or **wor-** before vowels) when the sense *what* + preposition is to be conveyed; this form combines with the preposition concerned to form a compound, thus *what . . . with?* is expressed by **womit?**, *what . . . on?* by **worauf?**

RELATIVE PRONOUNS

	SINGULAR			PLURAL
	MASC.	FEM.	NEUT.	ALL GENDERS
NOM.	der	die	das	die
ACC.	den	die	das	die
GEN.	dessen	deren	dessen	deren
DAT.	dem	der	dem	denen

The relative pronoun (*who, which, that*) agrees in gender and number with its antecedent (the noun it refers to), while its case is determined by its function within the clause. It is never omitted. The relative clause is always separated by commas from the rest of the sentence; the finite verb goes to the end of the clause. Examples: **die Illustrierte, die** (ACC.) **ich kaufen wollte** *the magazine (which) I wanted to buy,* **der Klub, dem ich angehöre** *the club I belong to (to which I belong).* (When the antecedent is a 1st or 2nd person pronoun, German repeats the pronoun concerned after the relative pronoun, e.g. **ich, der ich immer so geduldig bin** *I who am always so patient.*)

PRONOMINAL ADVERBS such as **womit, worin, worüber** occur, if the antecedent is a thing, in more formal prose as an alternative to the construction PREPOSITION + RELATIVE PRONOUN (e.g. **die Welt, worin**—instead of **in der**—**wir leben** *the world in which we live*); but they are now relatively uncommon —the combination of preposition and relative pronoun being generally preferred—*except* where the antecedent is a pronoun such as **das, alles, einiges, etwas, nichts**:

> **etwas, wofür man bezahlt werden sollte** *something for which one should be paid*
> **alles, worüber sie geschrieben hat** *everything about which she has written*

or a clause:

> **der Kugelstoßer hatte acht Stunden lang trainiert, wovon er ziemlich erschöpft war** *the shot-putter had been training for eight hours, as a result of which he was pretty worn out*

Was AS A RELATIVE: **Was** is used after **das** or neuter indefinites—e.g. **alles, was** *everything that,* **einiges, was** *some things that,* **etwas, was** *something that,* **nichts, was** *nothing that*—as well as neuter superlative adjectives used as nouns:

> **das Mindeste, was du tun kannst** *the least you can do*
> **das Beste, was Händel je komponiert hat** *the best thing Handel ever composed*

It is also used where a clause is the antecedent:

> **das Fußballspiel musste abgebrochen werden, was wir sehr bedauerten** *the football match had to be stopped, which (= which fact) we very much regretted*

DEMONSTRATIVE PRONOUNS

The forms are the same as those of the relative pronouns (above)—except that the *genitive plural* form **deren** is replaced by **derer** when followed by a relative clause, e.g. **die Gesichter derer, die jahrelang gewartet hatten** *the faces of those who had been waiting for years.* Translations vary according to context:

der/die mit der Perücke *the one* with the wig
**die Unfallrate der Aeroflot ist nicht höher als die vergleichbarer west-
licher Fluggesellschaften** *Aeroflot's accident rate is no higher than* **that**
of comparable Western airlines
Sorgen?—wir haben deren genug *worries?—we have enough of* **them/
those**
ach der! *oh him / that one!*
mein Rat ist der: . . . *my advice is* **this***: . . .*

The genitive forms **dessen** and **deren** are sometimes used in place of the possessive
adjectives **sein** (*his, its*) and **ihr** (*her, its, their*); they always refer back to the last-
mentioned noun. This substitution need only be employed where ambiguity could
arise, e.g. **am nächsten Tag besuchten sie sein Freund und dessen Sohn** (avoid-
ing the ambiguous **sein Sohn**) *the next day they were visited by his friend and the
latter's son.*

INDEFINITE PRONOUNS

(i) **man** *one, you, they, we, people:*[28]

This pronoun has no oblique cases, being replaced in the accusative by **einen**
and in the dative by **einem**; **sich** serves as its reflexive pronoun and **sein**
as its possessive adjective (*one's, your*) in the oblique cases.
    In some instances constructions with **man** are rendered by the English
passive. Examples of usage:

man weiß nie, was geschehen kann *one never knows what may happen*
man behauptet, er sei nach Australien ausgewandert *they say he has
(he is said to have) emigrated to Australia*
das tut einem gut *that does one good*
man hat mir gesagt, dass . . . *I've been told that . . .*

(ii) **jemand** *someone* and **niemand** *no-one, not . . . anyone*:

NOM.	jemand	niemand
ACC.	jemand(en)	niemand(en)
GEN.	jemand(e)s	niemand(e)s
DAT.	jemand(em)	niemand(em)

Someone/no-one + adjective is expressed by **jemand/niemand** + the
appropriate neuter adjectival noun, e.g. *someone interesting* **jemand Inte-
ressantes**, *with someone interesting* **mit jemand Interessantem**; *someone/
no-one else* is **jemand/niemand anders** (South German **anderer**).
    Einer and **keiner** are common alternatives to **jemand** and **niemand**
respectively.

(iii) **etwas** *something* and **nichts** *nothing, not . . . anything*:

---

[28] 'The overuse of **Leute** in German, where **man** would be appropriate, is very characteristic of
English learners' German' (Martin Durrell).

These pronouns are indeclinable and occur in the nominative and accusative, and after prepositions.

Etwas may be followed by a noun, with the sense *some*, e.g. **etwas (frische) Milch** *some (fresh) milk*; or it may be an adverb meaning *somewhat*.

(iv) **viel** *much*, **(ein) wenig** *(a) little*

These pronouns are indeclinable in the singular, but decline in the plural: **viele** *many*, **wenige** *few*. (The latter should not be confused with **weniger** (indeclinable) *less*.)

(v) **alles** *everything, all* and (plural) **alle** *all, everyone*:

NOM.	**alles**	**alle**
ACC.	**alles**	**alle**
GEN.	—	**aller**
DAT.	**allem**	**allen**

Colloquially **alles** may also signify *everyone*.

Adjectives and Adverbs

FORMS

In predicative use, the adjective in German is not inflected, e.g. **die Musik ist schön** *the music is beautiful*, **das Wasser ist heiß** *the water is hot.* Used attributively, i.e. preceding a noun, it is inflected (as shown below), e.g. **die schöne Musik** *the beautiful music*, **heißes Wasser** *hot water*.

Most adjectives may be used in the uninflected form as adverbs, e.g. **sie hat das Lied sehr schön gesungen** *she sang the song very beautifully.*

The adjective is declined as follows:

(i) WEAK DECLENSION. Following the definite article or other words declined like the definite article (**dieser, jeder, jener, mancher, solcher, welcher**):

SINGULAR

	MASC. (*the big dog*)	FEM. (*the big cat*)	NEUT. (*the big animal*)
NOM.	der groß*e* Hund	die groß*e* Katze	das groß*e* Tier
ACC.	den groß*en* Hund	die groß*e* Katze	das groß*e* Tier
GEN.	des groß*en* Hundes	der groß*en* Katze	des groß*en* Tieres
DAT.	dem groß*en* Hund	der groß*en* Katze	dem groß*en* Tier

PLURAL

NOM.	die groß*en* Tiere
ACC.	die groß*en* Tiere
GEN.	der groß*en* Tiere
DAT.	den groß*en* Tieren

(ii) MIXED DECLENSION. Following the indefinite article, **kein** *not a, no* or possessive adjective (**mein, dein**, etc.):

SINGULAR

	MASC.	FEM.	NEUT.
NOM.	ein groß*er* Hund	eine groß*e* Katze	ein groß*es* Tier
ACC.	einen groß*en* Hund	eine groß*e* Katze	ein groß*es* Tier
GEN.	eines groß*en* Hundes	einer groß*en* Katze	eines groß*en* Tieres
DAT.	einem groß*en* Hund	einer groß*en* Katze	einem groß*en* Tier

PLURAL

NOM.	meine groß*en* Katzen
ACC.	meine groß*en* Katzen
GEN.	meiner groß*en* Katzen
DAT.	meinen groß*en* Katzen

(iii) STRONG DECLENSION. Without article (here the adjective—through its ending—indicates the case of the noun):

SINGULAR

	MASC. (*good wine*)	FEM. (*warm milk*)	NEUT. (*fresh water*)
NOM.	gut*er* Wein	warm*e* Milch	frisch*es* Wasser
ACC.	gut*en* Wein	warm*e* Milch	frisch*es* Wasser
GEN.	gut*en* Weines	warm*er* Milch	frisch*en* Wassers
DAT.	gut*em* Wein	warm*er* Milch	frisch*em* Wasser

PLURAL

NOM.	gut*e* Weine
ACC.	gut*e* Weine
GEN.	gut*er* Weine
DAT.	gut*en* Weinen

These strong endings are also used after uninflected words (e.g. **viel/wenig heißes Wasser** *lots of/little hot water*, **welch glücklicher Zufall!** *what a happy coincidence!*, **trotz allerlei leckerer Torten** *in spite of all kinds of delicious gateaux*, **mit vier englischen Freunden** *with four English friends*), proper nouns in the genitive (e.g. **in Schillers großem Schreibtisch** *in Schiller's large desk*), and the genitive of the relative pronoun (e.g. **der Briefträger, dessen neues Fahrrad zehn Gänge hat** *the postman, whose new bicycle has ten gears*).

When personal pronouns are followed by attributive adjectives or adjectival nouns, these generally take a strong ending also, e.g. [**Da steh' ich nun,**] **ich armer Tor!** (*Faust I*) *poor fool that I am!*, **du Glücklicher!** *you lucky fellow!* A weak ending, however, is usual in the nominative plural, e.g. **wir (erfahrenen) Angestellten** *we (experienced) employees* (it is also preferred in the dative singular feminine); *we Germans* **wir Deutschen** (but **Deutsche** also occurs).

When inflected, adjectives ending in -el always drop e, e.g. **edel** *noble* but **ein edler Ritter** *a noble knight*, **miserabel** *awful* but **sein miserables Deutsch** *his awful German*. Adjectives in -**en** and -**er** usually retain e, although in elevated style it is sometimes elided. (Exceptions: adjectives of foreign origin in -**er**, e.g. **makaber** *macabre*, and those with a diphthong + -**er**, e.g. **sauer** *sour*, which regularly elide e, e.g. **eine makabre Geschichte** *a macabre story*, **saure Äpfel** *sour apples*.)

Two or more adjectives before a noun have the same ending, e.g. **ein großer, runder Tisch** *a large round table.*

The adjectives **viel** *much* and **wenig** *little* are not declined in the singular:

sie trinkt viel Milch *she drinks a lot of milk*
er kommt mit wenig Geld aus *he manages on little money*

but are declined in the plural:

viele Geschäftsleute *many businessmen*
mit wenigen Ausnahmen *with few exceptions*

Four categories of adjective take no ending:

(i) certain adjectives of foreign origin: **prima** (commercial) *first-class*, (coll.) *great* and the colour adjectives **beige, chamois, creme** *cream*, **lila** *purple*, **oliv** *olive*, **orange, rosa** *pink*; of these only **prima, lila**, and **rosa** are normally used attributively (e.g. **ein rosa Kleid** *a pink dress*), while the others are usually compounded with **-farben** or **-farbig** (*-coloured*) to avoid using the uninflected forms: **beigefarben, olivfarben**, etc.

(ii) **ganz** and **halb** before geographical names without the definite article, e.g. **ganz Zypern** *the whole of Cyprus*, **halb Europa** *half Europe.*

(iii) adjectives in **-er** derived from a place-name, e.g. **ein Wiener Walzer** *a Viennese waltz*, **die Londoner Theater** *the London theatres*, **Pariser Chic** [ʃɪk] *Parisian chic.*

(iv) adjectives in **-er** referring to a decade, e.g. **die neunziger Jahre** *the nineties* (such expressions may now also be written as one word: **die Neunzigerjahre** etc.).

The declension of ADJECTIVES FOLLOWING INDEFINITE ADJECTIVES (e.g. **alle, einige, mehrere**) is as follows:

(i) To adjectives following **einige** *some*, **ein paar** *a few*, **mehrere** *several*, **verschiedene** *various*, **viele** *many*, **wenige** *few*—all of which refer to a certain quantity (as opposed to all) of something—strong plural endings are added:

einige alte Lieder *some old songs*
die Werke mehrerer/vieler berühmter Komponisten *the works of several/ many famous composers*

Exceptionally, **manche** *some* is followed by adjectives with either strong or weak plural endings, e.g. **manche reiche(n) Leute** *some rich people.*

(ii) To adjectives following **alle** *all (the)* weak endings are added:

alle guten Nachschlagewerke *all good reference works*
die Ansichten aller ausländischen Studenten *the views of all foreign students*

Beide *both* and **sämtliche** *all (the)* are usually followed by adjectives with weak endings, but strong endings sometimes occur.

Alles Schöne, nichts Gutes, etc.:

(i) adjectives following **alles, manches, vieles, weniges** are written (with the exception of **ander**) with a capital letter and take the weak neuter singular endings, e.g. (NOM., ACC.) **alles Schöne** *everything beautiful,* (GEN.) **alles Schönen,** (DAT.) **allem Schönen;**

(ii) adjectives following **allerlei, etwas, manch, nichts, viel, wenig** are written (with the exception of **ander**) with a capital letter and take the strong neuter singular endings, e.g. (NOM., ACC.) **nichts Gutes** *nothing good,* (GEN., rare) **nichts Guten,** (DAT.) **nichts Gutem.**

POSSESSIVE ADJECTIVES

The possessive adjectives are: **mein** *my,* **dein** *your* (familiar form), **sein/ ihr/sein** *his/her/its,* **Ihr** *your,* **unser** *our,* **euer** *your* (familiar form, plural) and **ihr** *their;* they are declined like **kein** (p. 33). The possessive adjectives of the 3rd person singular agree in gender with the noun they refer to, thus *its* may be expressed by **sein** (referring to a masculine or neuter) or **ihr** (referring to a feminine), e.g. **die Partei hat ihre Anhänger enttäuscht** *the party has disappointed its supporters.*

COMPARISON OF ADJECTIVES AND ADVERBS

The comparative and superlative of adjectives is formed by adding **-er** and **-st (-est)** respectively:

> **langsam** *slow*—**langsamer** *slower*—**langsamst-** *slowest*
> **interessant** *interesting*—**interessanter** *more interesting*—**interessantest-** *most interesting*

(German has only this one way of forming the comparative and superlative —unlike English, which uses both *-er, -est* and *more . . . , most. . . .*)

The comparative of adverbs is identical with that of the corresponding adjective, e.g. **langsamer** *more slowly.* The superlative of adverbs is formed according to the pattern **am —sten,** e.g. **am langsamsten** *most slowly.*

Adjectives in **-el** drop the **e** in the comparative, e.g. **dunkel** *dark*—**dunkler** —**dunkelst-**; adjectives in **-en** and **-er** sometimes drop **e** in spoken German when inflected (but adjectives with a diphthong + **-er** always drop the **e,** e.g. **sauer** *sour*—**saurer**—**sauerst-, teuer** *expensive*—**teurer**—**teuerst-**).

In the superlative, **e** is inserted before **st,** for euphony's sake, in adjectives ending in **-d, -s, -sch, -sk, -ss, -ß, -t, -tz, -x, -z,** e.g. (**wild** *wild*) **wildest-,** (**hübsch** *pretty*) **hübschest-,** (**süß** *sweet*) **süßest-**—unless they have more than one syllable, e.g. (**praktisch** *practical*) **praktischst-,** (**bedeutend** *import-ant*) **bedeutendst-,** (**ausgezeichnet** *excellent*) **ausgezeichnetst-** (excep-tion: **berühmt** *famous*—with stress on the final syllable—which adds **e: berühmtest-**). After a diphthong or long vowel the insertion of **e** is optional, e.g. (**frei** *free*) **frei(e)st-,** (**früh** *early*) **früh(e)st-.**

The following common adjectives (and one adverb) mutate the stem vowel in the comparative and superlative, as **alt**—**älter**—**ältest-**:

alt *old*	**kurz** *short*
arm *poor*	**lang** *long*
dumm *stupid*	**oft** *often*
grob *coarse*	**scharf** *sharp*
hart *hard*	**schwach** *weak*
jung *young*	**schwarz** *black*
kalt *cold*	**stark** *strong*
klug *clever*	**warm** *warm*
krank *sick*	

With **fromm** *pious*, **gesund** *healthy*, and **rot** *red* mutation of the vowel is optional: in the case of **fromm** the form without umlaut is commoner, while **gesund** and **rot** usually have the umlaut.

Certain adjectives and adverbs are compared irregularly:

groß *big; tall; great*—**größer**—**größt-**
gut *good*—**besser**—**best-**
hoch *high*—**höher**—**höchst-**
nah *near, close*—**näher**—**nächst-**
viel *much*—**mehr**—**meist-**
bald *soon*—**eher**—**am ehesten**
gern *gladly*—**lieber**—**am liebsten**

-er and -er is expressed in German by **immer** + comparative, e.g. **immer schneller** *faster and faster*, **immer lauter** *louder and louder*.

The comparative form of some common adjectives has a second function, namely to indicate a fairly high degree of the quality concerned, without any comparison being made; this is known as the 'absolute comparative'. Examples: **eine größere Summe** *a largish sum*, **ein jüngeres Ehepaar** *a youngish couple*, **eine längere Reise** *a longish journey*, **seit längerer Zeit** *for some time now*; in adverbial use **öfter** *quite often*.

The predicative superlative—as in *which newspaper is the most interesting?* —occurs in two forms: **der/die/das —ste** and **am —sten**, e.g. **welche Zeitung ist die interessanteste / ist am interessantesten?** (i.e. of the newspapers being compared). Where items in the same category are compared but without their common denominator (**Zeitung** etc.) being stated, **am —sten** is used, e.g. **„Die Welt" ist interessanter als die „FAZ", aber die „Süddeutsche Zeitung" ist am interessantesten**. The form **am —sten** is also used when there is no comparison with others (English sometimes inserts *at its* before the superlative), e.g. **der Vierwaldstätter See ist im Frühling am schönsten** *the Lake of Lucerne is (at its) loveliest in spring*.

When *most* is used in an absolute sense (i.e. without a comparison being made) it may be expressed by **äußerst**, e.g. *I was most grateful* **ich war äußerst dankbar**; the adverbial construction **aufs —ste** is used when rendering statements such as *I was most pleasantly surprised* **ich war aufs angenehmste überrascht.**

ADJECTIVES USED AS NOUNS

German adjectives—and adjectival participles—may be used as nouns. They are written with a capital letter and are declined like ordinary adjectives, e.g. **der/die Erwachsene** *adult*:

SINGULAR

	MASCULINE		FEMININE
NOM.	**der Erwachsen***e*	**ein Erwachsen***er*	**die, eine Erwachsen***e*
ACC.	**den, einen Erwachsen***en*		**die, eine Erwachsen***e*
GEN.	**des, eines Erwachsen***en*		**der, einer Erwachsen***en*
DAT.	**dem, einem Erwachsen***en*		**der, einer Erwachsen***en*

PLURAL

NOM.	**die Erwachsen***en*	**Erwachsen***e*
ACC.	**die Erwachsen***en*	**Erwachsen***e*
GEN.	**der Erwachsen***en*	**Erwachsen***er*
DAT.	**den Erwachsen***en*	**Erwachsen***en*

Masculine, feminine, or plural adjectival nouns denote persons:

der/die Alte *old man/woman* (from **alt** *old*)
der/die Fremde *stranger* (from **fremd** *strange*)
der/die Deutsche *German* (from **deutsch** *German*)
der/die Reisende *traveller* (from **reisend** *travelling*)
der/die Geschiedene *divorcee* (from **geschieden** *divorced*)

Although without adjectival counterpart, **der Beamte** *official, civil servant* is included in this category as it is declined like an adjective. (Its feminine equivalent is, however, **die Beamtin**.)

Neuter adjectival nouns express abstract concepts:

das Gute *the good, that which is good* (from **gut** *good*)
das Edle *that which is noble* (from **edel** *noble*)

Sometimes the English equivalent is a full (abstract) noun, e.g. **sie hat einen ausgeprägten Sinn für das Schöne** *she has a keen sense of beauty.* They are also used to refer to a particular feature or quality, where English has *the . . . thing,* e.g. **das Interessante an diesem Buch** *the interesting thing about this book.* Neuter past participles used as nouns express what has been done or has happened, e.g. **das Erreichte** *what has been/was achieved*, **das soeben Geschehene** *what has just happened*.

Used without the article, neuter adjectival nouns are collective in sense, often being rendered by . . . *things*:

> **er hat auf diesem Gebiet Erstaunliches geleistet** *he has done amazing things in this field*

—likewise the neuter indefinite pronouns (spelt with a small letter), e.g. **manches** *some things*, **mehreres** *several things*. Neuter substantival past participles without the article are often used as collectives, e.g. **Geräuchertes** *smoked foods* (from **geräuchert** *smoked*), **Handgearbeitetes** *hand-made articles* (from **handgearbeitet** *handmade*), **Gefälschtes** *forgeries* (from **gefälscht** *forged*). All these words are in the singular and therefore take a singular verb, unlike their English translations, e.g. **manches war mir unklar** *some things were unclear to me*, **Wichtiges ist vernachlässigt worden** *important things have been neglected*.

MODAL PARTICLES

A number of German adverbs also serve as modal particles. The function of these heavily-used words—which also occur in a variety of combinations—is to indicate a speaker's *attitude* to what he or she is saying; while English has one or two words of this type such as *surely*, *just* it often relies on emphasis or tone of voice (or else phrases like *I suppose*, *I dare say*) to convey the same kind of nuance.

ABER
Reinforces an exclamation:

> **das ist aber originell!** *that is original, I must say!*
> **du kommst aber früh / bist aber gewachsen / siehst aber komisch aus!** *goodness, you are early / have grown / do look odd!*
> **das war aber ein Rennen!** *what a race!, that was some race!*

AUCH
Reinforces a statement:

> **das will auch etwas heißen** *that really means something*

Confirms:

> **sie sah krank aus und sie war es auch** *she looked ill, and she was*

States why something is only to be expected:

> **er spielt sehr gut—er übt aber auch in jeder freien Minute** *he plays very well—but then he uses every free minute to practise*

Corrects an erroneous impression:

> **das hat auch niemand behauptet** *nobody said it was / he would / you did* etc.

Expresses criticism, displeasure:

du bist auch zu gar nichts nütze! *you're absolutely useless!*
er kann auch nie den Mund halten *he never **can** keep his mouth shut*

Seeks reassurance:

hast du die Haustür auch richtig abgeschlossen? *are you sure you locked the front door properly?*
hast du es dir auch gut überlegt? *have you really given it careful thought?*

Conveys exasperation:

warum bist du auch so spät gekommen? *well, why **did** you come so late?*

Reinforces a command:

zieh dich auch immer warm an *make sure you always dress up warmly*
nun hör aber auch zu! *now listen!*

BLOSS (bloß)
Reinforces questions and commands:

warum haben wir unsere Aktien bloß nicht gestern verkauft? *why on earth didn't we sell our shares yesterday?*
wo bleibt er bloß so lange? *wherever has he got to?*
sag bloß nicht, du hast es vergessen *don't tell me you forgot it!*
geh mir bloß aus dem Weg! *get out of my way, will you!*
mach dir bloß keine Sorgen! *don't you worry!*

Expresses a wish:

wenn er bloß bald käme! *if only he'd come soon!*
hätte ich das bloß nicht gesagt! *if only I hadn't said that!*

DENN
Used chiefly in questions; has the effect of making them sound less abrupt:

wer ist denn da? *who's there?*
was ist denn heute mit ihm los? *what's the matter with him today?*
ist sie denn da gewesen? *was she there, then?*
wie geht's dir denn? *how are things?*
was sollen wir denn machen? *what **are** we to do?*
wozu denn? *what for?*

May contain a note of impatience or reproach:

bedient denn hier niemand? *isn't anyone serving here?*
bist du denn blind? *are you blind?*

DOCH
As a stressed particle, contradicts or rectifies:

er hat 'doch gelogen! *I tell you, he **was** lying!*
es ist 'doch wahr! *it **is** true!*

sie hat also 'doch keinen Pass! *so she **hasn't** got a passport!*
ihr wollt also 'doch heiraten? *so you **are** going to get married after all?*

As an unstressed particle, reinforces a statement:

ich bin doch kein Roboter! *I'm not a robot!*
sie fand, dass er im Pyjama doch schon recht alt aussah *she thought that he did look really rather old in his pyjamas*
es wäre doch gelacht, wenn ich das nicht schaffe! *it would be ridiculous if I didn't manage that!*
aber mein Schatz, du weißt doch, dass du bei mir immer an erster Stelle stehst! *but darling, you **know** that you always come first with me!*

Seeks reassurance:

das ist doch nicht dein Ernst! *surely you're not serious?*
du bist mir doch nicht etwa böse? *you're not cross with me, are you?*

Reinforces a command:

beeil dich doch! *do hurry!*
sei doch geduldig! *do be patient!*
reg dich doch nicht so auf! *don't get so worked up!*
(with **endlich**, more impatient) **hör doch endlich auf!** *do stop it, for heaven's sake!*
(with **mal**, encouraging) **schau doch mal vorbei!** *do drop by sometime*

Reinforces an exclamation:

das ist doch unerhört! *that's outrageous!*
wie schön es hier doch ist! *how lovely it is here!*

Expresses an urgent wish:

wenn doch die CDU mehr Mut hätte! *if only the CDU had more courage!*

Indicates an effort to recollect something:

wie heißt doch der Film? *what's the film called again?*

Indicates surprised recognition:

das ist doch Renate! *why, it's Renate!*

EBEN

States an inescapable fact:

wir müssen eben warten, bis der Briefträger kommt *we'll just have to wait till the postman comes*
er ist eben zu nichts zu gebrauchen *he's simply useless*
es ist eben so *that's how it is*
das *ist* es eben! *that's just it!*

In a command, indicates the lack of an alternative:

dann bleib eben zu Hause! *well, just stay at home, then*

ERST
Intensifies:

> **sie ist schon hübsch, aber du solltest erst ihre Schwester sehen!** *she is pretty, I'll grant you, but you should see her sister!*
> **wäre ich erst wieder zu Hause!** *if only I were back home again!*

ETWA
Occurs in questions which the speaker hopes will be contradicted by the person addressed:

> **bist du etwa krank?** *you're not ill, are you?*
> **hast du mich etwa vergessen?** *you don't mean to say you've forgotten me?*
> **Sie sind doch wohl nicht etwa beleidigt?** *surely you're not offended, are you?*

Underlines a negative statement:

> **du brauchst nicht etwa zu denken, ich hätte es nicht bemerkt** *you needn't think I hadn't noticed*

HALT
(*South German*) = **eben**.

JA
As a stressed particle, reinforces a command:

> **sei 'ja vorsichtig!** *do be careful!*
> **erzähl das 'ja nicht deiner Mutter!** *mind you don't tell your mother!*
> **vergiss 'ja nicht, die Rechnung zu bezahlen!** *whatever you do, don't forget to pay the bill!*

As an unstressed particle, draws the listener's attention to something he or she is assumed to know or agree with:

> **du weißt ja, wie er ist** *you know what he's like*
> **sie fährt ja immer Ski** *she's always skiing*
> **wir sind ja alle einmal jung gewesen** *(after all,) we were all young once*

May also give the reason for what is stated in the preceding clause:

> **wir können nicht gehen, sie ist ja noch nicht fertig** *we can't go—she isn't ready yet*
> **mach dir keine Sorgen, du hast ja genug Zeit** *don't worry, you've plenty of time*

In concessive use:

> **sein Plan ist ja interessant, aber unrealistisch** *his plan is interesting but unrealistic*
> **ich kann es ja versuchen, aber** . . . *I can of course try but* . . .

In an exclamation, underlines the utterance or expresses surprise:

> **das ist ja fürchterlich!** *that's just awful!*
> **du bist ja ganz nass!** *oh, you're all wet!*
> **es schneit ja!** *oh, it's snowing!*

or registers the expected arrival of someone or something:

da bist du ja! *ah,* **there** *you are!*

MAL

Used very widely in commands and requests, the tone of which is made less abrupt by its inclusion:

hier, probier mal meinen Stift *here—try my pencil*
hör mal! *listen!*
stell dir das mal vor! *just imagine*
Augenblick mal! *just a minute!*

For **doch mal** see **doch**.

NOCH

Indicates an effort to recollect something:

wie hieß er noch? *what was his name again?*

NUN MAL

Expresses resignation:

ich bin nun mal so *that's the way I am*
damit muss man nun mal rechnen *that's what you have to expect*

NUR

Reinforces questions and commands:

wo bleibt sie nur? *wherever has she got to?*
was hat er nur? *whatever is the matter with him?*
was soll ich nur mit dir anstellen? *what* **am** *I to do with you?*
sag mir nur nicht, du hast mich vergessen! *don't tell me you've forgotten me!*
stell dir nur vor! *just imagine!*
nur nicht so laut! *not so loud!*
nur keine Ausreden! *no excuses!*

Gives encouragement or reassurance:

kommen Sie nur herein! *do come in!*
nur keine Angst! *don't be afraid*

Expresses a wish:

wenn er nur nach Hause kommen würde! *if only he'd come home!*
hätte ich das nur nicht gesagt! *if only I hadn't said that!*

SCHON

Reinforces a statement:

Maria ist schon ein ganz besonderes Mädchen *Maria really is a very special girl*
das war schon erstaunlich / ein Erlebnis *that was quite extraordinary / an experience*

du hast schon Glück gehabt, dass du nicht umgekommen bist! *you're lucky you weren't killed!*

Expresses confidence or reassurance:

ich schaffe das schon *I'll manage(, don't worry)*
sie wird den Schlüssel schon finden *she'll find the key all right*

Expresses scepticism:

wer glaubt schon einem Astrologen? *whoever believes an astrologer?*
was weißt du schon von Informatik? *what do you know about computer science?*
was ändert das schon? *what difference does that make?*

Reinforces a command:

fang schon an! *do start!*
mach schon! *get a move on!*

Used concessively:

wenn ich schon gehen muss *if I **have** to go*
das ist schon wahr, aber . . . *that is true, but . . .*
das schon, aber . . . *yes, I do / she has / they will etc., but . . .*

Used in response to a question or negative assertion:

„Ob man das auch in Deutschland glaubt?"—„In Bayern schon" *'Do they believe that in Germany, too?'—'They do in Bavaria'*
„Das kann man einfach nicht machen!"—„Zu Hause schon!" *'You simply can't do that!'—'You can at home!'*

VIELLEICHT

Reinforces an exclamation:

das ist vielleicht originell! *that **is** original, I **must** say!*
du hast vielleicht Glück! *you **are** lucky!*
da habe ich vielleicht gelacht! *did I laugh!*
das war vielleicht eine Reise! *what a journey (that was)!, that was some journey!*

In yes/no questions, indicates that a negative answer is expected:

ist das vielleicht dein Ernst? *you're not serious, are you?*

WOHL

Expresses a supposition:

du glaubst wohl, ich entschuldige mich bei ihr? *I suppose you think I'm going to apologize to her?*
sie wird wohl den Zug verpasst haben *she's probably missed the train, I expect she's missed the train*
ich war wohl falsch verbunden *I must have got the wrong number*
es sieht wohl so aus *it would seem so*
Mensch, der ist wohl verrückt! *good Lord, he must be crazy!*

Used concessively:

das ist wohl möglich, aber . . . *that is no doubt possible, but* . . .

Reinforces a command:

wirst/willst du wohl damit aufhören! *will you stop that!*

In a question, expresses curiosity:

ob sie wohl mitkommt? *I wonder if she'll come with us?*

wie er wohl mit sechzig aussieht? *what will he look like at sixty, I wonder?*

Numerals

CARDINAL NUMBERS

0	null	21	einundzwanzig
1	eins	22	zweiundzwanzig
2	zwei	23	dreiundzwanzig etc.
3	drei		
4	vier	30	dreißig
5	fünf	40	vierzig ['fɪr-]
6	sechs [-ks]	50	fünfzig
7	sieben	60	sechzig [-ç-]
8	acht	70	siebzig
9	neun	80	achtzig [-xts-]
10	zehn	90	neunzig
11	elf	100	hundert
12	zwölf	101	hunderteins etc.
13	dreizehn	200	zweihundert
14	vierzehn ['fɪr-]	1000	tausend
15	fünfzehn	10 000	zehntausend
16	sechzehn [-ç-]	100 000	hunderttausend
17	siebzehn	1 000 000	eine Million
18	achtzehn [-xts-]	2 000 000	zwei Millionen
19	neunzehn	1 000 000 000	eine Milliarde
20	zwanzig	1 000 000 000 000	eine Billion

Note the omission of **s** in the spelling of **sechzehn** and **sechzig** and of **en** in **siebzehn** and **siebzig**.

Numbers are written as one word, starting with the greatest magnitude, but units—followed by **und**—precede tens, e.g. *2468* is **zweitausendvierhundertachtundsechzig**.

One is **eins**, unless prefixed to another number or **und** + another number, when **ein** is used, e.g. *seventy-one* is **einundsiebzig**. **Ein** is uninflected in **ein bis zwei**, **ein oder zwei** (e.g. **ein oder zwei Minuten lang** *for a minute or two*); also in **ein Uhr** *one o'clock*. Before a noun, **ein** is used with the same endings as those of the indefinite article, e.g. **er hat einen Onkel und eine Tante** *he has one uncle and one aunt* (unlike the indefinite article, **ein** *one* is stressed in spoken German). The pronoun *one* is rendered by **einer**, **eine**, **ein(e)s** (declined like **dieser** etc.), e.g. **einer der Männer sprach mit einer der Frauen** *one of the men was speaking to one of the women*, **ein(e)s der Fotos ist eine Fälschung** *one of the photos is a forgery*.

A special alternative to **zwei** exists in the shape of (the originally feminine) **zwo**, which is used—for example, on the telephone or when a judge announces a score at some sporting event—to avoid confusion between **zwei** and **drei**. **Zwei** and **drei** have genitive forms, **zweier** *of two* and **dreier** *of three*, but in everyday German **von zwei/drei** is usual.

Uninflected and written with a small letter, **hundert** and **tausend** may be used adjectivally, e.g. **hundert Menschen** *a hundred people*, **tausend Bücher** *a thousand books* (note that in **einige hundert/Hundert Menschen, mehrere tausend/Tausend Bücher**, etc. a capital letter is optional). Capitalized and with a plural in **-e**, they function as nouns, e.g. **Hunderte/Tausende von quakenden Fröschen** *hundreds/thousands of croaking frogs* (thus also compounds, e.g. **Hunderttausende von Käfern** *hundreds of thousands of beetles*); unless preceded by **einiger, mehrerer, vieler**, etc. indicating the genitive, they take **-er** in the genitive plural, e.g. **die Ansichten Hunderter** (but **vieler Hunderte**) **von Studenten** *the views of hundreds* (*many hundreds*) *of students*.

Eine Million, eine Milliarde *a billion*, and **eine Billion** *a million million*, U.S. *a trillion* are nouns and are always inflected in the plural, e.g. **zwei Millionen Einwohner** *two million inhabitants*, **Millionen von Sternen** *millions of stars*.

Like **das Hundert** and **das Tausend**, **das Dutzend** *dozen* forms the plural with **-e** (genitive **-er** unless preceded by **einiger, mehrerer, vieler**, etc.) (but after a numeral the singular form is used, e.g. **vier Dutzend Eier** *four dozen eggs*: see p. 38, (ii)).

DECIMALS are separated from whole numbers by a comma, e.g. *17.5* is **17,5** (read **siebzehn Komma fünf**).

Where English uses a comma in the numerical representation of thousands etc. German uses a space or full stop (period) (in numbers of more than four figures).

ORDINAL NUMBERS

1st   **erst-**
2nd **zweit-** (**zwot-**: see *Cardinal numbers*)
3rd **dritt-**

Other ordinals up to 19th are formed by adding **-t** to the cardinal number, e.g. **viert-** *fourth*; *seventh* is **siebt-**, *eighth* is **acht-** (with the loss of one **t**). Ordinals from 20th upwards are formed by adding **-st** to the cardinal, e.g. **zwanzigst-** *twentieth*, **tausendst-** *thousandth*.

When written as figures—Roman numerals included—they are followed by a full stop (period), e.g. **3. [dritter] Versuch** *3rd attempt*, **Heinrich VIII. [der Achte]** *Henry VIII*.

Being adjectives, the ordinal numbers are declined according to the standard adjectival patterns. Ordinals may combine with a superlative, e.g. **zweitgrößt-** *second largest*, **dritthöchst-** *third highest*.

FRACTIONS

Die Hälfte *half* is feminine; all others are neuter, and are formed by adding **-tel** (a reduced form of **Teil** *part*) to the ordinal (whose final **t** is suppressed), e.g. **ein Viertel** ['fɪr-] *a quarter, fourth*, **ein Sechstel** *a sixth*, **ein Zwanzigstel** *a twentieth*, **ein Tausendstel** *a thousandth*, **zwei Drittel** *two thirds*.

. . . *and a half* is expressed by **-(und)einhalb**, e.g. **sechs(und)einhalb** *six and a half*; *one and a half* is usually **anderthalb**, although **ein(und)einhalb** also occurs. (These forms are invariable.)

SUFFIXES ADDED

-ens added to the ordinal number = *-ly*, e.g. **drittens** *thirdly*.
-erlei (invariable) = . . . *kinds of*, e.g. **dreierlei** *three kinds of*.
-fach = *-fold*, e.g. **zweifach** *twofold*.
-mal = . . . *times*, e.g. **vierhundertmal** *four hundred times*.

USE AS NOUNS

Cardinal numbers may be used as nouns; they have feminine gender, and add **-en** to form the plural, e.g. **zwei römische Achten** *two Roman eights*, **die Eins ist gerade abgefahren** *the (number) one has just left*.

DATES

For the days of the month the ordinals are used, as in English, e.g. **der 17.** (pronounced **siebzehnte**) **Juli** *17th July*; as the date on a letter, this is written (e.g.) **Hamburg, den 17. Juli** (or **17.7.** i.e. **siebzehnten siebten**) **2001**. *On 17th July* is **am 17. Juli**. *In 19—, 20—, etc.* is expressed either by the date alone (e.g. **1920 trat er zurück** *in 1920 he resigned*) or by the phrase **im Jahre 1920** etc. A date in the 11th century begins **tausend** . . . , e.g. *1066* is **tausendsechsundsechzig**; in the same way 21st century dates begin **zweitausend**. . . .

The twenties etc. of a century are known as **die zwanziger** etc. **Jahre** (also spelt **Zwanzigerjahre** etc.). Here **-er** is added to the cardinal number (**zwanzig** etc.); the word so formed is invariable (**die zwanziger Jahre, in den zwanziger Jahren** *in the twenties*, etc.). *He's in his twenties* is **er ist in den Zwanzigern**; *she's in her early/mid-/late twenties* is **sie ist Anfang/ Mitte/Ende Zwanzig.**

Prepositions

(For detailed treatment of individual prepositions see pp. 117–154.)

Prepositions in German govern particular cases: accusative (e.g. **für** *for*, **ohne** *without*), genitive (e.g. **trotz** *in spite of*, **während** *during*) or dative (e.g. **aus** *out of, from*, **mit** *with*). Some prepositions govern two cases—accusative and dative—depending on circumstances. If the preposition indicates rest or motion within a place the dative is used:

> **der Rentner saß auf der Bank** *the pensioner was sitting on the bench*
> **das Bild hängt an der Wand** *the picture is hanging on the wall*
> **sie gingen im Garten spazieren** *they went for a walk in the garden*

while if movement to a place is involved the accusative is used:

> **der Rentner setzte sich auf die Bank** *the pensioner sat (down) on the bench*
> **er hängt das Bild an die Wand** *he is hanging the picture on the wall*
> **sie gingen in den Garten hinaus** *they went out into the garden*

In the case of **auf** and **über** the accusative is also the case normally used in figurative contexts, e.g. (with **auf** + ACC.) **eifersüchtig/stolz auf** *jealous/proud of*, **auf diese Weise** *in this way*, **warten auf** *to wait for*, **sich verlassen auf** *to rely on*; (with **über** + ACC.) **über alles Lob erhaben** *beyond praise*, **herrschen über** *to rule over*, **reden/schreiben über** *to talk/write about*, **sich wundern über** *to be surprised at*. (Two important exceptions are **beruhen auf** (+ DAT.) *to be based on* and **bestehen auf** (+ DAT.) *to insist on*.)

Some prepositions may follow the word they govern, e.g. **allen Erwartungen entgegen** *contrary to all expectations*, **der Schule gegenüber** *opposite the school*, **Ihren Anordnungen gemäß** *in accordance with your instructions*, **meiner Ansicht nach** *in my opinion*.

In other instances a preposition is used in conjunction with another word, either preceding the noun (in the case of **bis**, e.g. **bis zu** *as far as; until*) or enclosing it. Examples of the latter type are: **um . . . willen** *for the sake of*, the noun concerned being placed in the genitive, and phrases consisting of preposition (+ noun) + adverb, such as:

an . . . (DAT.) entlang *along* (coast etc.)
auf . . . (ACC.) zu *towards; up to*
hinter . . . (DAT.) her (run etc.) *after*
hinter/unter . . . (DAT.) hervor
  from behind/under
nach . . . hin *towards*

um . . . herum *round*
von . . . an *from . . . (onwards)*
von . . . aus *from*
zu . . . hinaus *out of*
  (door, window)

Some prepositions combine with the definite article in contracted forms:

am = an dem	überm (coll.) = über dem
ans = an das	übers (coll.) = über das
aufs = auf das	ums = um das
beim = bei dem	unterm (coll.) = unter dem
durchs = durch das	unters (coll.) = unter das
fürs = für das	vom = von dem
hinterm (coll.) = hinter dem	vorm (coll.) = vor dem
hinters (coll.) = hinter das	vors (coll.) = vor das
im = in dem	zum = zu dem
ins = in das	zur = zu der

German does not always use a preposition where English has one:

(i) Sometimes German uses a GRAMMATICAL CASE where English has a preposition to indicate the relationship between words, notably:

(a) the DATIVE as the equivalent of *to* (with verbs of giving etc. to indicate the indirect object, e.g. *why did you give it to him?* **warum hast du es ihm gegeben?**, *she wrote to him often* **sie hat ihm oft geschrieben**; also such verbs as *to belong to* **gehören** + DAT., *to correspond to* **entsprechen** + DAT., *to listen to* **zuhören** + DAT., *it seems to me that* . . . **mir scheint, dass** . . . ; usages such as *she was a good mother to him* **sie war ihm eine gute Mutter**; and with some adjectives such as *similar to* **ähnlich** + DAT., *superior to* **überlegen** + DAT., *loyal to* **treu** + DAT., *unknown to* **unbekannt** + DAT., e.g. *their intentions are unknown to me* **ihre Absichten sind mir unbekannt**);
(b) the GENITIVE where English has *of* (e.g. *the coast of Italy* **die Küste Italiens**, *a sense of relief* **ein Gefühl der Erleichterung**), *in* (e.g. *a bend in the road* **eine Biegung der Straße**, *a change in the weather* **eine Änderung des Wetters**), *to* (e.g. *visitors to the museum* **die Besucher des Museums**, *to be witness to a scene* **Zeuge einer Szene sein**).

(ii) In other cases a PREFIX is the German equivalent of an English preposition; thus *from* may be expressed by the separable prefix **ab-** in **ich habe ihm das alte Radio abgekauft** *I bought the old radio from him*, and by the inseparable prefix **ent-** in **sie entriss ihm die Handtasche** *she snatched the handbag from him*, while *at* may be rendered by the separable prefix **zu-** in **sie lächelte ihm zu** *she smiled at him*.

(iii) In certain instances APPOSITION occurs in German where English has *of*, e.g. *a glass of water* **ein Glas Wasser**, *the city of Cologne* **die Stadt Köln**, *the University of Edinburgh* **die Universität Edinburg**, *the Isle of Man* **die Insel Man**, *in the month of May* **im Monat Mai**.
  If (in *a glass of water* etc.) the second noun is qualified by an adjective, German has two possibilities: (a) apposition (with case agreement)—the

usual construction, thus *a glass of cold water* **ein Glas kaltes Wasser,** *I'd like a cup of hot coffee* **ich möchte eine Tasse heißen Kaffee,** *with a piece of French cake* **mit einem Stück französischem Kuchen;** (*b*) the genitive —sometimes encountered in literary style, e.g. **ein Glas kalten Wassers.**

(iv) German often has a COMPOUND NOUN where English has two nouns linked by a preposition, most frequently *of*:

OF

corner of the mouth
   der Mundwinkel
side of the street **die Straßenseite**
year of manufacture **das Baujahr**
colour of (one's) skin **die Hautfarbe**
work of art **das Kunstwerk**
voyage of discovery **die Entdeckungsfahrt**
head of state **das Staatsoberhaupt**
point of departure/view **der Ausgangspunkt / Standpunkt**
sense of direction **der Ortssinn**
knowledge of English **die Englischkenntnisse**

FOR

need for adventure
   das Abenteuerbedürfnis
suggestion for improvement
   der Verbesserungsvorschlag

IN

difference in meaning
   der Bedeutungsunterschied

TO

claim to power
   der Machtanspruch
damage to property **der Sachschaden**

(v) In TIME PHRASES signifying *at the beginning / in the middle / at the end of* German dispenses with a preposition, e.g. *at the beginning of May / this month* **Anfang Mai / dieses Monats,** *in the middle of next week* **Mitte nächster Woche,** *at the end of 1984 / the eighties* **Ende 1984 / der achtziger Jahre.** Similarly, *in* in dates is not translated, thus *in 2003* is simply **2003** (see also p. 65).

The converse is sometimes true:

(i) The sense of the preposition **bei** is often expressed in English by a conjunction:

   beim Überqueren der Straße *when/while crossing the road*
   bei ausgeschalteter Maschine *when the machine is/was switched off*
   bei nasser Fahrbahn *if the road is/was wet*

(ii) Where German uses an intransitive verb with **mit** to express certain acts carried out using a part of the body (or something held in the hand, e.g. a stick or whip) English employs a transitive verb:

   ich nickte mit dem Kopf *I nodded my head*
   wir stampften mit den Füßen *we stamped our feet*
   sie wackelte mit den Hüften *she wiggled her hips*
   der Spaniel wedelte mit dem Schwanz *the spaniel wagged its tail*
   er knallte mit der Peitsche *he cracked his whip*

(iii) **in** (+ ACC.) and **zu** denoting a change of state have no equivalent in English in instances such as:

ein britischer General hat Fort Duquesne in Pittsburgh umbenannt
a British general renamed Fort Duquesne Pittsburgh
er wurde zum Bundeskanzler gewählt *he was elected Federal Chancellor*

Verbs

German verbs, like English verbs, fall broadly into two groups: weak and strong verbs. WEAK verbs form the past tense by adding -te to the stem, and the past participle by prefixing ge- to the stem and adding -t; there are also some irregular verbs that are conjugated weak but which also exhibit vowel change in the past tense and past participle. STRONG verbs change the stem vowel in the past tense and, in most cases, the past participle; the latter has the prefix ge- and ends in -en.

Examples:

WEAK. **leben** *to live* (stem: **leb-**), past **lebte** *lived*, past participle **gelebt** *lived*
IRREGULAR WEAK. **nennen** *to name*, past **nannte** *named*, past participle **genannt** *named*
STRONG. **singen** *to sing*, past **sang** *sang*, past participle **gesungen** *sung*

CONJUGATION OF VERBS

The conjugation of weak and strong verbs is as follows:

INDICATIVE

	WEAK (Examples: **leben** *to live*, **arbeiten** *to work*)		STRONG (Examples: **singen** *to sing*, **graben** *to dig*)	
PRESENT TENSE				
ich	lebe	arbeite	singe	grabe
du	lebst	arbeitest	singst	gräbst
er/sie/es	lebt	arbeitet	singt	gräbt
wir	leben	arbeiten	singen	graben
ihr	lebt	arbeitet	singt	grabt
sie, Sie	leben	arbeiten	singen	graben
PAST TENSE				
ich	lebte	arbeitete	sang	grub
du	lebtest	arbeitetest	sangst	grubst
er/sie/es	lebte	arbeitete	sang	grub
wir	lebten	arbeiteten	sangen	gruben
ihr	lebtet	arbeitetet	sangt	grubt
sie, Sie	lebten	arbeiteten	sangen	gruben

PERFECT TENSE

= present tense of the auxiliary **haben** (p. 74) + past participle (usually at end of clause); in the case of verbs of motion or change of state (e.g. **kommen** *to come*, **einschlafen** *to fall asleep*), verbs meaning *to happen* (e.g. **geschehen**) or *to succeed* or *fail* (e.g. **gelingen, misslingen: es gelingt, misslingt**),[29] **bleiben** *to remain*, and **sein** *to be*, the auxiliary **sein** (p. 74) is used instead of **haben** (cf. archaic English *I am come, Christ is risen*, etc.); e.g.:

> **ich habe** etc. . . . **gelebt** *I have* etc. *lived*
> **ich bin** etc. . . . **gekommen** *I have* etc. *come*

In the South, **sein** is also used with **liegen** *to lie*, **sitzen** *to sit*, and **stehen** *to stand*, e.g. **da ist die Leiche gelegen** *that's where the body was lying*.

Some verbs of motion take **sein** if indicating movement to a place or distance covered (e.g. **ich bin zur Insel / hundert Meter geschwommen** *I swam to the island / a hundred metres*), but **haben** or **sein** if an activity as such is referred to (e.g. **ich habe/bin zwei Stunden geschwommen** *I've been swimming for two hours*, **wir haben/sind in diesem Sommer viel gesegelt** *we've done a lot of sailing this summer*). The verbs concerned are: **paddeln** *to paddle* (a canoe), **reiten** *to ride*, **rudern** *to row*, **schwimmen** *to swim*, **segeln** *to sail*, **tauchen** *to dive*.

PLUPERFECT TENSE

= past tense of the auxiliary **haben** (or **sein** where appropriate) + past participle (usually at end of clause), e.g.:

> **ich hatte** etc. . . . **gelebt** *I* etc. *had lived*
> **ich war** etc. . . . **gekommen** *I* etc. *had come*

FUTURE TENSE

= present tense of the auxiliary **werden** (p. 74) + infinitive (usually at end of clause), e.g.:

> **ich werde** etc. . . . **leben** *I shall* etc. *live*
> **ich werde** etc. . . . **kommen** *I shall* etc. *come*

FUTURE PERFECT TENSE

= present tense of the auxiliary **werden** + (usually at end of clause) past participle + **haben** (or **sein** where appropriate), e.g.:

> **ich werde** etc. . . . **gelebt haben** *I shall* etc. *have lived*
> **ich werde** etc. . . . **gekommen sein** *I shall* etc. *have come*

NOTES on verb forms:

(i) WEAK VERBS IN -**eln**, -**ern**: The stem of these verbs is obtained by removing the final n; thus **rudern** *to row* has as its stem **ruder-** (present indicative **rudere, ruderst, rudert**, pl. **rudern, rudert, rudern**; past **ruderte** etc.; past participle **gerudert**). In

---

[29] Exception: **klappen** *to work out all right* (**es hat geklappt**).

the 1st singular present the **e** is often omitted in verbs in **-eln** (e.g. **ich hand(e)le** *I act*), seldom in **-ern** verbs.

(ii) VERBS WITH STEM ENDING IN **d** OR **t**: (*a*) In weak verbs of this type the stem is followed by **e** throughout (present indicative -e, -est, -et, pl. -en, -et, -en; past -ete etc.; past participle ge—et), e.g. **arbeiten** (see tables above), **reden** *to talk*. (*b*) In the present tense of strong verbs which do not change the stem vowel (e.g. **leiden** *to suffer*) the stem is likewise followed by **e** (thus 2nd and 3rd singular **leidest, leidet**). Those that do change the stem vowel, e.g. **halten** *to hold, keep*, etc., **raten** *to advise, guess*, **gelten** *to be valid* etc., add **-st, -** (zero ending) to the stem in the 2nd and 3rd singular respectively, thus **hältst, hält; rätst, rät; giltst, gilt**; but several verbs deviate slightly from this pattern, namely **bersten** *to burst*, **laden** *to load*, **treten** *to step*, **werden** *to become*: **birst, birst; lädst, lädt; trittst, tritt; wirst, wird**. In the past tense, **e** is inserted in the 2nd plural (e.g. **littet, hieltet, ludet**).

(iii) WEAK VERBS WITH STEM ENDING IN A CONSONANT (EXCEPT **l, r**) + **m, n**: As with weak verbs in the preceding category, the stem is followed throughout by **e**, e.g. (with the same endings as those shown at (ii) for weak verbs) **widmen** *to dedicate*, **atmen** *to breathe*, **leugnen** *to deny*, **öffnen** *to open*, **zeichnen** *to draw*.

(iv) VERBS WITH STEM ENDING IN (*a*) **s, ss, ß, tz, z**: the 2nd singular present normally has the ending **-t** and thus coincides with the 3rd singular, e.g. (**wachsen** *to grow*) **wächst**, (**beißen** *to bite*) **beißt**, (**schwitzen** *to sweat*) **schwitzt**; (*b*) **sch**: the 2nd singular present retains the **s** of the normal **-st** ending, e.g. (**waschen** *to wash*) **wäschst**. The 2nd singular past of strong verbs (*a, b*) has **-est**, e.g. (**wachsen**) **wuchsest**, but informally the ending may be reduced to **-t**, e.g. **wuchst**.

(v) Many STRONG VERBS CHANGE THE STEM VOWEL in the 2nd and 3rd singular present (**a > ä, e > i** or **ie, o > ö, au > äu**), e.g. (**graben**, see above) **gräbst, gräbt**; (**helfen** *to help*) **hilfst, hilft**; (**lesen** *to read*) **liest, liest**; (**stoßen** *to push*) **stößt, stößt**; (**laufen** *to run*) **läufst, läuft**.

SUBJUNCTIVE

	PRESENT		PAST	
	(WEAK)	(STRONG)	(WEAK)	(STRONG)
ich	lebe*	grabe*	lebte	grübe
du	lebest*	grabest*	lebtest	grüb(e)st
er/sie/es	lebe	grabe	lebte	grübe
wir	leben*	graben*	lebten	grüben
ihr	lebet*	grabet*	lebtet	grüb(e)t
sie, Sie	leben*	graben*	lebten	grüben

*The asterisked forms of the present subjective do not normally occur in practice, being replaced by the corresponding forms of the past subjunctive.

The traditional terms for the two basic tenses of the subjunctive—the 'present subjunctive' and 'past subjunctive', parallel to the present and past indicative—are here retained as they are widely used and familiar to many readers. It should, however, be borne in mind that (unlike in the indicative) no difference of time is implied. (It is for this reason that German grammarians nowadays refer to the two tenses as **Konjunktiv I** and **II**.)

The PAST SUBJUNCTIVE OF STRONG VERBS is formed with the endings shown above (**grübe** etc.). Where possible, the vowel of the past indicative is mutated (e.g. **sang** *sang*, subjunctive **sänge**); in certain instances a mutated vowel not corresponding to that of the indicative is used (e.g. **half** *helped*, subjunctive **hülfe**; **starb** *died*, subjunctive **stürbe**; **schalt** *scolded*, subjunctive **schölte**), while in a few cases both forms of past subjunctive exist side by side (e.g. **stand** *stood*, subjunctive **stünde**, **stände**). The PAST SUBJUNCTIVE—rarely used—OF THE IRREGULAR WEAK VERBS **brennen**, **kennen**, **nennen**, and **rennen** has the same vowel as the present tense (**brennte** etc.); **senden** and **wenden** have **sendete**, **wendete**; **bringen** and **denken** mutate the vowel of the indicative: **brächte**, **dächte**.

The COMPOUND TENSES are formed as for the indicative, except that the subjunctive forms of the auxiliaries **haben**, **sein**, and **werden** are used in place of the indicative forms.

IMPERATIVES: e.g. (singular) **leb(e)!**, **grab(e)!**; (plural) **lebt!**, **grabt!**; (**Sie** form) **leben Sie!**, **graben Sie!** Where the ending -e is optional the form without -e is generally preferred except in more elevated style, e.g. **frag deinen Onkel!** *ask your uncle!*, **schlaf gut!** *sleep well!*

Verbs such as **atmen**, **öffnen** (see p. 72, Note (iii)) do not drop the ending, e.g. **atme!** *breathe!*, **öffne!** *open!*; verbs in -eln likewise retain it, but often omit the penultimate e, e.g. **hand(e)le!** *act!* Strong verbs that change e to i or ie in the 2nd and 3rd singular present also have this change of vowel in the imperative singular (-e is not added, except in **siehe** (direction in or to a book etc.) *see*), e.g. (**helfen**) **hilf!**, (**lesen**) **lies!** (Strong verbs that mutate other vowels in the 2nd and 3rd singular, on the other hand, do not mutate in the imperative, e.g. (**blasen**) **blas(e)!**, (**laufen**) **lauf(e)!**)

PARTICIPLES: e.g. (present) **lebend**, **grabend**; (past: weak) **gelebt**, **gearbeitet**, (strong) **gesungen**, **gegraben**.

PAST PARTICIPLES:

(i) The prefix **ge-** is omitted from the past participle of verbs not stressed on the first syllable, i.e. verbs with an inseparable prefix (e.g. **beginnen** *to begin*, past participle **begonnen**), those ending in -ieren (e.g. **halbieren** *to halve*, past participle **halbiert**) and a handful of other verbs such as **offenbaren** *to reveal*, **prophezeien** *to prophesy*, **schmarotzen** *to sponge*. It is also omitted where a separable prefix is attached to such verbs, e.g. **anerkennen** *to acknowledge*, **ausrangieren** *to discard* (past participles **anerkannt**, **ausrangiert**).

(ii) The *modal verbs* (**dürfen**, **können**, etc.—see below) have *two past participles*: one formed with ge- (**gedurft**, **gekonnt**, etc.) and one identical with the infinitive, used when a dependent infinitive precedes the past participle. A few other verbs also have a second past participle analogous to those of the modal verbs, notably **brauchen** (with a negative, e.g. **er hat nicht zu schießen brauchen** *he didn't need to shoot*), **hören** *to hear* and **sehen** *to see* (e.g. **ich habe ihn kommen sehen** *I saw him come*), and **lassen** (e.g. **er hat die Teller fallen lassen** *he dropped the plates*, **sie hat es auf der Fensterbank liegen lassen** *she left it on the window-sill*—although the participle with **ge-** (**fallen gelassen** etc.) may, and in the passive must, be used).

PASSIVE VOICE

The passive is formed by using the appropriate tense of **werden** together with the past participle of the verb concerned (which usually goes to the end of the clause). In the perfect and pluperfect tenses the past participle of **werden** takes the form **worden**. The future passive is often replaced by the present passive.

PRESENT TENSE

e.g. **ich werde** etc. . . . **gefragt** *I am* etc. *asked*

PAST TENSE

e.g. **ich wurde** etc. . . . **gefragt** *I was* etc. *asked*

PERFECT TENSE

e.g. **ich bin** etc. . . . **gefragt worden** *I have* etc. *been asked*

PLUPERFECT TENSE

e.g. **ich war** etc. . . . **gefragt worden** *I* etc. *had been asked*

FUTURE TENSE

e.g. **ich werde** etc. . . . **gefragt werden** *I shall* etc. *be asked*

FUTURE PERFECT TENSE

e.g. **ich werde** etc. . . . **gefragt worden sein** *I shall* etc. *have been asked*

CONJUGATION OF **HABEN**, **SEIN**, AND **WERDEN**

	haben		sein		werden	
	INDIC.	SUBJ.	INDIC.	SUBJ.	INDIC.	SUBJ.
PRESENT TENSE						
ich	habe	habe*	bin	sei	werde	werde*
du	hast	habest*	bist	sei(e)st	wirst	werdest*
er/sie/es	hat	habe	ist	sei	wird	werde
wir	haben	haben*	sind	seien	werden	werden*
ihr	habt	habet*	seid	seiet*	werdet	werdet*
sie, Sie	haben	haben*	sind	seien	werden	werden*

*The asterisked forms are in practice normally replaced by the past subjunctive.

PAST TENSE

ich	hatte	hätte	war	wäre	wurde	würde
du	hattest	hättest	warst	wär(e)st	wurdest	würdest
er/sie/es	hatte	hätte	war	wäre	wurde	würde
wir	hatten	hätten	waren	wären	wurden	würden
ihr	hattet	hättet	wart	wär(e)t	wurdet	würdet
sie, Sie	hatten	hätten	waren	wären	wurden	würden

The COMPOUND TENSES are formed in the usual way (**sein** and **werden** take the auxiliary **sein**): (perfect) **ich habe** etc. . . . **gehabt, ich bin** etc. . . . **gewesen, ich bin** etc. . . . **geworden**; (pluperfect) **ich hatte** etc. . . . **gehabt, ich war** etc. . . . **gewesen, ich war** etc. . . . **geworden**; (future) **ich werde** etc. . . . **haben/sein/werden**; (future perfect) **ich werde** etc. . . . **gehabt haben / gewesen sein / geworden sein**. (For the subjunctive substitute the corresponding subjunctive forms of the auxiliaries **haben** or **sein** as appropriate.)

IMPERATIVES: (singular) **hab(e)!, sei!, werde!**; (plural) **habt!, seid!, werdet!**; (Sie form) **haben Sie!, seien Sie!, werden Sie!**

PARTICIPLES: (present) **habend, seiend, werdend**; (past) **gehabt, gewesen, geworden** or (in passive constructions) **worden**.

CONJUGATION OF MODAL VERBS AND **WISSEN**

German has a set of verbs called 'modal' verbs—related to the English modals *can, may*, etc.—which, unlike their English cognates, also have an infinitive form. They are **dürfen** *to be allowed to* (present *darf* etc. also *may*), **können** *to be able to* (**kann** etc. also *can*), **mögen** *to like (to)* (**mag** etc. also *may*), **müssen** *to have to* (**muss** etc. also *must*), **sollen** *to be (supposed) to*, **wollen** *to want (to)*. These verbs (the meanings and uses of which are treated more fully on p. 95) exhibit several special features: (*a*) the 1st and 3rd singular present forms are identical (like their English counterparts: *I can, he can*); (*b*) the vowel of the present singular differs from that of the plural and infinitive (except in the case of **sollen**); (*c*) each modal verb has two past participles, one with **ge-** and one (used with a dependent infinitive) identical with the infinitive; (*d*) a dependent infinitive is used without **zu**, e.g. **er wollte es nicht lesen** *he did not want to read it*.

The conjugation of the modal verbs is shown together with that of the similarly-conjugated **wissen** *to know*:

	dürfen	können	mögen	müssen	sollen	wollen	wissen

PRESENT TENSE (INDICATIVE)

ich	darf	kann	mag	muss	soll	will	weiß
du	darfst	kannst	magst	musst	sollst	willst	weißt
er/sie/es	darf	kann	mag	muss	soll	will	weiß
wir	dürfen	können	mögen	müssen	sollen	wollen	wissen
ihr	dürft	könnt	mögt	müsst	sollt	wollt	wisst
sie, Sie	dürfen	können	mögen	müssen	sollen	wollen	wissen

The PRESENT SUBJUNCTIVE is regular, having the vowel of the infinitive throughout: (dürfen) ich dürfe, du dürfest, er/sie/es dürfe, wir dürfen, ihr dürfet, sie and Sie dürfen; (können) ich könne etc.; (mögen) ich möge etc.; (müssen) ich müsse etc.; (sollen) ich solle etc.; (wollen) ich wolle etc.; (wissen) ich wisse etc. (The plural forms are in practice normally replaced by the past subjunctive.)

PAST TENSE (INDICATIVE)

ich	durfte	konnte	mochte	musste	sollte	wollte	wusste
du	durftest	konntest	mochtest	musstest	solltest	wolltest	wusstest
er/sie/es	durfte	konnte	mochte	musste	sollte	wollte	wusste
wir	durften	konnten	mochten	mussten	sollten	wollten	wussten
ihr	durftet	konntet	mochtet	musstet	solltet	wolltet	wusstet
sie, Sie	durften	konnten	mochten	mussten	sollten	wollten	wussten

The PAST SUBJUNCTIVE is conjugated like the indicative, but (except in the case of sollen, wollen) with the vowel mutated: (dürfen) ich dürfte etc.; (können) ich könnte etc.; (mögen) ich möchte etc.; (müssen) ich müsste etc.; (sollen) ich sollte etc.; (wollen) ich wollte etc.; (wissen) ich wüsste etc.

The COMPOUND TENSES are regular. A special feature of the *perfect* and *pluperfect* is that they are constructed with either (*a*) a past participle of the type ge—t, e.g. ich habe ihn nie gemocht *I never liked him*, or (*b*) (if another infinitive is dependent on the modal) a past participle identical with the infinitive, e.g. ich habe es nicht lesen können *I was unable to read it*, sie hatte es bezahlen müssen *she had had to pay for it*. In the *future* the modal verb follows its infinitive, e.g. ich werde kommen können *I shall be able to come*.

IMPERATIVES of wissen: wisse!; wisst!; wissen Sie!

PAST PARTICIPLES: (*a*) gedurft, gekonnt, gemocht, gemusst, gesollt, gewollt, gewusst; (*b*) (modal verbs only: with dependent infinitive) dürfen, können, mögen, müssen, sollen, wollen.

USE OF TENSES

Unlike English, German does not have both simple and continuous forms; the context normally makes clear whether, for example, sie isst Pfannkuchen means *she eats pancakes* or *she is eating pancakes*.

(i) The PRESENT tense may refer not only to present actions and events but very often also—as sometimes in English—to those in the future when the context makes it clear that future time is meant:

ich bin gleich wieder da *I'll be right back*
ich fahre morgen nach Köln *I'm going to Cologne tomorrow*
sie findet es nie *she'll never find it*

As the historic present it may also 'bring alive' past occurrences in vivid narrative style:

der Prinz ist zwölf Jahre alt, als sein Vater stirbt *the prince was twelve years old when his father died*

An important difference in usage between the two languages is that an action begun in the past and still going on is expressed in English by the perfect tense, in German by the present tense:

ich bin seit 3 Uhr / seit Jahren hier *I've been here since 3 o'clock / for years*

In negative statements both languages have the perfect:

ich habe ihn seit Jahren nicht (mehr) gesehen *I haven't seen him for years*

(ii) Reporting the past:

(*a*) The PAST tense reports past actions and events, and is the tense in which most narrative prose is written:

Im Herbst des Jahres 1787 unternahm Mozart in Begleitung seiner Frau eine Reise nach Prag (Mörike) *In the autumn of 1787 Mozart, accompanied by his wife, went on a journey to Prague*
Sie warf mir einen scheuen feindseligen Blick zu und blickte sich suchend um (Ernst Penzoldt) *She gave me a shy, hostile glance and looked round in search of something*

It may also describe a past state or situation:

sie sah krank aus *she looked ill*
er saß in der Ecke und las *he sat in the corner reading*

In addition, the past tense is used in: **es wirkten mit** . . . *those taking part were* . . . , **Sie hörten/sahen** . . . *you have been listening to/watching.* . . .

In sentences such as:

ich wartete seit 3 Uhr/seit Jahren *I'd been waiting since 3 o'clock/for years*

the use of the past tense—where English has the pluperfect—is analogous to the use of the present described in (i) above, 2nd paragraph. In negative statements both languages have the pluperfect:

ich hatte ihn seit Jahren nicht (mehr) gesehen *I hadn't seen him for years*

(*b*) The PERFECT tense is used, like its English counterpart, to refer to past events that have a bearing on the present:

er hat viele Romane gelesen *he has read many novels*
es hat geschneit! *it's been snowing!*
ist er schon angekommen? *has he arrived yet?*

In spoken German it is also extensively used to refer to past actions and events (where English has the past tense):

wir sind letztes Jahr nach Indien getrampt *last year we hitch-hiked to India*
**in Piräus haben sie Schilder mit der Aufschrift „Not inside the grass"
entdeckt** *in Piraeus they discovered signs saying 'Not inside the grass'*
sie hat in einem Hotel gearbeitet *she worked in a hotel*

Here the perfect tense has made considerable inroads on the territory of the past tense; but past tense forms (including those of **haben, sein, werden,** the modal auxiliaries and such widely used verbs as **denken, sagen, gehen, kommen, stehen**) are still common—except in the South, where the colloquial perfect reigns supreme.

Just as the present tense is often used to indicate future time, so the perfect is commonly employed in place of a future perfect:

bis du zurückkommst, habe ich das Buch zu Ende gelesen *by the time you return I'll have finished the book*

In subordinate clauses the perfect may be used in both English and German with the force of a future perfect:

ich möchte lieber warten, bis wir genug gespart haben *I'd prefer to wait until we've saved enough*

USED TO, WOULD: The force of *used to* is usually conveyed by the adverb **früher**:

Südtirol gehörte früher zu Österreich *South Tyrol used to be part of Austria*
er hat früher bei der Post gearbeitet *he used to work for the Post Office*
sie kommen nicht so oft wie früher *they don't come as often as they used to*

—except where another adverb of time makes **früher** redundant. *Would* indicating habitual action as in *she would visit her two nieces every year* is expressed by the past tense:

sie besuchte jedes Jahr ihre beiden Nichten

(c) The PLUPERFECT tense is used like its English counterpart:

ich hatte den Wecker nicht gehört *I hadn't heard the alarm clock*
sie waren beim Fernsehen eingenickt *they had nodded off while watching TV*

(iii) Future time is often expressed by the present tense (see (i), 1st paragraph). The FUTURE tense may be used to indicate a future event:

die Messe wird nächstes Jahr in Mailand stattfinden *the fair will be held in Milan next year* to predict:

die Preise werden wohl wieder steigen *prices will probably go up again*

to express an intention:

ich werde es mir überlegen *I'll think about it*

(In this last function **werden** competes with **wollen: ich will es mir über-legen**. But only **wollen** is used (*a*) to express the idea of willingness to do something, e.g. **willst du mir helfen?** *will you help me?*, **die Russen wollen nicht unterschreiben** *the Russians won't sign*, (*b*) to make a suggestion, e.g. **wollen wir ins Museum gehen?** *shall we go to the museum?*)

The future tense, often supported by the adverbs **schon** or **wohl**, may also suggest a probability:

sie wird schon recht haben *I expect she's right*
es wird schon so sein, wie er sagt *it'll be as he says*

This is also true of the future perfect:

er wird (wohl) zu viel gegessen haben *I expect he's eaten too much*
sie werden inzwischen abgereist sein *they'll have left by now*
es wird ihm doch nichts passiert sein? *I trust nothing's happened to him?*

THE PASSIVE

In the passive the direct object of an active construction (e.g. *the article* in *I wrote the article*) becomes the subject (*the article was written by me*).

The German passive is formed with the auxiliary **werden** + the past participle of the verb:

die Brücke wird gebaut *the bridge is being built*
das Haus wurde selten angestrichen *the house was rarely painted*
er ist/war angegriffen worden *he has/had been attacked*
(with the present passive indicating future time):
der neue Bahnhof wird am Montag eröffnet *the new station will be opened on Monday*
wann werde ich abgeholt? *when will I be collected?*

Unlike English *to be*, **sein**—which normally denotes a state, not an action —is *not* used to form the passive.[30] A clear distinction needs to be made between, for example, *the bridge was built* (= the construction of the bridge was carried out) **die Brücke wurde gebaut** and *the bridge was built* (= was complete) **die Brücke war gebaut**. (In the latter statement the past participle functions like an adjective.)

---

[30] **Werden** is, however, replaced by **sein** as the auxiliary for passive statements (*a*) in the imperative and present subjunctive, e.g. **es sei darauf hingewiesen, dass . . .** *attention is drawn to the fact that . . .* , (*b*) (sometimes) in the infinitive, when used with a modal verb, e.g. **das will vorsichtig gemacht sein** *that needs to be done carefully.*

The AGENT (the subject of the verb in an active construction, the 'doer') in a passive construction is usually indicated by the preposition **von** by:

> **die Buchdruckerkunst ist von Gutenberg erfunden worden** *printing was invented by Gutenberg*
>
> **er wurde von seiner Mutter geweckt** *he was awoken by his mother*

Although used chiefly with a person as agent, **von** may also occur with an inanimate agent if it is perceived as the 'doer' of the action:

> **Guernica wurde von Hitlers Bombern zerstört** *Guernica was destroyed by Hitler's bombers*

The MEANS by which an action is carried out is usually indicated by **durch** (also *by*):

> **er wurde durch den Lärm geweckt** *he was woken by the noise*
>
> **Guernica wurde durch Hitlers Bomben zerstört** *Guernica was destroyed by Hitler's bombs*

Following a verbal noun the agent is, exceptionally, indicated by **durch**:

> **die Erfindung der Buchdruckerkunst durch Gutenberg** *the invention of printing by Gutenberg*

Points about the passive:

(i) *I WAS OFFERED, TOLD, ETC.*: A significant difference between English and German usage lies in the fact that in English the indirect object of the verb (in the active) can become the subject of the passive (e.g. *I was offered a place at London University*), whereas in German this is not possible—only the direct object (here *a place*, which is what is really being offered) can become the subject of the passive: **mir wurde ein Studienplatz an der Universität London angeboten**; cf. *I was told that that was not true* **mir wurde** (or **es wurde mir**) **gesagt, dass das nicht stimmte**, *I was ordered to shoot* **mir wurde** (or **es wurde mir**) **befohlen zu schießen** (**befehlen** *to order* takes the dative).

(ii) *ALTERNATIVES TO THE PASSIVE*: Often where the passive is used in English, German employs some other construction. Very commonly, when no agent is specified, **man** is used with an active verb:

> **man hat gesagt, dass** . . . *it has been said that* . . .
>
> **man hörte ihn singen** *he was heard singing*

In the case of verbs taking an indirect object in the active, an active construction with **man** may be preferred:

> **man hat mir einen Studienplatz angeboten** *I was offered a place*
>
> **man versprach uns bessere Arbeitsbedingungen** *we were promised better working conditions*
>
> **man hat ihr einen anderen Arzt empfohlen** *she was recommended another doctor*

while sometimes a construction with **bekommen** + past participle is used:

sie hat das Buch zugeschickt bekommen *she was sent the book*
ich habe einen Studienplatz angeboten bekommen *I was offered a place*

To be given something and *to be told something* are often expressed in German by the active verbs **bekommen** and **erfahren**, e.g. *I was given a present by them* **ich habe von ihnen ein Geschenk bekommen**, *at the airport I was told that the plane was two hours late* **am Flughafen erfuhr ich, dass das Flugzeug zwei Stunden Verspätung hatte**.

Sometimes German uses a REFLEXIVE VERB, in 'cases where things come about of themselves' (George O. Curme), e.g. **sich widerspiegeln in** *to be reflected in*, **sich erfüllen** (of wish etc.) *to be fulfilled*, **sich bestätigen** (of suspicion etc.) *to be confirmed*; and sometimes an INTRANSITIVE VERB, e.g. **heißen** *to be called*, **gelten als** *to be regarded as*, **erschrecken** *to be frightened*, **ertrinken** *to be drowned*, **umkommen** *to be killed*, **verloren gehen** (of thing) *to get lost*, **heiraten** *to get married*.

Where English has *can* + passive, German very frequently uses **lassen** + **sich** + infinitive:

das lässt sich machen *that can be done*
Prousts Werke lassen sich nicht leicht zusammenfassen *Proust's works cannot easily be summarized*

NOTE: An active construction with inverted word order (see p. 105) in German frequently corresponds to a parallel passive construction in English, e.g. **schon am nächsten Tag besuchten ihn seine Freunde aus Neapel** *the very next day he was visited by his friends from Naples*, **mich fasziniert der Gedanke, dass . . .** *I'm fascinated by the thought that . . .*

(iii) THE IMPERSONAL PASSIVE: A widely-used construction in German is the impersonal passive, which is used with *intransitive* verbs to indicate an activity without reference to a specific agent:

es wurde gestreikt *there was a strike*
freitags wurde getanzt *on Fridays there was dancing*
wann wird geheiratet? *when's the wedding?*

(with a personal subject—*someone*—supplied in the English translation):

er muss immer fürchten, dass mitgehört wird *he always has to fear that someone is listening in*

(with a prepositional object, again with a personal subject supplied in the translation):

an der neuen Schule wird bereits zwei Jahre gebaut *they've already been working on the new school for two years*

Note that the impersonal **es** is omitted when not in initial position.

THE SUBJUNCTIVE

The subjunctive mood survives in English only in a limited number of constructions of the type *they requested that he **withdraw** from the contest* and in a few petrified usages such as *be that as it may*, *if I **were** you*, **suffice** *it to say* or indeed *Britannia **rule** the waves*. In German, by contrast, it continues to play a major role as the second mood of the verb alongside the indicative; and the student of German needs to be familiar with its forms and uses.

Chief uses of the subjunctive:

(i) INDIRECT (or REPORTED) SPEECH: In *written* German, e.g. in newspaper reports, when the verb in the main clause (the 'verb of saying') is in the *past* tense, the verb in the subordinate clause goes into the subjunctive (**dass** is very frequently omitted); unlike its English counterpart, it retains the tense of the original statement or question:

> **sie sagte, er *habe* sie missverstanden** (original statement: **er hat mich missverstanden**) *she said he had misunderstood her*
> **ich fragte ihn, ob er teilnehmen *könne*** (original question: **können Sie teilnehmen?**) *I asked him if he could take part*

Where, however, the present subjunctive forms are identical with the indicative forms (e.g. **ich habe**, **wir spielen**) and therefore not distinctive, the past subjunctive is used instead:

> **sie sagte, ich *hätte* sie missverstanden** *she said I had misunderstood her*
> **er behauptete, wir *spielten* kein Tennis** *he maintained we did not play tennis*

A common alternative—although not in newspaper reports—is the indicative with (except in the case of questions) **dass**, again with the verb in the tense of the original utterance:

> **sie sagte, dass er sie missverstanden *hat***
> **ich fragte ihn, ob er teilnehmen *kann***

In *spoken* German the present subjunctive is avoided, and either the past subjunctive or the present indicative (the tense of the original utterance) used instead:

> **sie sagte, er *hätte/hat* sie missverstanden**
> **ich fragte ihn, ob er teilnehmen *könnte/kann***

When the verb of saying is in the *present* tense, it is usually followed by the indicative:

> **er sagt, dass er an einem Reiseführer *schreibt*** *he says he is writing a guidebook*

but the subjunctive (again often without **dass**) may also be used:

> **er sagt, dass er an einem Reiseführer *schreibe***

—implicit here, as always, in the subjunctive of indirect speech is an attitude of detachment on the part of the speaker or writer: no view is expressed as to the truth or otherwise of the words reported.

As the subjunctive reports what has been said, it is naturally much used in newspaper reports where someone's opinion or account of something is being quoted; and since the subjunctive forms are clearly recognizable as indicating indirect speech, German is able to dispense with the phrases (of the type *he said, they maintained*, and so on) that from time to time may need to be used in an English text to indicate that indirect speech is continuing. The following extract from a newspaper report illustrates the use of the subjunctive to express indirect speech:

Vor Journalisten sagte er, er *werde* solange in Frankreich bleiben, bis sein Volk dem Weg der Demokratie *folge*. ,,Ich bin hier, um den Widerstand meines Volkes zu ermutigen." Er *habe* seit seiner Amtsenthebung in T. gelebt, und es *sei* ihm sogar möglich gewesen, ,,in den Straßen umherzugehen, ohne entdeckt zu werden".

*Speaking to journalists he said that he **would** stay in France until such time as his people **followed** the path of democracy. 'I am here to encourage the resistance of my people.' He **had** [, he went on,] been living in T. since his removal from office, and it **had** even been possible for him 'to walk about the streets without being discovered'.*

Sometimes verbs of saying are omitted altogether, since the subjunctive itself implies that a person's words are being reported (which in translation is conveyed by phrases of the *he/she said* type):

Er hat mir schon beim ersten Telefongespräch einen Besuch in W. ausgeredet. Da *sei* nichts zu sehen *He talked me out of visiting W. in our very first phone call. **He said** there wasn't anything to see there*

The subjunctive is also used following verbs (or their corresponding nouns) referring to an *opinion* or *belief* from which the writer or speaker wishes to distance him- or herself:

er bildet sich ein, er *sei* Napoleon *he imagines he is Napoleon*
der Glaube, dass der Krieg unabwendbar *sei* *the belief that war is (was) inevitable*
es ist ein Irrtum zu meinen, dass Umweltschutz wenig Geld *koste* *it's a mistake to think that conservation doesn't cost much money*

Where an assumption has subsequently been proved false, the subjunctive is again used:

ich dachte, du *hättest* meinen Brief bekommen *I thought you'd received my letter*

(ii) CONDITIONAL STATEMENTS (so-called 'unreal condition'—referring to an improbable eventuality, expressed by the past subjunctive, or one that was but is no longer possible, expressed by the pluperfect subjunctive):

(past subjunctive) **wenn ich ein Wörterbuch *hätte*, könnte ich das Wort nachschlagen** *if I had a dictionary I could look the word up*
(pluperfect subjunctive) **wenn er *gekommen wäre*, hätten wir viel Spaß gehabt** *if he had come we'd have had a lot of fun*

(If the verb in the *if* clause is in the present tense ('open condition') the indicative is used, e.g. **wenn es regnet, können wir ins Theater gehen** *if it rains we can go to the theatre.*)

The past subjunctive forms that are in regular use are **hätte** and **wäre**, the modal auxiliaries **dürfte, könnte, möchte, müsste, sollte, wollte** (and South German **bräuchte**) and those of the commonest strong verbs (e.g. **ginge, käme, ließe, täte**) together with **wüsste**. (Past subjunctives of other strong verbs are confined to formal prose.) Otherwise, in spoken German and extensively in the written language, the past subjunctive is replaced (and in the case of the commonest strong verbs, may be replaced) by the construction **würde** + infinitive:

> **wenn er härter** *arbeiten würde*, **wäre seine Familie besser dran** *if he worked harder his family would be better off*
> **wenn ich das Geld** *abheben würde*, **könnte ich morgen in die USA fliegen** *if I withdrew the money I could fly to the USA tomorrow*

In the **wenn**-clause **sollte** + infinitive sometimes replaces the subjunctive, e.g. **wenn die Vorstellung später beginnen sollte** *if the performance were to begin later.*

(iii) IN *AS IF* CLAUSES: The (usually past) subjunctive is used in clauses introduced by **als ob/wenn** or (in literary usage) **als** with inversion:

> **sie sieht (so) aus, als ob sie krank wäre** *she looks as if she were ill*
> **ihm war, als müsste er davonlaufen** (literary) *he felt as if he had to run away*

(iv) IN CLAUSES INTRODUCED BY **damit**: In literary German the subjunctive is sometimes used instead of the indicative in clauses introduced by **damit** *so that.*

(v) IN CONCESSIVE CLAUSES: The subjunctive is used in set expressions: **wie dem auch sei** *be that as it may,* **koste es, was es wolle** *cost what it may,* **komme, was da wolle** *come what may.*

(vi) EXPRESSING A WISH, COMMAND, ETC.: The present subjunctive is used to express:

(*a*) a *wish* in certain set phrases (3rd person singular, e.g. **es lebe . . . !** *long live . . . !,* **Dein Reich komme** *Thy kingdom come,* **Gott behüte!** *heaven forbid!,* **hol ihn der Teufel!** *to hell with him!,* also the South German greeting **grüß Gott!**); the present subjunctive of **mögen** is used in all persons to express *may . . . ,* e.g. **mögen Sie lange leben!** *may you live long!*

(*b*) an *exhortation* or a *command*: in the 3rd person singular, the subjunctive may serve to exhort (in literary language, e.g. **Edel sei der Mensch, hilfreich und gut** (Goethe) *Let man be noble, helpful, and good*); it may be used with imperative force (e.g. **wer dagegen ist, der trete vor!** *anyone not in favour step forward!,* (with **man** as subject) **man wende sich an . . .** *apply to . . . ,* in recipes etc. **man nehme . . .** *take . . .*) or to express a proposition (e.g. **ABC sei ein gleichschenkliges Dreieck** *let ABC be an isosceles triangle*); in the 1st person plural[31] it is used in the sense of *let's . . . !*:

seien wir ehrlich! *let's be honest!*
also fangen wir an! *let's start then!*

The past and pluperfect subjunctives, accompanied by **doch** (or **bloß, nur, doch bloß/nur**), express a (heartfelt) wish that the speaker cannot expect to see realized, *if only . . .* :

wenn sie doch käme! *if only she would come!*
hätte ich doch mehr Zeit! *if only I had more time!*
wenn er das nur nicht gesagt hätte! *if only he hadn't said that!*

(vii) VARIOUS USES in which the subjunctive, always less direct than the indicative, adds a nuance of caution, tentativeness to a statement:

(*a*) making a *polite utterance*, e.g. **eine Frage hätte ich noch** *there's one more thing I'd like to ask*, **ich hätte gern sechs Eier** *I'd like six eggs*, **ich hätte gern Herrn X gesprochen** *I wonder if I might speak to Mr X?*, **hätten Sie sonst noch einen Wunsch?** (in a shop) *is there anything else I can get you?*;
(*b*) referring to the *completion* of something, e.g. **das wär's!** *that's that!*, **da wären wir endlich!** *here we are at last!*;
(*c*) **ich wünschte**: the past subjunctive has the special sense *I wish*, e.g. **ich wünschte, ich hätte ihn nie getroffen** *I wish I'd never met him*;
(*d*) with **beinahe, fast** *almost*, e.g. **das Auto wäre beinahe umgekippt** *the car nearly tipped over*, **fast hätte ich den Fehler übersehen** *I almost overlooked the mistake*;
(*e*) in clauses introduced by **(an)statt dass** *instead of (-ing)*, **nicht dass** *not that*, **ohne dass** *without (-ing)*, **(zu . . . ,) als dass** *(too . . .) to*; in these instances the (less tentative, more direct) indicative may also be used.

THE INFINITIVE

The position of the infinitive is treated on p. 107.

(i) The infinitive is in most cases preceded by **zu,** in the same way that *to* precedes the English infinitive:

sie versucht zu schlafen *she's trying to sleep*
du brauchst nicht zu warten *you needn't wait*
er beabsichtigte den Brief am nächsten Tag zu schreiben *he intended to write the letter the next day*

Where the verb concerned has a separable prefix, **-zu-** is inserted between the prefix and the simple verb:

er beabsichtigte dieses Hobby aufzugeben *he intended to give up this hobby*

---

[31] The forms are indistinguishable from the indicative except in the case of **sein** (**seien wir**).

The infinitive with **zu** has *passive sense* when used with the verb **sein** (cf. English *the house is to let*):

kein Laut war zu hören *not a sound was to be heard*
diese Hitze ist nicht zu ertragen *this heat is (not to be borne =) unbearable*
diese Frage ist leicht zu beantworten *this question is (easily to be answered =) easy to answer*
die Personalausweise sind am Eingang vorzuzeigen *identity cards are to be shown at the entrance*

The infinitive with **zu** is used in combination with certain prepositions: **um . . . zu** *(in order) to*, **(an)statt . . . zu** *instead of (-ing)*, **ohne . . . zu** *without (-ing)*, e.g. **um/ (an)statt/ohne die Tür abzuschließen** *(in order) to lock the door / instead of locking the door / without locking the door*. **Um . . . zu** is also sometimes used without any implication of purpose, like English *to* + infinitive, to indicate someone's destiny, e.g. **sie trennten sich, um einander nie wiederzusehen** *they parted, never to see each other again.*

(ii) INFINITIVE WITHOUT **zu**: used after certain verbs, notably:

(*a*) the modal verbs (**dürfen, können, mögen, müssen, sollen, wollen**):

sie darf die Bibliothek nicht benutzen *she is not allowed to use the library*
ich wollte ihn sprechen *I wanted to speak to him*

(*b*) the auxiliary **lassen** *to let (do something)*:

sie ließ den Gepard entkommen *she let the cheetah escape*

(with infinitive in passive sense) *to have (something done)*:

er ließ die Nationalhymne fünfmal spielen *he had the national anthem played five times*

(*c*) the verbs of perception **hören** *to hear*, **sehen** *to see*, **fühlen** *to feel*, **spüren** *to feel, sense*:

sie hörte ihn kommen *she heard him coming*
ich fühlte mein Herz schlagen *I felt my heart beating*

(*d*) **bleiben** (denoting a situation) and **gehen** (referring to an activity), e.g. **stehen bleiben** *to remain standing; to stop*, **schwimmen gehen** *to go swimming*;

(*e*) (if the infinitive stands on its own, without an object etc.) **helfen** (+ DAT.) *to help*, **lehren** *to teach*, **lernen** *to learn*:

sie half mir abtrocknen *she helped me to dry up*
er muss erst schwimmen lernen *he must learn to swim first*

Contrast: **man lehrte uns alle Fremdwörter nachzuschlagen** *we were taught to look up all the foreign words.*

The simple infinitive is also used as an *imperative* to convey brief directions, e.g. **weitermachen!** *carry on!*, **alles aussteigen!** *all change!*, **rückwärts**

einsteigen! (on Austrian tramcars) *board at the rear,* **Einfahrt freihalten!** *keep entrance clear,* (with suppression of the reflexive pronoun) **nicht hinauslehnen!** *do not lean out of the window.*

The infinitive may be used as a *noun,* in which case it has neuter gender and is written with a capital letter, e.g. **das Reisen** *travel(ling),* **das Lesen** *reading;* it may form part of a compound, e.g. **das Kopfschütteln** *shaking/shake of the head,* **das Menschsein** *being human, humanity,* **das Zuhörenmüssen** *having to listen.* The infinitive—in an infinitive phrase with **zu**—may also play a nominal role as, for example, the subject of the verb in:

> **einen Eisbären zu füttern ist gefährlich** (here **zu** is optional) *feeding a polar bear is dangerous*
> **zu sagen, dass sie Glück hatten, ist unrealistisch** *to say that they were lucky is unrealistic*

or as the complement in:

> **sein Ziel war eine Goldmedaille zu gewinnen** *his goal was to win a gold medal*

PARTICIPLES

The present and past participles may, as in English, be used adjectivally:

> **ein lächelndes Gesicht** *a smiling face*
> **ein ausgebildeter Dolmetscher** *a trained interpreter*
> **sie ist einfach reizend** *she's simply delightful*
> **ich war entsetzt** *I was horrified*

Examples of adverbial use:

> **fragend/entsetzt schaute sie ihn an** *she looked at him questioningly / in horror*
> **überraschend früh** *surprisingly early*

The participles may occur (chiefly in written German) in a participial phrase preceding the noun (see p. 111, *Adjectival and participial phrases*):

> **die im Teich schwimmenden Hechte** *the pike swimming in the pond*
> **der als Verbrecher entlarvte Präsident** *the president (who was) exposed as a criminal*

The construction with **zu** + present participle has passive force (the so-called gerundive):

> **das zu lösende Problem** *the problem to be solved*

In literary style—the construction is rather less common than its English counterpart—the present participle sometimes occurs in a participial phrase with adverbial force (with the participle coming last):

**die Route verläuft, etwa der tschechischen Grenze folgend, durch
den Bayrischen Wald** *roughly following the Czech border, the route runs
through the Bavarian Forest*
(with this literary-sounding construction used to telling ironic effect):
... **Dettmar Cramer, der nichts sagte, dies aber perfekt artikulier-
end** (from a review of a TV programme) ... *Dettmar Cramer, who said
nothing, albeit with perfect articulation*

The similar past participle construction may have the participle at the beginning or the end:

von seiner schauspielerischen Anlage überzeugt (or **überzeugt von
seiner schauspielerischen Anlage**) **ging er zum Theater** *convinced of
his talent as an actor, he went on the stage*

The English present participle (-*ing*) is rendered by other constructions
in German in a number of situations:

(i) (=**relative clause**) e.g. *a teacher driving a minibus* **ein Lehrer, der einen
Kleinbus fährt/fuhr**
(causal: **da** ...) e.g. *having nothing to do, I went for a walk* **da ich nichts zu tun
hatte, ging ich spazieren,** *this being the case,* ... **da dies der Fall ist/war,** ...
(temporal: **als** ... , **nachdem** ... , **während** ...) e.g. *hearing the doorbell, he went
to open the door* **als er die Klingel hörte, ging er die Tür öffnen,** *having written
the article, I went to bed* **nachdem ich den Artikel geschrieben hatte, ging ich ins
Bett,** *and then, raising his baton, he looks up at the box* **und dann sieht er, während
er den Dirigentenstab hebt, zur Loge hinauf**; sometimes two clauses linked by **und**
are used, e.g. *taking out his knife, he opened the letter* **er nahm sein Messer heraus
und öffnete den Brief,** *he left early, only later realizing that he had left his umbrella
behind* **er ging früh und merkte erst später, dass er seinen Schirm vergessen
hatte,** (simultaneous actions) *there she stood waiting* **da stand sie und wartete,** *he
sat peeling potatoes* **er saß und schälte Kartoffeln**

(ii) WITH VERBS OF PERCEPTION: expressed by the infinitive, e.g. *she heard him coming*
sie hörte ihn kommen (see p. 86, *The infinitive* (ii) (*c*)); frequently, especially with
more complex sentences, a clause with **wie** is used, e.g. *he could see Donald being
propped against the wall* **er sah, wie Donald gegen die Wand gelehnt wurde,** *he
heard the rain falling* **er hörte, wie der Regen fiel**

(iii) *spend time -ing, be busy -ing*: here the participle is rendered by **mit** + infinitive
noun or, if followed by an object etc., by **damit** + infinitive phrase, e.g. *he spends
most of his time reading / collecting beer-mats* **er verbringt die meiste Zeit mit Lesen
/ damit, Bierdeckel zu sammeln,** *she was busy hanging out the washing* **sie war damit
beschäftigt, Wäsche aufzuhängen**

(iv) *come -ing*: translated by **kommen** + past participle of the verb of motion concerned, e.g. *they came running along* **sie kamen angelaufen**

The German past participle is also used as an *imperative*, to express
peremptory—especially military—commands, e.g. **stillgestanden!** *attention!* (from **stillstehen** *to stop*), **abgesessen!** *dismount!* (from **absitzen** *to
dismount*).

SEPARABLE AND INSEPARABLE VERBS

The German vocabulary contains a large number of verbs formed with prefixes, either separable and stressed (e.g. **auf-** in **aufgeben** *to give up*) or inseparable and unstressed (e.g. **be-** in **bekommen** *to get*). Eight prefixes are inseparable: **be-, emp-, ent-, er-, ge-, miss-** (normally), **ver-, zer-**; the rest are or (in the case of variable prefixes) may be separable. The variable prefixes **durch-, hinter-, über-, um-, unter-, voll-, wider-, wieder-** may occur as either separable or inseparable prefixes; in some instances the same verb occurs in both separable and inseparable forms, e.g. **úmfahren** *to knock down* as opposed to **umfáhren** *to go/drive/sail round*.

SEPARABLE VERBS

These have no exact counterpart in English, but may be compared with phrasal verbs such as *give up, take over, stick out*. Unlike the adverbial element in these English verbs, however, the German separable prefix *goes right to the end* in a main clause in the present and past tenses, e.g. **ich gehe heute abend mit meiner Freundin *aus*** *I'm going out with my girl-friend tonight*; but where (in a subordinate clause) the verb itself is in final position, the prefix is reunited with the simple verb in the sequence prefix–verb, e.g. w**enn ich mit meiner Freundin *ausgehe*** *if/when I go out with my girl-friend*, **wusstest du nicht, dass sie mit ihm *ausgeht*?** *didn't you know she's going out with him?*

Separable prefixes precede, and are joined to, the verb in the infinitive (e.g. **ausgehen**) and the present participle (e.g. **ausgehend**); where the infinitive is used with **zu** the latter is inserted between the prefix and the simple verb (e.g. **auszugehen**); in the past participle the prefix precedes the **ge-** element (e.g. **ausgegangen**).

Examples:

aufgeben *to give up* (ich gebe . . . auf, (wenn etc.) ich . . . aufgebe, ich habe . . . aufgegeben)

einzahlen *to pay in* (ich zahle . . . ein, (wenn etc.) ich . . . einzahle, ich habe . . . eingezahlt)

mithalten *to keep up* (ich halte . . . mit, (wenn etc.) ich . . . mithalte, ich habe . . . mitgehalten)

Some separable verbs are formed by prefixing a noun or adjective to the simple verb, e.g. **teilnehmen** *to take part* (from **Teil** *part* and **nehmen** *to take*), **fernsehen** *to watch television* (from **fern** *far* and **sehen** *to see*). These are handled in exactly the same way as other separable verbs, thus **ich nehme . . . teil, (wenn etc.) ich . . . teilnehme, ich habe . . . teilgenommen; ich sehe . . . fern, (wenn etc.) ich . . . fernsehe, ich habe . . . ferngesehen.**

NOTE: The beginner needs to remember that before looking up a verb in the dictionary one should first look at the end of the clause (usually marked in German by some form of punctuation) to see whether a separable prefix is there. If so, it is the entry for the *compound verb* (consisting of prefix + (simple) verb) that must be consulted; thus in the case of a sentence such as **der Mond übt auf die Erde eine Kraft aus** it is **ausüben** *to exert* etc., and not **üben** *to practise* etc., that should be looked up: *the moon exerts a force on the earth.*

INSEPARABLE VERBS

Some verbs are formed with inseparable prefixes, e.g. **erreichen** *to reach*, **vergessen** *to forget*. As their name suggests, these prefixes cannot be detached from the verb. The past participle of such verbs, unlike that of separable verbs, has no **ge-**; **ge-** may, however, itself be an inseparable prefix, as in **genehmigen** *to approve*.

There is in addition a class of compound verbs—they may conveniently also be termed inseparable—some of which are derived from compound nouns (e.g. **frühstücken** *to have breakfast*, **handhaben** *to handle* from **das Frühstück, die Handhabe**) while others are formed by other means (e.g. **schlafwandeln** *to walk in one's sleep*). All are stressed on the first syllable and conjugated weak; their past participles are formed with the prefix **ge-** (in contrast with the inserted **-ge-** in the past participles of separable verbs like **teilnehmen**—see above): **gefrühstückt, gehandhabt, geschlafwandelt.**

REFLEXIVE VERBS

Reflexive verbs—for their conjugation see *Reflexive pronouns*, p. 45—are verbs whose subject and object refer to the same person or thing:

> **ich wasche mich jeden Tag** *I wash (myself) every day*
> **das Fenster öffnet sich** *the window opens* (literally: *itself*)
> **wir haben uns verteidigt** *we defended ourselves*

With the reflexive pronoun in the dative, as the indirect object:

> **ich will mir einen Volvo kaufen** *I'm going to buy (myself) a Volvo*
> (when referring to a part of one's body):
> **ich wasche mir die Hände vor jeder Mahlzeit** *I wash my hands before every meal*
> **sie hat sich das Bein gebrochen** *she's broken her leg*

Some verbs exist only in the reflexive form, e.g. **sich beeilen** *to hurry*, **sich auskennen** *to know one's way around*. Others are strictly speaking verbs that may also be used reflexively, e.g. **(sich) rasieren** *to shave*, **(sich) anpassen** *to adapt*; semantically the reflexive use may be quite unconnected with that of its non-reflexive counterpart, e.g. **sich betragen** *to behave*, cf. **betragen** *to amount to*.

A number of reflexive verbs are followed by: (*a*) the GENITIVE, e.g. **sich schämen** *to be ashamed of*, **sich bemächtigen** *to take possession of*; (*b*) the DATIVE, e.g. **sich anvertrauen** *to confide in*, **sich nähern** *to approach*, **sich widersetzen** *to resist*;

(c) a PREPOSITION, e.g. **sich erinnern an** (+ACC.) *to remember,* **sich verlassen auf** (+ACC.) *to rely on,* **sich auseinandersetzen mit** *to grapple with* (a problem etc.), **sich sehnen nach** *to long for,* **sich wundern über** (+ACC.) *to be surprised at.*

The scope of the reflexive verb is wider in German than in English, and its English equivalent may be (apart from a parallel reflexive construction):

(i) an INTRANSITIVE VERB (the reflexive sense being implied), e.g. **sich anziehen/ ausziehen** *to dress/undress,* **sich konzentrieren** *to concentrate,* **sich leeren** (of a room etc.) *to empty,* **sich zeigen** (of fear etc.) *to show.*

(ii) a TRANSITIVE VERB + NOUN OBJECT, e.g. **sich kämmen** *to comb one's hair,* **sich räuspern** *to clear one's throat,* **sich bessern** *to mend one's ways,* **sich versuchen als** *to try one's hand as.*

(iii) a VERB IN THE PASSIVE, e.g. **sich bestätigen** (of a suspicion etc.) *to be confirmed,* **sich erfüllen** (of a wish, prophecy) *to be fulfilled,* **sich wieder finden** (of a lost object) *to be found.*

(iv) a TRANSITIVE VERB USED INTRANSITIVELY WITH PASSIVE FORCE, e.g. **das wird sich nie in Kanada verkaufen** *that'll never sell in Canada,* **der Roman liest sich gut** *the novel reads well;* with **leicht** and **schwer** the reflexive verb is translated by *to be easy/hard to . . . ,* e.g. **das Lied singt sich leicht/schwer** *the song is easy/hard to sing,* **das sagt sich leicht** *that's easy to say.*

(v) *to . . . one's way,* e.g. **sich** (**zum Fenster** etc.) **tasten** *to feel one's way,* **sich durchkämpfen** *to fight one's way through.*

Certain verbs are used in an impersonal construction with adverbs such as **gut, leicht,** e.g. **hier fährt/schläft es sich gut** *this is a good road for driving on / a good place to sleep,* **es schreibt sich so schwer mit einem ausgetrockneten Filzstift** *it's so hard writing with a dried-out felt pen.*

RECIPROCAL USE

A second function of reflexive verbs (in the plural) is to express reciprocity; the reflexive pronoun here is equivalent to English *one another, each other.* Examples:

sie lieben sich *they love each other*
wann sehen wir uns wieder? *when will we see each other again?*

Again, the reflexive pronoun is often left untranslated in English, e.g. **die Kinder schlugen sich um das neue Spielzeug** *the children fought* (i.e. *each other*) *over the new toy,* **schreibt ihr euch** (DAT.) **noch?** *do you still write* (i.e. *to each other*)?

The reflexive verb with reciprocal force can even, in certain instances, be used with a singular subject, usually in combination with **mit,** e.g. **er duzt sich mit ihr** *he is on first-name terms with her* (cf. **sie duzen sich** *they are on first-name terms*).

An alternative to the reciprocal reflexives **uns/euch/sich** in both the accusative and the dative is **einander**, which is invariable. It is, however, restricted to more elevated style—except after a preposition, when only **einander** is possible; the preposition and **einander** join to form one word (with the stress remaining on the second syllable of **einander**), e.g. **wir tanzten miteinander** *we danced with one another*, **seid nett zueinander!** *be nice to one another!*

In cases where the reflexive pronoun might be ambiguous—e.g. **sie trösteten sich** *they comforted themselves/each other*—reciprocal **uns/euch/ sich** may be reinforced by **gegenseitig** (literally *mutually*): **sie trösteten sich gegenseitig.**

IMPERSONAL VERBS AND CONSTRUCTIONS

A number of German verbs are used impersonally (i.e. in the 3rd person singular with the impersonal pronoun **es**), some of which have impersonal equivalents in English:

> **es regnet** *it rains/is raining*
> **es handelt sich um** . . . *it is a matter of* . . . ; *it is about* . . . ; *he/she/it is* . . . , *they are* . . .

Other examples have *there is* . . . in the translation:

> **es klopft** *there is a knock at the door*
> **es zieht** *there is a draught*
> **es riecht nach Gas** *there is a smell of gas*
> **es knallte** *there was a bang*

Yet other examples have a noun subject where the German sentence has **es**:

> **es klingelt** *the doorbell is ringing*
> **es wimmelte von Insekten/Touristen** *the place was swarming with insects/tourists*

How a person feels may also be expressed by an impersonal construction:

> **es ist mir** (or **mir ist**) **warm/kalt** *I'm (feeling) warm/cold*
> **es graut mir** (or **mir graut**) **vor** (+ DAT.) *I dread*
> **es ist mir** (or **mir ist**), **als ob** . . . *I feel as if* . . . ; *it seems to me that* . . .

Note that **es** is omitted if it does not begin the sentence.

TRANSLATION OF 'THERE IS/ARE . . .': These are translated by **es gibt** (+ACC.), when the existence of something or someone is referred to and/or when one could logically insert *in the nature of things* in the sentence concerned:

> *there are spiders throughout Africa* **es gibt Spinnen überall in Afrika**
> *are there people on Mars?* **gibt es Menschen auf dem Mars?**
> *there wasn't much snow this winter* **es gab in diesem Winter wenig Schnee**
> *there was nothing to eat* **es gab nichts zu essen**

there's always a lot to do before Christmas **vor Weihnachten gibt es immer viel zu tun**
there are several reasons for it **es gibt mehrere Gründe dafür**

Es ist/sind, on the other hand, is concerned not with existence but with presence, namely in a specified, limited place:

there is nobody there at the moment **es ist im Augenblick niemand da**
there were many clouds in the sky **es waren viele Wolken am Himmel**
there are too many tourists in the town **es sind zu viele Touristen in der Stadt**

Es is omitted when not in initial position:

im Augenblick ist niemand da
ich nehme an (*I assume*), **dass im Augenblick niemand da ist**

There is a certain amount of overlap between the two constructions, and it is not always possible to draw hard and fast distinctions.

In many contexts other translations are used, e.g. (LOCATION: **stehen**) *there are three apple trees in the garden* **es stehen drei Apfelbäume im Garten**, (**liegen**) *there were many books on the table* **auf dem Tisch lagen viele Bücher**; (PREVALENCE: **herrschen**) *there is uncertainty as to whether . . .* **es herrscht Ungewissheit darüber, ob . . .**, *there was great excitement* **es herrschte große Aufregung**; (EXISTENCE: **bestehen**) *there is the possibility/danger that . . .* **es besteht die Möglichkeit/Gefahr, dass . . .**, *there is no reason to suppose/no doubt that . . .* **es besteht kein Grund zur Annahme / kein Zweifel, dass . . .** ; (COLLECTIVE ACTIVITY: impersonal passive—see p. 81) *there was a strike* **es wurde gestreikt**, *on Fridays there was dancing* **freitags wurde getanzt**; (PHENOMENA: **es** + verb used impersonally—see above) *there is a draught* **es zieht**.

THE MODAL VERBS AND *BRAUCHEN*

The modal verbs are used, chiefly in conjunction with a dependent infinitive, to express possibility, permission, necessity, obligation, inclination, or volition. (For their conjugation see p. 75.) The relationship between the German modals and their English counterparts (*can*, *may*, etc.) is complicated partly by the fact that the English verbs are defective—the infinitives, for example, are lost—and by the absence from English of an equivalent to **dürfen**, and partly because their usage coincides in some respects, but differs in others.

A feature common to all German modal verbs is the use of *elliptical constructions* involving the omission of: (*a*) VERBS OF MOTION (**gehen, fahren, kommen**), e.g. **sie will in die Stadt / zu ihrer Mutter** *she wants to go into town / to her mother*, **muss er mit?** *must he come too?*, **ich durfte nicht zurück** *I wasn't allowed (to go) back*, **ich kann nicht weiter** *I can't go on*, **er soll nach Hause** *he is to go home*, **wo willst du hin?** *where do you want to go?* (cf. in English *the truth will out*); (*b*) **tun**, e.g. **ich darf es** *I'm allowed to do it*, **er kann alles** *he can do everything*, **was soll ich hier?** *what am I doing here?*, (for **ich habe es tun können/müssen**) **ich habe es gekonnt/**

gemusst *I was able/had to do it.*[32] (For other ellipses specific to **können** and **sollen** see those verbs below.)

For the special word order that applies when a compound tense of a modal occurs in a subordinate clause (e.g. . . . **dass ich habe kommen können**) see p. 107, *Subordinate clauses*, exception (iii).

INDICATIVE AND SUBJUNCTIVE

The distinction between indicative and subjunctive forms is especially noteworthy in the past tense of modal verbs, where the indicative refers to a real event in the past while its subjunctive counterpart may express a possibility (usually conveyed in English by *would*):

INDICATIVE	SUBJUNCTIVE
durfte *was allowed to*	**dürfte** *would be allowed to*
konnte *was able to, could*	**könnte** *would be able to, could; might*
musste *had to; was bound to*	**müsste** *would have to; would be bound to*

NOTE: English *could* so to speak straddles this dividing line in that it has two senses, one relating to a past event (*was able to*), the other to a possibility (*would be able to*; *might*): (*a*) (*was able to* **konnte**): *how could you do this to me?* **wie konntest du mir das bloß antun?** (*b*) (*would be able to* **könnte**): *I could sell the piano* **ich könnte das Klavier verkaufen;** (*might* **könnte**): *it could rain tomorrow* **es könnte morgen regnen** (For further examples see **können** (i) and (iii), below.)

COULD HAVE, SHOULD HAVE, ETC.

An unrealized possibility, expressed in English by constructions such as *could have, should have,* is conveyed in German by the pluperfect subjunctive: **hätte . . . können, hätte . . . sollen,** etc.:

> **ich *hätte* kommen *können*, wenn ich genug Zeit gehabt hätte** *I could have come if I'd had enough time*
> **du *hättest* daran denken *sollen*, bevor du Mitglied wurdest** *you should have thought of that before you joined*

The other forms are **hätte . . . dürfen** *would have been allowed to,* **hätte . . . mögen** *would have liked to,* **hätte . . . müssen** (1) *would have had to / been bound to,* (2) *ought to / should have,* **hätte . . . wollen** *would have wanted to;* for examples see the verbs concerned below.

All these constructions carry the implication . . . *but did not.* (Contrast the following two translations of *he could have written it:* **er hätte es schreiben können** (but did not), **er könnte es geschrieben haben** (he might have done, and quite possibly did).)

---

[32] Cf. Martin Luther's defiant **Hier stehe ich, ich kann nicht anders** *Here I stand, I cannot do otherwise* (spoken at the Diet of Worms, 1521).

Elliptical constructions from which an infinitive is omitted (see above) also occur, e.g. **ich hätte sonst nach Hause gemusst** (for **gehen müssen**) *I would otherwise have had to go home*, **er hätte es nicht gekonnt** (for **tun können**) *he wouldn't have been able to do it.*

DÜRFEN PERMISSION

(i) *to be allowed to, (I etc.) may*:

darf ich rauchen? *may I smoke?*

das Mädchen durfte erst abends fernsehen *the girl wasn't allowed to watch TV till the evening*

wir dürften am nächsten Tag das Land verlassen *we would be allowed to leave the country the next day*

sie haben die Moschee nicht besuchen dürfen *they weren't allowed to visit the mosque*

das hättest du nicht erklären dürfen *you wouldn't have been allowed to explain that*

This verb also occurs in various polite utterances, e.g. **ich darf Sie im Namen der Stadt begrüßen** *may I welcome you on behalf of the town*, **was darf es sein?** (asked by shop assistant) *can I help you?*, (by a waiter or waitress) *what will you have?*, **darf es etwas in Seide sein?** *may I show you something in silk?* (cf. in a formal letter **wir dürfen Ihnen mitteilen, dass** . . . *we have pleasure in informing you that* . . .); and in remarks such as **ich darf Sie daran erinnern/darauf hinweisen, dass** . . . *may I remind you/point out that* . . .

In negative use: (prohibition) e.g. **Ärzte dürfen hier nicht rauchen** *doctors are not allowed to smoke here.* Commonly (*I etc.*) *must not* is the English equivalent, e.g. **du darfst die Kinder nicht allein lassen** *you mustn't leave the children on their own*, **das darf man nicht laut sagen** *one mustn't say that out loud.*

(ii) *to have reason to, (I etc.) can*:

du darfst stolz auf ihn sein *you can be proud of him*

wenn man es ein Haus nennen darf *if one can call it a house*

man darf annehmen, dass . . . *one can assume that* . . .

das dürfen Sie mir ruhig glauben *you can take my word for it*

(iii) PROBABILITY (past subjunctive) **dürfte** *should, ought to*:

es dürfte einfach sein, ihren neuen Roman ins Deutsche zu übersetzen *it should be easy to translate her new novel into German*

Sometimes *probably* catches the flavour:

das dürfte stimmen *that's probably true*

The past subjunctive may also express a polite request:

dürfte ich dieses Buch mitnehmen? *may I take this book with me?*

dürfte ich Sie um Feuer bitten? *could I trouble you for a light?*

(iv) **hätte nicht . . . dürfen** *should not have, ought not to have,* e.g. **das hättest du nicht schreiben dürfen** *you shouldn't have written that.*

Bedürfen (+GEN.) *to need* is conjugated like **dürfen.**

KÖNNEN ABILITY, POSSIBILITY

(i) *to be able to, (I etc.) can; to manage to:*

ich kann Auto fahren *I can drive,* **kannst du mir helfen?** *can you help me?,* **wie kann er so etwas sagen?** *how can he say such a thing?*

wir konnten nachts nicht schlafen *we couldn't sleep at night,* **wie konnte ich nur so dumm sein!** *how could I be so stupid!,* **von unseren Springreitern konnte nur einer eine Medaille gewinnen** *only one of our show-jumpers managed to win a medal*

ich könnte Sie am Bahnhof abholen *I could meet you at the station,* **könntest du mir einen Gefallen tun?** *could you do me a favour?*

er hat sie nie vergessen können *he's never been able to forget her*

ich hätte kommen können, wenn ich genug Zeit gehabt hätte *I could have come if I'd had enough time*

(For the distinction between **konnte** and **könnte** see p. 94, *Indicative and subjunctive.*)

May be used with verbs of perception in the sense *to be able to stand*:

sie kann kein Blut riechen/sehen *she can't stand the smell/sight of blood*
ich kann das nicht mehr hören! *I can't bear to hear that any longer!*

Also used with a direct object with reference to a skill:

Ute kann (gut) Englisch *Ute can speak (good) English*
Erich kann dieses Gedicht auswendig *Erich knows this poem by heart*

The passive construction is very common in the past tense, e.g. (*it was possible to . . .*) **mit dem neuen Ventilator konnte eine gute Wärmeverteilung garantiert werden** *with the new fan it was possible to guarantee a good distribution of heat,* (*. . . managed to . . .*) **der Verbrecher konnte schnell gefasst werden / von der Polizei gefasst werden** *they / the police soon managed to catch the criminal;* cf. **das will gekonnt sein** *you have to have the knack.*

(ii) PERMISSION, SANCTION, ETC. (*I etc.) can:*

kann ich nach Hause gehen? *can I go home?*
meinetwegen können sie zu Ostern kommen *as far as I'm concerned they can come at Easter*
das kannst du unmöglich tragen! *you can't possibly wear that!*

(iii) POSSIBILITY (*I etc.) may:*

das kann sein *that may be,* **ich kann mich irren** *I may be wrong,* **der Arzt kann jeden Augenblick kommen** *the doctor may come any moment,* **sie kann es getan haben** *she may have done it,* **das Paket kann**

verloren gegangen sein *the parcel may have got lost;* cf. **man kann nie wissen** *you never know, you never can tell*
es könnte durchaus stimmen *it could well be true,* **du könntest recht haben** *you could be right,* **er könnte krank / in Lissabon sein** *he could be ill / in Lisbon,* **sie könnte mich gesehen haben** *she could have seen me,* **es könnten hundert gewesen sein** *it could have been a hundred* (see also p. 94, *Could have, should have, etc.*)

(iv) POTENTIAL (*I* etc.) *can:*

sie kann sehr freundlich sein *she can be very friendly*
die Winter können dort sehr kalt sein *the winters can be very cold there*
das kann jedem passieren *that can happen to anyone*

MÖGEN INCLINATION; POSSIBILITY

(i) *to like* (often reinforced by **gern**; the commonest sense—used most frequently in the past subjunctive **möchte** *would like*):

(*a*) with noun or pronoun object:

ich mag seine Schwiegermutter *I like his mother-in-law,* **magst du Kaffee?** *do you like coffee?,* **sie mag kein Bier** *she doesn't like beer*
wir mochten ihn alle gern *we all liked him*
ich möchte noch etwas Wein *I'd like some more wine,* **er möchte nicht, dass sein Angebot missverstanden wird** *he wouldn't like his offer to be misunderstood*
ich habe diesen Tizian nie gemocht *I've never liked this Titian*

(*b*) with an infinitive (often in negative use):

ich mag keinen Knoblauch essen *I don't like to eat garlic*
sie mochte es ihm nicht sagen *she didn't like to tell him*
ich möchte am liebsten nach Spanien fahren *I'd like most of all to go to Spain,* (in weakened sense) **man möchte meinen, er sei der Chef** *you'd think he was the boss*
er hatte nicht fragen mögen *he hadn't liked to ask*
das hätte ich hören mögen *I'd have liked to hear that*

(ii) SUPPOSITION (chiefly in literary style) (*I* etc.) *may:*

(in general use) **(das) mag sein** *that may be so*
das Stück mag schon vor dem Krieg entstanden sein *the play may have been written before the war*
diese Romane mochten an Intellektuelle gerichtet sein *these novels may have been aimed at intellectuals*

In questions, *can* (*I* etc.):

was mag der Verfasser damit gemeint haben? *what can the author have meant by that?*
was mochte sie dazu bewogen haben, so zu handeln? *what could have induced her to act like that?*

Estimating, (*I* etc.) *would*:

sie mag/mochte zehn Jahre alt sein *she would be/have been about ten years old*
es mochte 3 Uhr gewesen sein, als die Polizei erschien *it would have been about 3 o'clock when the police appeared*

(iii) CONCESSIVE USE (*I* etc.) *may*:

was ich auch tun mag *whatever I may do*

However . . . ; . . . though . . . :

die schwarzen Polizisten mochten auf ihren Pfeifen trillern, soviel sie wollten . . . *however much the black policemen blew their whistles . . .*
mochte ich mich hierin auch geirrt haben . . . *mistaken though I may have been about this . . .*

(iv) WISH, REQUEST
In formal German the present subjunctive **möge** may express a wish, *may . . . , let . . .* :

möge es ihm gelingen! *may he succeed!*
das möge dir zur Warnung dienen *let that be a warning to you,* **das mögen andere beurteilen** *let others be the judge of that*

In subordinate clauses (. . . **möge** . . . or past subjunctive . . . **möchte** . . .) a request may be expressed:

sagen Sie ihm, er möge/möchte sofort kommen *ask him to come at once*

Vermögen (literary) *to be able to* is conjugated like **mögen**.

MÜSSEN OBLIGATION, NECESSITY

(i) *to have to*, (*I* etc.) *must*, NECESSITY also *to need*:

sie muss den Aufsatz bis Freitag abgeben *she has to hand in the essay by Friday,* **ich muss unbedingt einen Dolmetscher holen** *I really must fetch an interpreter,* **man muss sich nur sein Bild ansehen** *one has only to / need only look at his picture,* **das muss nachgestellt / gestrichen / gut überlegt werden** *that needs adjusting / a coat of paint / careful consideration*
nach dem Anschluss mussten Wiener Fußballer für Deutschland spielen *after the Anschluss Viennese footballers had to play for Germany,* **musste es soweit kommen?** *did it have to come to that?*
er müsste sich einen neuen Job suchen *he'd have to look for a new job*
die Russen haben sehr lange warten müssen *the Russians have had to wait a very long time*
ich hätte unter diesen Umständen ein neues Thema wählen müssen *under these circumstances I'd have had to choose a new topic*

NOTE: When used with a negative, **müssen** retains the sense of compulsion (contrast English *must not*, which indicates a prohibition and has to be translated by **nicht dürfen**, e.g. *I mustn't read it* **ich darf es nicht lesen**):[33]

> **das muss nicht der Fall sein** *that doesn't have to / needn't be the case*,
> **man muss kein Sozialdemokrat sein, um diese Politik zu verstehen**
> *you don't have to / needn't be a Social Democrat to understand this policy*
> **sie musste es nicht tun / hat es nicht tun müssen** *she didn't have/need to do it*

(ii) INEVITABILITY *to be bound to*:

> **das muss er ja sagen** *he's bound to say that*
> **früher oder später musste es so kommen** *sooner or later it was bound to happen*, **acht Briefe, die ihre Mitschuld an der Ermordung Darnleys erweisen mussten** *eight letters which were bound to prove her complicity in Darnley's murder*
> **eine solche Ausstellung müsste großes Aufsehen erregen** *an exhibition like that would be bound to cause a great stir*
> **seine Wiederwahl hätte zu einer wirtschaftlichen Krise führen müssen** *his re-election would have been bound to lead to an economic crisis*

(iii) LOGICAL DEDUCTION (*I* etc.) *must*:

> **sie muss schon sehr krank sein, wenn ihre Mutter ein Telegramm schickt** *she must be very ill for her mother to send a telegram*
> **das Flugzeug muss auf Zypern gelandet sein** *the aircraft must have landed in Cyprus*, **Kolumbus muss Nordamerika entdeckt haben** *Columbus must have discovered North America*
> **das Flugzeug musste im Dschungel abgestürzt sein** *the aircraft must have crashed in the jungle* (in narrative; **musste** because the assumption was made in the past)

(iv) INNER COMPULSION *to have to*, (*I* etc.) *cannot help –ing*:

> **ich muss immer daran denken, wenn sie diese Melodie spielen** *I can't help thinking of it whenever they play this tune*
> **wir mussten lachen** *we had to laugh/couldn't help laughing*

(v) EMOTIVE USE *to have to*, (*I* etc.) *would (have to)*:

> **gerade an meinem Geburtstag muss es natürlich regnen** *of course it would (have to) rain on my birthday*, **warum musste das ausgerechnet mir passieren?** *why did it have to happen to me of all people?*

(*He* etc.) *will*:

> **er muss ständig dazwischenreden** *he will keep interrupting*

---

[33] In North German usage, however, the 2nd person may be used like English *must not*, e.g. **du musst nicht traurig sein** *you mustn't be sad.*

(vi) **müsste, hätte . . . müssen**: The past and pluperfect subjunctive may also signify *ought to, should* and *ought to/should have* respectively:

> **sie müssten heute in London sein** *they ought to be in London today,* **es müsste doch möglich sein** *it ought to be possible,* **Gerlinde ist hübsch, nur sie müsste schlanker sein** *Gerlinde is pretty, only she ought to be slimmer*
>
> **sie hätte Lehrerin werden müssen** *she ought to have been a teacher*

The meaning of these subjunctive forms is not identical with that of **sollte** and **hätte . . . sollen** (although they share the same translations with them). **Müsste** and **hätte . . . müssen** do not carry the implication of an obligation that characterizes the latter; rather, they refer to what may be reasonably thought or assumed in the circumstances.

Müsste also expresses wishful thinking:

> **reich müsste man sein!** *wouldn't it be nice to be rich!*
> **hier müsste man wohnen!** *this is the place to live!*
> **so müsste das Wetter den ganzen Sommer lang bleiben!** *the weather should stay like this right through the summer!*

SOLLEN OBLIGATION, INTENTION, REPORT

(i) *to be to; to be supposed to*:

> **ich soll um 4 Uhr dort sein** *I'm (supposed) to be there at 4 o'clock,* **die Soldaten sollen das Land verteidigen** *the soldiers are supposed to defend the country,* **was soll man darunter verstehen?** *what is one (supposed) to understand by that?*
>
> **wir sollten das Buch lesen / haben das Buch lesen sollen** *we were (supposed) to read the book,* **was sollte ich machen?** *what was I (supposed) to do?,* **wie sollte er das wissen?** *how was he (supposed) to / could he know that?*

NOTE: English usage differs from German in saying e.g. *I don't know what to do, she didn't know who(m) to ask* = **ich weiß nicht, was ich tun soll, sie wusste nicht, wen sie fragen sollte.**

In 1st-person questions *shall* is sometimes used, e.g. **soll ich mitkommen?** *shall I come too?,* **was soll ich ihm sagen?** *what shall I tell him?,* (making a suggestion) **sollen wir nach Hause gehen?** *shall we go home?*

When the emphasis is on the fact that it is someone's wish—often that of the speaker or writer—that is involved, the English translation is usually *. . . want(s)* (someone or something) *to . . .* :

> **sie soll sich hier wie zu Hause fühlen** *I/we want her to feel at home here*
> **meine Bücher sollen preiswert sein** *I want my books to be good value for money*
> **ich soll das alles heute nachmittag tippen?** *you want / he wants etc. me to type all that this afternoon?*

Sollen often expresses an instruction, e.g. **er soll sofort nach Hause kommen** *he's to come home at once,* **du sollst nicht stehlen** etc. (Bible) *thou shalt not steal* etc. **Man soll . . . one should . . .** may occur in exhortations instead of **man sollte . . .** , e.g. **man soll immer die Wahrheit sagen** *one should always tell the truth.*

A note of warning or challenge (*let . . .*) is sounded in e.g. **das soll dir eine Warnung sein** *let that be a warning to you,* **das sollen sie nur versuchen!** *just let them try!*

(ii) WHAT IS INTENDED *to be to; to be supposed to; to be intended/meant to:*

ein neues Krankenhaus soll hier gebaut werden *a new hospital is to be built here,* **die Gesamtschulen in Großbritannien sollen der jungen Generation die Möglichkeit bieten, eine auf individuelle Fähigkeiten abgestimmte Ausbildung zu erhalten** *Britain's comprehensive schools are intended to offer the younger generation the opportunity of receiving an education geared to pupils' individual abilities*

diese Figuren sollten lebenslustige Schäferinnen darstellen *these figures were supposed to represent shepherdesses full of the joys of life,* **sein letztes Werk sollte eine Warnung vor dieser Ideologie sein** *his last work was intended to be / intended as a warning against this ideology*

Compare also the promise **es soll nicht wieder vorkommen** *it won't happen again.*

Elliptical use: **Was soll . . . ?** *what's the point of . . . ?,* e.g. **was soll das ganze Geld?** *what's the point of all this money?*

(iii) REPORT, RUMOUR *to be said/reported to:*

jeder zweite Deutsche soll Übergewicht haben *every second German is said to be overweight,* **Renate soll zuviel getrunken haben / sehr intelligent gewesen sein** *Renate is said to have drunk too much / been very intelligent*

(iv) OBLIGATION (past and pluperfect subjunctive) **sollte** *ought to, should,* **hätte . . . sollen** *ought to/should have:*

du solltest dich schämen *you ought to be ashamed of yourself,* **wir sollten einfach weggehen** *we should just go away*
er hätte früher daran denken sollen *he should have thought of that earlier*

(v) WHAT IS DESTINED TO HAPPEN (past indicative) **sollte** *was (destined) to, would:*

kurz danach sollte er den Thron besteigen *soon afterwards he was to ascend the throne*
sie sollte Polen nie wiedersehen *she would never again see Poland*
Compare also **es hat so/nicht sein sollen** *it was meant/not to be.*

(vi) POSSIBILITY (past subjunctive) **sollte . . . ?** *could . . . ?:*

sollte er recht haben? *could he be right?,* **sollte ich das wirklich vergessen haben?** *could I really have forgotten that?*

(vii) CONDITIONAL (past subjunctive) **sollte** *should, were to*:

wenn es schneien sollte, (dann) bleiben wir zu Hause *if it should/were to snow we'll stay at home*
solltest du meine Hilfe brauchen *should you need/if you should need my help*

(viii) IN IDIOMATIC EXPRESSIONS **sollte** *would, should*:

man sollte glauben/meinen, dass . . . *you would think that . . .* , **es sollte mich wundern, wenn . . .** *I should be surprised if . . .*

WOLLEN VOLITION

(i) *to want to*:

ich will Arzt werden *I want to be a doctor*
er wollte den Grund nicht wissen/hat den Grund nicht wissen wollen *he didn't want to know the reason*
sie hatte nicht lange bleiben wollen *she hadn't wanted to stay long*
das hätte er bestimmt als Ausrede benutzen wollen *I'm sure he would have wanted to use that as an excuse*

If the emphasis is on someone's willingness to do something, *will* (past *would*) is usual, e.g. **willst du mir helfen?** *will you help me?*, **sie will nicht unterschreiben** *she won't sign*, **er wollte es nicht zugeben** *he wouldn't admit it*. In negative use **wollen** may also occur with an inanimate subject, e.g. **die Tür will nicht zugehen** *the door won't shut*, **die Wunde wollte nicht heilen** *the wound wouldn't heal*, **der Motor wollte nicht anspringen** *the engine wouldn't/refused to start*. (Compare also **es will mir nicht eingehen, dass . . .** *I can't grasp the fact that . . .* , **die Arbeit will mir heute nicht schmecken** *I don't feel like work today*, **der Film wollte kein Ende nehmen** *the film went on for ever*, **nicht enden wollender Beifall** *unending applause*.)
Wollen is often used with a direct object: *to want*:

willst du Kartoffelpüree? *do you want mashed potatoes?*
sie wollten keine Kinder *they didn't want any children*
ich habe doch nur dein Bestes gewollt *I only wanted what was best for you*
(with **dass**-clause) **ich will, dass sie mitkommt** *I want her to come with us*

To like in e.g. **wenn du willst** *if you like*, **ganz wie du willst** *just as you like*.
Ich wollte (past subjunctive) expresses a wish, e.g. **ich wollte, ich hätte mehr Zeit** *I wish I had more time*.

(ii) SUGGESTION OR REQUEST (*a*) **wollen wir . . . ?** *shall we . . . ?*, e.g. **wollen wir gehen?** *shall we go?*; **wir wollen . . .** *let's . . .* , e.g. **komm, wir wollen es noch einmal versuchen!** *come on, let's try again!*, **wir wollen uns doch nichts vormachen** *let's not kid ourselves*; (*b*) **wollen Sie bitte . . .** *will/would you please . . .* , e.g. **wollen Sie bitte Platz nehmen** *will you please take a seat*, **wollen Sie bitte so freundlich sein und mir den Weg zeigen** *would you please be so kind as to show me the way* (a different tone is heard in **willst du / wollt ihr wohl ruhig sein!** *will you be quiet!*).

(iii) INTENTION (*I* etc.) *will, to be going to, to plan to*:

ich will sie morgen früh anrufen *I'll ring her tomorrow morning,* **wie willst du ihm das erklären?** *how will you / how are you going to explain that to him?,* **wir wollen im Sommer nach Teneriffa segeln** *we plan to sail to Tenerife in the summer*
sie wollte mich ursprünglich nächsten Freitag besuchen *she was originally going to visit me next Friday*

(iv) IMMINENT ACTION *to be about to, to be going to*:

wir wollten gerade einkaufen gehen, als Karls Onkel auftauchte *we were just about to go shopping when Karl's uncle turned up*
die Sonne wollte eben untergehen *the sun was just about to go down,* **es sieht aus, als wollte es regnen** *it looks as if it's going to rain*

(v) *to be intended/meant to*:

seine Bilder wollen die rätselhafte Beschaffenheit des Menschen dokumentieren *his pictures are intended to record man's enigmatic nature*
die Sendung wollte vor den Gefahren des Massentourismus warnen *the programme was meant to alert us to the dangers of mass tourism*

(vi) NECESSITY: . . . **will** + past participle + **sein**[34] (*a*) . . . *must/has to be* + past participle, e.g. **Geld will erst mal verdient sein, ehe man es ausgibt** *money must first be earned before you spend it;* (*b*) . . . *needs* + gerund, e.g. **diese Entscheidung will überlegt sein** *this decision needs thinking about.*

(vii) *to claim*:

sie will Visagistin sein *she claims to be a make-up artist*
er will seine Frau 1939 kennen gelernt haben *he claims to have met his wife in 1939,* **sie will zur Party eingeladen worden sein** *she claims to have been invited to the party*
Compare the idioms **ich will nichts gehört/gesehen haben** *I didn't hear/see a thing* (i.e. pretending that I didn't), **keiner/niemand will es gewesen sein** *no-one wants to admit it was him.*

(viii) CONCESSIVE (present subjunctive) **wolle** in **komme, was da wolle** *come what may,* **koste es, was es wolle** *cost what it may.*

(ix) CONDITIONAL (past subjunctive) **wollte** = *were to*:

wenn man alles glauben wollte, was der Minister sagt *if one were to believe everything the minister says*

---

[34] Regarding this use of **sein** with passive force see p. 79, footnote 30.

es wäre tragisch, wollte man die Rechte dieses Stammes außer Acht lassen *it would be tragic if the rights of this tribe were to be disregarded*

(x) IN IDIOMATIC EXPRESSIONS: **das will ich hoffen/meinen!** *I should hope/think so!*, **das will ich dir gern glauben** *I quite believe it.*

The quasi-modal **BRAUCHEN** *to need (to)*
This verb, although not itself a modal verb, is included here since it resembles such verbs in several ways: (*a*) The past participle formed with **ge-** (**gebraucht**) is replaced by the infinitive form when a dependent infinitive precedes, e.g. **sie hätte nicht zu kommen brauchen** *she needn't have come.* (*b*) In subordinate clauses an auxiliary verb precedes a dependent infinitive, e.g. **wenn sie nicht hätte zu kommen brauchen** *if she hadn't needed to come* (see p. 107, *Subordinate clauses* (iii)). (*c*) While the infinitive is preceded by **zu** in established usage (e.g. **niemand braucht es zu wissen** *nobody need know*, **du brauchst nur seinen Namen zu sagen** *you need only say his name*), **zu** is omitted colloquially by some speakers—a construction that is widely regarded as unacceptable. (*d*) Finally, although in standard usage the past subjunctive is, as with all other weak verbs, identical with the indicative form (**brauchte**), a second, distinctively subjunctive form **bräuchte** has evolved in southern German.

Its use as an auxiliary is limited to constructions with a negative or **nur**; otherwise **müssen** is used. Examples:

I need to do it **ich muss es tun**
it needed to be done **es musste getan werden**
I don't need to do it **ich brauche es nicht zu tun**
it didn't need to be done **es brauchte nicht getan zu werden**

Like the true modals, **brauchen** may also be used elliptically, e.g. **ich brauche heute nicht in die Stadt** *I don't need to go into town today.*

Word Order

MAIN CLAUSES

In a main clause (except in the case of a question or command) the finite verb forms the *second element* in the sentence. It may, as usually in English, follow the subject, e.g. **der Mann reitet auf dem Pferd** *the man is riding the horse*; but it may also follow another element, in which case the subject comes after the finite verb, as happens in English in cases like *no sooner was she . . . , only later did they . . .* —this is known as *inversion*.

Examples:

(finite verb follows adverb) **gestern** *habe* **ich im Garten gearbeitet** *yesterday I worked in the garden*

(finite verb follows complement) **ein Experte** *ist* **er nicht, aber . . .** *he's no expert, but . . .*

(finite verb follows object) **dieses Wort** *kenne* **ich nicht** *I don't know this word*

(finite verb follows appositional phrase) **Däne von Geburt,** *lebt* **er jetzt auf Kreta** *a Dane by birth, he now lives in Crete*

(finite verb follows past participle: i) **viele haben diesen Roman gelesen, verstanden** *haben* **ihn nur wenige** *many people have read this novel, but few have understood it*

(finite verb follows past participle: ii) **sie forderten, dass die Wiedervereinigung Deutschlands aufgegeben werden solle; begründet** *wurde* **diese Forderung mit dem Argument, dass . . .** *they demanded that the reunification of Germany should be abandoned, basing their demand on the argument that . . .*

(finite verb follows infinitive) **,,Setzen wir Deutschland, sozusagen, in den Sattel! Reiten** *wird* **es schon können"** (Bismarck, 1867) *'Let us put Germany, so to speak, in the saddle! She'll be able to ride all right'*

(finite verb follows subordinate clause) **weil es heute so warm ist, können wir draußen essen** *because it's so warm today we can eat outdoors*

Inverted word-order is often used (as in the second example above) to emphasize the word or phrase placed before the verb, and may serve to underline a contrast (fifth example); not all inversion, however, is emphatic (see e.g. the first and last examples). Inverted order may also establish a link with the preceding sentence or clause (sixth example).

Exceptionally, inversion does not occur in main clauses *following a concessive clause* beginning with the equivalent of *whatever, whoever, however,* etc.:

was (immer) du auch sagst, ich halte an meiner Meinung fest *whatever you say, I'm sticking to my opinion*

The verb precedes the subject in the *imperative* (**Sie** form) and *direct questions* (unless the subject is an interrogative pronoun):

stehen Sie auf! *get up!*
warum hast du es getan? *why did you do it?*

Similarly in the 1st person plural present subjunctive used in exhortations:

gehen wir nach Hause! *let's go home*

Inverted order occurs in some *exclamations*:

hab ich's mir doch gedacht! *I thought as much!*
war das eine Hetze! *what a rush that was!*
hat die aber Glück gehabt! *was she lucky!*
wären wir doch in Leipzig geblieben! *if only we'd stayed in Leipzig!*

While it is quite usual for an English sentence to begin with two adverbs (or adverbial phrases), in German the position of the finite verb as the second element rules out such a word order, and in an equivalent German sentence the verb stands *between* the adverbs, e.g. *two weeks ago, under similar circumstances, she would not have hesitated to do it* **vor zwei Wochen** hätte sie **unter ähnlichen Umständen** nicht gezögert es zu tun. (Compare, however, *on the right, next to the piano, stood the two American ladies* **rechts, neben dem Klavier, standen die beiden amerikanischen Damen**: adverbs of the same type, which effectively form a unit, are not separated.)

SUBORDINATE CLAUSES

In a subordinate clause the finite verb *goes to the end*:

wir wussten, dass sie nicht kommen konnten *we knew that they couldn't come*
ich fragte, wann er angekommen sei *I asked when he had arrived*
das Mädchen, das eine blaue Bluse anhatte *the girl (who was) wearing a blue blouse*
sobald ich die Grenze erreichte *as soon as I reached the border*

Exceptions to this rule:

(i) After the conjunction **denn** the word order is that of a main clause, e.g. **sie gingen langsam, denn es war sehr heiß in der Wüste** *they walked slowly, it being very hot in the desert.*

(ii) When the conjunction **dass** is omitted after **sagen, glauben**, etc., the word order is that of a main clause, e.g. **er sagte, er habe von dieser Grammatik kein Wort verstanden** *he said he hadn't understood a word of this grammar.*

(iii) The auxiliary **haben** precedes the dependent infinitive in constructions with modal verbs (or other verbs having a second past participle identical with the infinitive), e.g. **wenn ich das** *hätte* **aussprechen können** *if I'd been able to pronounce that,* **sie beklagte sich, dass sie die Insel nicht** *habe* **besuchen dürfen** *she complained that she hadn't been allowed to visit the island.* The auxiliary **werden** likewise precedes the dependent infinitive in constructions with modal verbs, e.g. **es stellte sich heraus, dass ich den Laden** *würde* **behalten können** *it turned out that I would be able to keep the shop.*

(iv) Inversion occurs:

(*a*) when in a conditional clause **wenn** *if* + verb at the end of the clause is replaced by inversion of subject and verb, e.g. **kommt der Pianist nicht, dann kann das Konzert nicht stattfinden** *if the pianist doesn't come the concert can't take place,* **wäre ich sofort aufgestanden, hätte ich den Zug noch erreicht** *if I'd (had I) got up immediately I would have caught the train.*

(*b*) when **als** is used in the sense of *as if,* e.g. **es sieht aus, als würde es bald regnen** *it looks as if it'll rain soon.*

(*c*) (in literary style) when used with **doch** to convey causal force, e.g. **das Dorf ist sehr ruhig, liegt es doch abseits der Hauptverkehrsstraßen** *the village is very quiet, situated as it is away from the main roads.*

If two (or more) clauses have compound tenses *with the same auxiliary,* the latter is 'held over' until the end of the second (last) clause, e.g. **nachdem ich gebadet und mein Haar gewaschen** *hatte,* **machte ich mir ein Omelett** *after I'd had a bath and washed my hair I made myself an omelette.*

It follows from the rule regarding the position of the verb in a subordinate clause that when *one subordinate clause is enclosed within another* the verb goes to the end in both clauses, e.g. **er wusste, dass sich das junge Paar, das sehr wenig Geld** *hatte,* **die neue Sitzgarnitur nicht leisten** *konnte* he knew that the young couple, who had very little money, could not afford the new suite.

INFINITIVES, PAST PARTICIPLES, AND SEPARABLE PREFIXES

Infinitives, past participles, and separable prefixes go to the end of a main clause:

> (infinitive) **Indonesien wird auf seinen Anspruch nicht** *verzichten* Indonesia will not give up her claim
> (past participle) **wir haben viel Geld** *verloren* we've lost a lot of money
> (separable prefix) **der Schäferhund hielt die Herde** *zusammen* the sheepdog kept the flock together

(An infinitive follows a past participle, e.g. **die Räder müssen ausgewuchtet werden** the wheels need balancing.)

This rule, helpful though it is as a general guideline for the student of German, is not rigidly observed in that:

(i) one or more prepositional phrases sometimes follow such words:

er wird sich bestimmt entschuldigen *für seinen Fehler* he's sure to apologize for his mistake

dieses Auto wird gern gekauft *wegen der geringen Unterhaltungskosten* this car sells well because of its low maintenance costs

wir schalten um *nach München* (TV announcement) we're going over to Munich

This phenomenon is particularly common in the spoken language, but may also be encountered in written German. It is a question of style whether one writes e.g. **ein Film, in dem scharfe Kritik am Leben der oberen Zehntausend Roms geübt wird** *a film in which the life of Rome's high society is sharply criticized* or . . . **in dem scharfe Kritik geübt wird am Leben der oberen Zehntausend Roms**.

(ii) phrases of comparison introduced by **als** *than* and **wie** *as, like* follow them:

sie hätte keinen besseren Begleiter haben können *als diesen schneidigen jungen Flieger* she could have had no better escort than this dashing young aviator

man muss den Kopf drehen *wie ein Flamingo* you have to turn your head like a flamingo

Note that when a subordinate clause follows a main clause containing an infinitive, past participle, or separable prefix as final element, the latter separates the subordinate clause from the word it refers back to:

all das war in einer Nation *entstanden,* **die** . . . all this had come into being in a nation which . . .

er sprach die Hoffnung *aus,* **dass** . . . he expressed the hope that . . .

In a subordinate clause infinitives and past participles occupy the penultimate position, immediately before the finite verb (e.g.—to return to the examples given under *Subordinate clauses* above— . . . **dass sie nicht kommen konnten,** . . . **wann er** *angekommen* **sei**); separable prefixes are compounded with the verb (e.g. . . . **das eine blaue Bluse** *an*hatte).

COMPLEMENTS

Complements—both nouns and adjectives—come last:

er ist seit vielen Jahren *Dirigent* he's been a conductor for many years

sie ist nach meiner Meinung *eine bewundernswerte Frau* she's an admirable woman in my opinion

Pferde sind in der Regel *gehorsam* horses are obedient as a rule

die Tage sind im Winter *kurz* the days are short in winter

POSITION AND ORDER OF OBJECTS AND ADVERBS

(i) POSITION OF THE PRONOUN OBJECT (INCLUDING REFLEXIVE PRONOUN):

(*a*) In a main clause with the subject first, it comes immediately after the finite verb:

man hat es in Sambia entdeckt *it was discovered in Zambia*
der Werbespot rentiert sich nicht mehr *the commercial no longer pays*

(*b*) In a subordinate clause or when there is inversion in the main clause, it generally precedes the subject if the latter is a noun (or indefinite pronoun such as **jemand, nichts**) but always follows if it is a personal pronoun:

da mir der Zollbeamte (but **da er mir**) **den Pass wegnehmen wollte**
as the customs officer (*he*) *wanted to take away my passport*
letztes Jahr hat ihn ein Hund (but **hat er ihn**) **gebissen** *last year a dog*
(*it*) *bit him*
plötzlich öffnete sich sein Fallschirm (but **öffnete er sich**) *suddenly his*
parachute (*it*) *opened*
kann sich ein Rentner (but **kann er sich**) **so ein großes Haus leisten?**
can a pensioner (*he*) *afford such a big house?*[35]

(ii) DIRECT AND INDIRECT OBJECTS OF THE VERB:

(*a*) two nouns: dative precedes accusative:

er gab dem Jungen ein Spielzeug *he gave the boy a toy*
die Prinzessin gewährte der Presse ein weiteres Interview *the princess*
granted the press another interview

A dative object denoting a thing normally follows an accusative object denoting a person, e.g. **sie überließ ihren Partner seinem Schicksal** *she left her partner to his fate.*

(*b*) two pronouns: accusative precedes dative:

er gab es ihm *he gave it to him*

(*c*) pronoun precedes noun:

er gab es dem Jungen *he gave it to the boy*
er gab ihm ein Spielzeug *he gave him a toy*

(iii) ADVERBS AND ADVERBIAL PHRASES: The usual order is Time–Manner–Place (although this is not rigidly applied and variations may occur for the sake of emphasis):

sie sind gestern (T) **mit dem Bus** (M) **nach Zürich** (P) **gefahren** *they*
went by bus to Zurich yesterday

Where there are two or more adverbs (or adverbial phrases) of time the more general precedes the more specific, e.g. **sie kommt jeden Abend um 8 nach Hause** *she comes home at 8 every evening.*

---

[35] It is not uncommon, however, for the pronoun object (including the reflexive pronoun) to follow the noun subject, e.g. **da der Zollbeamte mir den Pass wegnehmen wollte**.

Numerous adverbial phrases are used in conjunction with a verb to form a set phrase of the type **in Betracht ziehen** *to take into account.* (Other examples are **in Frage** (or **infrage**) **stellen** *to call in question,* **zur Folge haben** *to lead to,* **zu Stande** (or **zustande**) **bringen** *to bring about, achieve.*) They may be compared to separable prefixes, occupying the same position in the sentence as the latter (e.g. **hinzu kam, dass der Vulkanausbruch in ganz Europa Wetterveränderungen zur Folge hatte** *added to which the eruption of the volcano led to changes in the weather throughout Europe*).

(iv) ADVERBS AND NOUN OBJECTS: When both an adverb (or adverbial phrase) and a direct noun object are present, the former generally precedes the latter:

> **wir erwarten seit fünf Monaten eine Gehaltserhöhung** *we've been expecting a salary increase for five months*
> **Amnesty International erhielt 1977 den Friedensnobelpreis** *Amnesty International received the Nobel peace prize in 1977*

Emphasis may, however, reverse this order, e.g. (with the time stressed) **wir erwarten eine Gehaltserhöhung seit fünf Monaten.**

(v) POSITION OF **nicht** *not*:

(*a*) **Nicht** is normally placed after an object (but before an infinitive, past participle, or separable prefix) when it negates an entire sentence or clause:

> **wir brauchen seine Hilfe nicht** *we don't need his help*
> **ich habe es nicht gesehen** *I haven't seen it*
> **sag das nicht!** *don't say that!*
> **warum liest du das Buch nicht?** *why don't you read the book?*

But it precedes a complement:

> **diese Bemerkung war nicht sehr freundlich** *that remark was not very friendly*
> **das ist nicht meine Schuld** *that's not my fault*

or a prepositional phrase:

> **steig nicht auf den Berg!** *don't climb the mountain!*

(*b*) If a particular word or phrase is negated, **nicht** then precedes that word or phrase:

> **nicht jeder kann das** *not everyone can do that*
> **ich habe nicht dich gemeint, sondern Jürgen** *I didn't mean you, I meant Jürgen*
> **ich bin nicht im geringsten beleidigt** *I'm not in the least offended*

(*c*) Common combinations (with **nicht** placed second): **auch nicht** *not . . . either,* **noch nicht** *not yet,* **gar/überhaupt nicht** *not at all.*

ADJECTIVAL AND PARTICIPIAL PHRASES (ATTRIBUTIVE)

A common feature of written German is the adjectival or participial phrase preceding the noun, e.g. **der für die Schulen zuständige Minister** *the minister responsible for schools* (literally *the for schools responsible minister*), **ein nach Kapstadt bestimmtes Schiff** *a ship bound for Cape Town* (literally *a for Cape Town bound ship*), **diese Fußball spielenden Mädchen** *these girls playing football* (literally *these football playing girls*).

This construction can be a stumbling-block for the beginner, not only because the order of words is unfamiliar but also because the article is separated (sometimes considerably) from the noun it refers to. To translate the construction it is necessary first to identify and translate the article (or similar word) and the noun it refers to, which will always follow the adjective or participle concerned:

1	4	3	2
der	[für die Schulen	zuständige]	Minister
ein	[nach Kapstadt	bestimmtes]	Schiff
diese	[Fußball	spielenden]	Mädchen

The adjective or participle (3) is then translated, and finally any words (4) that come between the article etc. and the adjective or participle.

The adjectival or participial phrase may immediately follow an adjective (plus comma), whereas in English their equivalents would be separated by the noun concerned, e.g. **auf jene sorglose, für die Jugend typische Weise** *in the carefree manner typical of the young.*

This construction may also occur where an adjective or participle functions as a noun, e.g. **der von der Polizei Gesuchte** *the man wanted by the police*, **die Hoffnungslosigkeit der politisches Asyl Suchenden** *the hopelessness of those seeking political asylum* (**politisches Asyl** = object).

Word Formation

NOUN SUFFIXES

-CHEN (pl. same), N. DIMINUTIVE suffix (making the noun neuter and usually causing the stem-vowel to be mutated where possible), e.g. **das Lämmchen** *little lamb* (**Lamm** *lamb*); nouns in -e and -en lose these endings before -chen, e.g. **das Schürzchen** *little apron* (**Schürze** *apron*), **das Fädchen** *little thread* (**Faden** *thread*).

-EI (with verbs ending in -eln, -ern), **-erei** (pl. -en), F.

1. —*ing* (ACTIVITY OR PRODUCT OF AN ACTIVITY), e.g. **die Schnitzerei** *(wood-)carving* (**schnitzen** *to carve*); denoting a continual or repeated activity, the suffixes often have a pejorative flavour, e.g. **die Schreiberei** *(endless) writing* (**schreiben** *to write*), **die Fragerei** *(tiresome) questioning* (**fragen** *to ask*). (The neuter prefix Ge- may be used in the same way, e.g. **das Gegacker** *(constant) cackling* (**gackern** *to cackle*), **das Gesinge** *(irksome) singing* (**singen** *to sing*).)

2. (-**erei** only) —*ery*, e.g. **die Bäckerei** *bakery* (**Bäcker** *baker*).

-ER (pl. same), M.

1. (from verbs). Denotes a PERSON ENGAGED IN AN ACTIVITY, e.g. **der Brauer** *brewer* (**brauen** *to brew*), or a TOOL, e.g. **der Öffner** *opener* (**öffnen** *to open*).

2. (added to place-names). Denotes an INHABITANT, e.g. **der Berliner** *Berliner*, **der Stockholmer** *inhabitant of Stockholm*.

-EREI: see **-ei**.

-HEIT, F. Denotes a QUALITY: —*ness*, —*ity*, etc., e.g. **die Faulheit** *laziness* (**faul** *lazy*), **die Gleichheit** *equality* (**gleich** *equal*). Some nouns also function as countables (pl. -en), e.g. **die Schönheit** *beauty* (= quality or woman).

-IN (pl. -nen), F. FEMININE suffix (usually with mutation of stem-vowel where possible): *female . . .* ; *woman . . .* ; —*ess*; *she-*; e.g. **die Arbeiterin** *(female/woman) worker* (**Arbeiter** *male worker*), **die Ärztin** *(woman) doctor* (**Arzt** *male doctor*), **die Französin** *Frenchwoman* (**Franzose** *Frenchman*), **die Russin** *Russian (woman)* (**Russe** *(male) Russian*), **die Gräfin** *countess* (**Graf** *earl, count*), **die Füchsin** *vixen* (**Fuchs** *fox*), **die Hündin** *bitch* (**Hund** *dog*).

-KEIT, -igkeit, F. Denotes a QUALITY: —*ness*, —*ity*, etc., e.g. **die Einsamkeit** *loneliness* (**einsam** *lonely*), **die Ewigkeit** *eternity* (**ewig** *eternal*), **die Hoffnungslosigkeit** *hopelessness* (**hoffnungslos** *hopeless*), **die Genauigkeit** *accuracy, precision* (**genau** *accurate, precise*). Some nouns also function as countables (pl. -en), e.g. **die Unzulänglichkeit** *inadequacy*.

-LEIN (pl. same), N. Chiefly poetic: DIMINUTIVE suffix making the noun neuter and causing the stem-vowel to be mutated where possible, e.g. **das Bächlein** *little stream* (**Bach** *stream*).

-LING (pl. **-e**), M.
1. Used (often pejoratively) to refer to INDIVIDUALS WITH A PARTICULAR QUALITY, e.g. **der Neuling** *novice* (**neu** *new*), **der Schwächling** *weakling* (**schwach** *weak*), **der Primitivling** *primitive person.*
2. Used of PERSONS UNDERGOING SOMETHING, e.g. **der Prüfling** *examinee* (**prüfen** *to examine*), **der Lehrling** *apprentice* (**lehren** *to teach*).
3. **der Zwilling** *twin*, **der Drilling** *triplet*, **der Vierling** *quadruplet*, etc.

-SCHAFT (pl. **-en**), F.
1. Denotes a GROUP OF PERSONS, e.g. **die Studentenschaft** *student body.*
2. Denotes a ROLE or OFFICE: —*ship* etc., e.g. **die Urheberschaft** *authorship*, **die Vaterschaft** *paternity* (**Vater** *father*), **die Präsidentschaft** *presidency* (**Präsident** *president*).

-TUM, N. (except **der Irrtum** *error*, **der Reichtum** *wealth*)
1. . . . *world*, . . . *civilization*, e.g. **das Germanentum** *the Germanic world.*
2. —*ism*, —*ry*, e.g. **das Nomadentum** *nomadism*, **das Luthertum** *Lutheranism*, **das Heldentum** *heroism*, **das Rittertum** *chivalry* (**Ritter** *knight*).
3. Denotes an OFFICE, e.g. **das Papsttum** *papacy* (**Papst** *pope*).
4. Forms a COLLECTIVE NOUN, e.g. **das Beamtentum** *officialdom, civil servants* (**Beamte(r)** *official, civil servant*).

-UNG (pl. **-en**), F. Forms VERBAL NOUNS: —*ing*, —*tion*, etc., e.g. **die Atmung** *breathing* (**atmen** *to breathe*), **die Erklärung** *explanation* (**erklären** *to explain*).

ADJECTIVAL SUFFIXES

-ARTIG. —*like*, e.g. **schlangenartig** *snake-like*; *of a* . . . *kind*, e.g. **andersartig** *of a different kind.*

-BAR (added to verb stems). —*able*, —*ible*, e.g. **übersetzbar** *translatable* (**übersetzen** *to translate*), **essbar** *edible* (**essen** *to eat*).

-FÄHIG.
1. *able to*, e.g. **arbeitsfähig** *able to work.*
2. —*able*, —*ible*, e.g. **transportfähig** *transportable*; *capable of*, e.g. **entwicklungsfähig** *capable of development*; also indicates ELIGIBILITY, e.g. **gesellschaftsfähig** *socially acceptable.*

-HAFT. Forms adjectives indicating a QUALITY, e.g. **vorteilhaft** *advantageous* (**Vorteil** *advantage*), **damenhaft** *lady-like* (**Dame** *lady*), **greisenhaft** *senile* (**Greis** *old man*), **episodenhaft** *episodic* (**Episode** *episode*).

-IG. Forms adjectives indicating a QUALITY (often with vowel mutation), e.g. **sandig** *sandy* (**Sand** *sand*), **wässerig** *watery* (**Wasser** *water*), **mutig** *courageous* (**Mut** *courage*). Referring to time, indicates duration, e.g. **dreistündig** *lasting three hours, three-hour* (**Stunde** *hour*).

-ISCH.
 1. Forms (especially pejorative) adjectives indicating a QUALITY (sometimes with vowel mutation), e.g. **kindisch** *childish* (**Kind** *child*), **herrisch** *imperious* (**Herr** *master*), **bäurisch** *boorish* (**Bauer** *farmer, peasant*).
 2. (in words of foreign origin) —*ic(al)*, e.g. **historisch** *historic(al)*, **dramatisch** *dramatic*, **mathematisch** *mathematical*.
 3. Forms ADJECTIVES FROM PROPER NOUNS, e.g. **platonisch** *Platonic, platonic*, **europäisch** *European*, **israelisch** *Israeli*.

-LICH (often with mutation of the stem-vowel).
 1. Forms adjectives indicating a QUALITY, e.g. **tödlich** *fatal* (**Tod** *death*), **menschlich** *human* (**Mensch** *human being*), **mündlich** *oral* (**Mund** *mouth*). Referring to time, indicates periodic recurrence: —*ly*, e.g. **zweistündlich** *two-hourly*.
 2. (especially with COLOUR WORDS) —*ish*, e.g. **bläulich** *bluish* (**blau** *blue*), **rötlich** *reddish* (**rot** *red*).
 3. (ADDED TO VERB STEMS) —*able*, —*ible*, e.g. **erhältlich** *obtainable* (**erhalten** *to obtain*), **unglaublich** *incredible* (**glauben** *to believe*).

-LOS. —*less, without . . .* , e.g. **hoffnungslos** *hopeless* (**Hoffnung** *hope*), **widerstandslos** *without resistance* (**Widerstand** *resistance*).

-MÄSSIG (-mäßig).
 1. In the sense *in accordance with* (sometimes -**gemäß** is used instead), e.g. **verfassungsmäßig** *constitutional* (**Verfassung** *constitution*), **gewohnheitsmäßig** *habitual* (**Gewohnheit** *habit*).
 2. *in terms of, as regards,* e.g. **qualitätsmäßig** *in terms of / as regards quality*.
 3. In the sense *in the nature of,* e.g. **behelfsmäßig** *makeshift* (**Behelf** *makeshift*).
 4. In adverbial use, denotes MANNER, e.g. **karteimäßig** (record etc.) *on index cards* (**Kartei** *card index*), **zahlenmäßig** (express etc.) *in figures* (**Zahl** *figure*).

-SAM. Forms adjectives indicating a QUALITY, e.g. **gewaltsam** *violent* (**Gewalt** *force, violence*), **sparsam** *thrifty* (**sparen** *to save*), **bedeutsam** *significant* (**bedeuten** *mean, signify*).

COMPOUND NOUNS

The German convention of writing compounds (including long ones) as single words sometimes leads beginners to regard them—or German— as difficult; and Mark Twain complains, in his tongue-in-cheek essay on 'The Awful German Language', of these 'mountain-ranges stretching across the page', suggesting they should only be allowed to be uttered with intervals. (One wonders what he would have made of some of the coinages current in present-day computerese, for instance **das Unterbrechungs-anforderungsflipflop,** alias *interrupt request latch.*) In fact, however, English and German are not so different here—it is merely a matter of orthography: English does not always join up the elements to make a formal compound, whereas German does, e.g. *life insurance company* **die Lebensversicherungsgesellschaft,** *media research* **die Medienforschung.** A more substantial difference between the two languages in the matter of compounds lies in the fact that German often has a compound where English uses something else, for example a phrase with nouns linked by *of* (*work of art* **das Kunstwerk**), adjective + noun (*man-made fibre* **die Kunstfaser,** *human geography* **die Kulturgeographie**), or a word consisting of one element only (*desk* **der Schreibtisch,** *skunk* **das Stinktier**).

German compound nouns may be composed of the following elements: (*a*) NOUN + NOUN, e.g. **der Marktplatz** *market-place*; (*b*) ADJECTIVE OR PARTICIPLE + NOUN, e.g. **der Billigflug** *cheap flight,* **der Gebrauchtwagen** *used car*; (*c*) NUMERAL + NOUN, e.g. **der Dreifuß** *tripod*; (*d*) VERB-STEM + NOUN, e.g. **das Rennpferd** *racehorse*; (*e*) PREPOSITION + NOUN, e.g. **der Nachsommer** *Indian summer*; (*f*) PRONOUN + NOUN, e.g. **das Selbstvertrauen** *self-confidence.*

Not even the largest dictionary can include all possible compound nouns, and if a word is not given in a dictionary it should be broken down into its component parts, consideration of which should suggest a possible translation. In this connection, it is helpful to have a knowledge of how compounds of type (*a*) (noun + noun: the commonest type) are put together:

(i) NOUN 1 + NOUN 2, directly joined: e.g. **der Milchmann** *milkman,* **die Hausfrau** *housewife,* **das Zahnfleisch** *gums.*

(ii) NOUN 1 (WITH LOSS OF FINAL **-e**) + NOUN 2: e.g. **die Kirschblüte** *cherry blossom* (cf. **die Kirsche**), **das Endstadium** *final stage* (cf. **das Ende**).

(iii) NOUN 1 + LINKING ELEMENT + NOUN 2:
(*a*) **-e-:** e.g. **die Mausefalle** *mousetrap* (cf. **die Maus**), **das Tagebuch** *diary* (cf. **der Tag**).
(*b*) **-(e)n-:** e.g. **der Schwanengesang** *swan-song* (cf. **der Schwan**), **die Sonnenuhr** *sundial* (cf. **die Sonne**), **die Menschenrechte** *human rights* (cf. **der Mensch**).
(*c*) **-(e)ns-:** e.g. **der Schmerzensschrei** *scream of pain* (cf. **der Schmerz**), **die Willensfreiheit** *free will* (cf. **der Wille**).
(*d*) **-er-:** e.g. **der Kinderschuh** *child's shoe* (cf. **das Kind**), **die Bildersprache** *imagery* (cf. **das Bild**), **der Eierlikör** *advocaat* (cf. **das Ei**).
(*e*) **-s-,** also **-es-:** e.g. **der Geburtstag** *birthday* (cf. **die Geburt**), **der Produktions-ausfall** *loss of production* (cf. **die Produktion**), **die Schönheitskönigin** *beauty queen* (cf. **die Schönheit**), **das Volkslied** *folk-song* (cf. **das Volk**), **das Hilfsverb** *auxiliary (verb)* (cf. **die Hilfe**); **der Freundeskreis** *circle of friends* (cf. **der Freund**), **die Bundesregierung** *the (Federal) Government* (cf. **der Bund**), **das Liebesgedicht** *love-poem* (cf. **die Liebe**).

Sometimes the first noun appears in different forms: e.g. (**die Geburt** *birth*) **die Geburtenkontrolle** *birth control,* **der Geburtsort** *place of birth*;

(der Mann *man*) **das Mannloch** *manhole,* **das Mannesalter** *manhood,* **die Männerstimme** *male voice.*

A few regional variations occur: North German **Rinder-, Schweine-** and **Gänse-** (followed by e.g. **-braten** *roast beef, pork, goose*) become **Rinds-, Schweins-** and **Gans-** on southern menus. Austrian usage replaces **e** by **s** in words such as **die Aufnahmsprüfung** *entrance examination,* **der Ausnahmsfall** *exception(al case),* **die Einnahmsquelle** *source of income;* and inserts linking **s** in e.g. **der Fabriksarbeiter** *factory hand,* **der Gesangsverein** *choral society,* **die Zugsverbindung** *train connection.*

COMPOUND ADJECTIVES

German compound adjectives may be composed of the following elements:

(i) NOUN + ADJECTIVE (OR PARTICIPLE)—sometimes directly joined, sometimes connected by a linking element or with the loss of final -e: e.g. (with noun as object of present participle) **atemberaubend** *breathtaking;* (corresponding to genitive construction) **siegessicher** *sure of victory,* (to dative construction) **umweltfeindlich** *damaging to the environment;* (corresponding to prepositional constructions) **kalorienreich** *rich in calories,* **schrankfertig** *washed and ironed* (literally *wardrobe-ready*); (with participles: instrumental) **efeuumrankt** *ivy-clad,* **computergestützt** *computer-assisted,* **handgemalt** *hand-painted,* **fetttriefend** *dripping with fat;* (with participles: locative) **stadtbekannt** *known all over the town,* **endbetont** *with final stress;* (comparison, intensification) **stocksteif** *stiff as a poker,* **splitter(faser)nackt** *stark naked.*[36]

(ii) ADJECTIVE + ADJECTIVE: e.g. **kleinlaut** *subdued,* **dunkelrot** *dark red;* ('copulative' compounds with two elements of equal weight) **nasskalt** *cold and wet,* **bittersüß** *bitter-sweet,* **schwarzweiß** *black and white;* (colour adjectives denoting a particular shade) **blaugrün** *bluish-green;* ('parasynthetic' compounds in -**ig**, the second elements of which do not exist as independent adjectives) **blauäugig** *blue-eyed,* **kurzlebig** *short-lived,* **viertürig** *four-door.*

(iii) VERB-STEM + ADJECTIVE: e.g. **kauflustig** *in a buying mood* (cf. **kaufen**), **experimentierfreudig** *keen on experimenting* (cf. **experimentieren**), **schreibfaul** (literally *writing-lazy*) **sein** *to be a poor correspondent* (cf. **schreiben**).

Hyphenated adjectival combinations represent a looser kind of association of two adjectives, the hyphen indicating that they retain their separate force, e.g. **seine nüchtern-kalte Beurteilung der Situation** *his sober, cold assessment of the situation.* The hyphen is used in combinations such as **deutsch-englisch** (of relations etc.) *Anglo-German.* Note also **römisch-katholisch** *Roman Catholic,* **griechisch-orthodox** *Greek Orthodox,* **maria-theresianisch** *of the reign of Empress Maria Theresa* [German **Theresia**].

---

[36] Certain compounds which combine a noun with a past participle are neither instrumental nor locative in sense. A number of formations with -**betont** are used in the sense *with . . . emphasized,* e.g. **taillenbetont** *with the waist emphasized,* i.e. *emphasizing the waist,* **gefühlsbetont** *emotional, emotive;* in the similar formation **hirnverbrannt** *hare-brained* the French *cerveau brûlé hothead* is reproduced, in form if not in meaning.

Guide to Prepositions

AB (+ dative)

1. (indicating time) FROM (. . . ONWARDS):

ab **Mitte der achtziger Jahre** (also **Achtzigerjahre**) *from the mid-eighties*
ab **Ostern** *from Easter*
Kinder *ab* **sechs Jahren** *children from the age of six*

When the article is omitted the accusative may also be used in e.g. *ab* **nächstem/nächsten Montag** *(as) from next Monday*.

2. (indicating place) FROM (. . . ONWARDS):

die Lok, die den ,,Schweiz-Express" *ab* **Basel zog** (*Spiegel*) *the engine that pulled the 'Swiss Express' from Basle*

3. (indicating lower limit) FROM . . . UPWARDS:

ab **$50** *from $50 upwards*
die Dienstgrade *ab* **Oberst** *ranks from colonel upwards*

AN

I. (+ dative)

1. (indicating place)

(*a*) ON (the side of):
an der Wand *on the wall*
am Berg *on the hill/mountain*
Wir lagen . . . **an der Bahnböschung** (Ch. Wolf) *We lay on the railway embankment*

(*b*) (proximity) AT:
  er stand *am* Fenster *he stood **at** the window*
  Da standen sie . . . *an* der Gartenpforte (Ch. Wolf) *There they stood **at** the garden gate*
  BY:
  sie wärmten sich die Hände *am* Ofen *they warmed their hands **by** the stove*

(*c*) ON (the edge of):
  ***an* der Grenze** *on the border*
  ***am* Stadtrand** *on the outskirts of the town/city*
  Trier liegt *an* der Mosel *Trier is **on** the Moselle*
  der Laden liegt direkt *an* der Hauptstraße *the shop is right **on** the main street*
  ***an* der Südküste von Island** (Brecht) *on the southern coast of Iceland*

(*d*) (with part of the body) ON:
  ***An* einer Hand fehlte dem Kerl ein Finger** (Zwerenz) ***On** one hand the fellow was missing a finger*

(*e*) ***am* Himmel** *in the sky* (as opposed to ***im* Himmel** *in heaven*)

(*f*) AGAINST:
  Rita lehnte zum Sterben müde *an* einem Baum (Ch. Wolf) *Rita, dead tired, was leaning **against** a tree*

(*g*) . . . **an** . . . . . . TO . . . :
  Rücken *an* Rücken *back **to** back*
  Wange *an* Wange *cheek **to** cheek*
  Stoßstange *an* Stoßstange *bumper **to** bumper*

(*h*) AT:
  der Ort, *an* dem es passierte *the place **at** which it happened*
  ***An* allen größeren Kreuzungen sind Panzer aufgefahren** (*Spiegel*) ***At** all the major crossroads tanks have moved into position*
  ***am* Ausgang der Zeile** *at the end of the line*
  ***an* der Spitze der Kolonne** *at the head of the column*
  im ersten Stock des Schulgebäudes, *an* strategischer Stelle (Kempowski) *on the first (U.S. second) floor of the school building, **at** a strategic point*
  ***an* den amerikanischen Universitäten** *at American universities*

(*i*) (suspension) FROM:
  die Lampe hängt *an* der Decke *the lamp hangs **from** the ceiling*

(*j*) (creative activity in progress) expressed by English continuous tense:
  sie schreibt *an* einem Roman *she is writing a novel*
  er webte *an* einem Teppich *he was weaving a carpet*

(*k*) (nibbling, sipping, sniffing, etc.) AT, or expressed by transitive verb:
  die Maus hat *am* Käse geknabbert *the mouse has nibbled **at** the cheese*
  sie nippte *am* Wein *she sipped **(at)** the wine*

der Dalmatiner schnupperte *am* Laternenpfahl *the Dalmatian sniffed (at) the lamp-post*

2. (indicating time)

(*a*) ON:

Es hat *am* Montag geregnet (Wohmann) *It rained on Monday*

Aber *an* anderen Tagen speiste er in Restaurants (Hesse) *But on other days he dined in restaurants*

But often not translated by a preposition:

***Am* nächsten Morgen, als ich aufwachte, war die Weimarer Republik verschwunden** (Zwerenz) *The next morning, when I woke up, the Weimar Republic had disappeared*

IN:

***am* Tage** *in the daytime, by day*

in der Imbissstube, in der ich *am* Morgen gefrühstückt hatte (Böll) *in the café in which I had had breakfast in the morning*

(*b*) (*South German*) (with festivals) AT:

***an* Ostern/Pfingsten/Weihnachten** *at Easter/Whitsun/Christmas*

3. (with part of the body) BY:

Zwei Offiziere ergreifen ihn *an* den Armen (Weiss) *Two officers grab him by the arms*

4. (indicating means) BY:

sie erkannte ihn *an* seiner Stimme *she recognized him by his voice*

***An* seiner Nase habe ich gesehen, dass er ein Russe war** (Böll) *I could tell by his nose that he was Russian*

BY MEANS OF:

er hat es *an* einem Beispiel gezeigt *he demonstrated it by means of an example*

Gerade wollte er . . . den heimlichen Charakter der Stadt *an* den Regeln des Ruderns erläutern (Lenz) *He was just about to explain the secret character of the town by means of the rules of rowing*

5. (indicating cause) OF, FROM:

Das . . . Kind war *an* einem Hitzschlag gestorben (Wohmann) *The child had died of heat-stroke*

Etwa 85 Prozent aller *an* Lungenkrebs Erkrankten waren Raucher (*Aktuell*) *About 85 per cent of all those suffering from lung cancer were smokers*

BY:

die Partei scheiterte *an* der Fünfprozentklausel *the party was defeated by the five-per-cent rule*

***An* der polnischen Frage entzündete sich der Zweite Weltkrieg** (Kleiner Brockhaus) *The Second World War was sparked off by the Polish question*

6. (indicating inherent quality) ABOUT:

> **Das Wichtige** *an* **Felice war, dass es sie gab** (Canetti) *The important thing about Felice was that she existed*
> **was so deutsch ist** *an* **der deutschen Kunst** (*FAZ*) *what is so German about German art*
> **was mir** *an* **ihnen auffiel** *what struck me about them*
>
> IN:
>
> **es ist nichts** *an* **dem Gerücht** *there is no truth in the rumour*
> **ich weiß nicht, was du** *an* **ihm findest** *I don't know what you see in him*

7. (*in respect of*) IN:

> **reich** *an* **Vitaminen** *rich in vitamins*
> **er ist uns** *an* **Intelligenz überlegen** *he is superior to us in intelligence*
> **Zugleich gewinnt der Islam** *an* **politischer Bedeutung** (*Aktuell*) *At the same time Islam is gaining in political importance*
>
> OF:
>
> **das Angebot** *an* **Gemüse** *the selection of vegetables*
> **ein hohes Maß** *an* **moralischer Integrität** (*SZ*) *a high degree of moral integrity*
>
> BY WAY OF:
>
> **was** *an* **Dokumenten zur Verfügung stand** (*Welt*) *what was available by way of documents*
>
> (with object of action) OF:
>
> **der Export** *an* **Kaffee** *the export of coffee*
> **Verrat** *an* **einem Freund** *betrayal of a friend*
> **die Kritik** *an* **den herkömmlichen psychiatrischen Institutionen** (*Aktuell*) *the criticism of traditional psychiatric institutions*
> **das Massaker** *an* **französischen Zivilisten** (*Spiegel*) *the massacre of French civilians*

II. (+ accusative)

1. (indicating motion) TO:

> **Die sowjetische Flotte rückt immer näher** *an* **das amerikanische Hoheitsgebiet** (*MM*) *The Soviet fleet is moving closer and closer to American territory*
> **Der Pförtner legte sein Ohr** *an* **das Fenster** (Lenz) *The porter put his ear to the window*
>
> ON (the side of):
>
> **er schrieb die Formel** *an* **die Tafel** *he wrote the formula on the blackboard*
> **sie klopften** *an* **ihre Tür** *they knocked on her door*
>
> AGAINST:
>
> **der Hagel prasselte** *an* **die Fenster** *the hail beat against the windows*
> **sie wurden** *an* **die Wand gestellt** *they were stood against the wall*

AT, BY:

sie setzte sich *an* den Tisch / das Feuer *she sat down at the table / by the fire*

2. (in figurative use) TO:

er schreibt nie *an* seine Mutter *he never writes to his mother*

Tuzzi, *an* den diese Frage . . . gerichtet war (Musil) *Tuzzi, to whom this question was addressed*

eine Rückgabe des Landes *an* die Ureinwohner (*Spiegel*) *a return of the land to its original inhabitants*

Er will wissen, wer ihn *an* die Stasi verraten hat (*Zeit*) *He wants to know who betrayed him to the Stasi*

Lawrence verstand es, sich *an* arabische Verhältnisse anzupassen (*PersonenLexikon*) *Lawrence knew how to adapt to Arabian conditions*

ON:

ihre Ansprüche *an* das Leben (Ch. Wolf) *her demands on life*

die deutsche Kriegserklärung *an* Russland *the German declaration of war on Russia*

OF:

Er dachte nicht *an* die verlorene Chance (Lenz) *He did not think of the lost opportunity*

Es war die Erinnerung *an* eine sonderbar ausgegangene Leidenschaft (Musil) *It was the memory of a passion that had ended strangely*

3. (usually with definite article) ROUGHLY:

an die 500 Bewerber pro Monat (*Spiegel*) *roughly 500 applicants per month*

ANSTATT = statt

AUF

I. (+ dative)

1. (indicating place)

(*a*) ON:

das Glas steht *auf* dem Tisch *the glass is on the table*

Hier, *auf* dem Primrose Hill, ging Marx spazieren (Weiss) *Here, on Primrose Hill, Marx would go for walks*

(*b*) AT:

ich habe sie *auf* der Post / einer Party getroffen *I met her at the post office/a party*

ich habe *auf* der Tagung schlecht geschlafen *I didn't sleep well at the conference*

das rätselhafte Geschehen *auf* Schloss Fenimore *the mysterious events at Castle Fenimore*

die Ampel stand *auf* Rot *the lights were at red*

(c) IN:

Ihretwegen hatte die Mutter *auf* **den Feldern . . . gearbeitet** (Ch. Wolf)
For their sake their mother had worked **in** *the fields*
Und draußen *auf* **der Straße kamen sie vorbeigezogen** (Böll) *And out*
in *the street they came marching past*
auf **Bahn sechs** *in lane six*
auf **Ferrari** *in a Ferrari*

Also with names of islands:

auf **Zypern/Teneriffa/den Bahamas** *in Cyprus/Tenerife/the Bahamas*

2. ON (holiday, journey, etc.):

Er befand sich *auf* **einem kurzen Urlaub in Luxor** (C. W. Ceram) *He was*
on *a short holiday in Luxor*
auf **ihrem Spaziergang durch Venedig** (Th. Mann) *on their walk through*
Venice
auf **dem Weg zum Pol** *on the way to the Pole*

II. (+ accusative)

1. (indicating motion)

(a) ON:

er stellte das Glas *auf* **den Tisch** *he put the glass* **on** *the table*
sie setzte sich *auf* **die Mauer** *she sat down* **on** *the wall*
Eine Haarnadel fiel *auf* **den Teppich** (A. Zweig) *A hairpin fell* **on** *the carpet*
Er lachte und tippte ihr *auf* **die Nase** (Ch. Wolf) *He laughed and tapped*
her **on** *the nose*

Also used when someone writes, draws, etc. something on something:

der einzige, der den Einfall gehabt hat, *auf* **eine Banane zu schreiben:**
es lebe Togo (Böll) *the only one to have the idea of writing* **on** *a banana:*
Long live Togo

(b) INTO:

er ging *auf* **die Straße / das Feld** *he went* **into** *the street/field*

(c) TO:

sie ging *auf* **die Post / eine Party** *she went* **to** *the post office / a party*

2. AT:

er zielte *auf* **die Scheibe** *he aimed* **at** *the target*
indem sie misstrauisch *auf* **die Preise sah** (Bachmann) *by looking askance*
at *the prices*
Ernst Wendland . . . deutete *auf* **den Zug** (Ch. Wolf) *Ernst Wendland*
pointed **at** *the train*

3. (indicating time)

(a) FOR (prospective period):

der Bundestag wird *auf* **vier Jahre gewählt** *the Bundestag is elected* **for**
four years

Compare **auf immer** *for ever*, **auf unbestimmte Zeit** *indefinitely*.

(*b*) ... **auf** ...... AFTER ... :
  Monat *auf* **Monat** *month **after** month*

4. (indicating manner) IN:
  auf **diese Weise** *in this way*
Also with names of languages:
  auf **Deutsch** *in German*

5. (in figurative use)
(*a*) **auf den ersten Blick** *at first sight*
(*b*) (*in response to*; often supported by following **hin**) AT:
  auf **meinen Wunsch (hin)** *at my request*
  ON:
  auf **meinen Rat (hin)** *on my advice*
(*c*) FOR:
  Bestellungen *auf* **Trauerkränze werden sorgfältig und prompt ausgeführt** (florist's notice) *Orders **for** wreaths carefully and promptly carried out*
  Horst Rudolf, der . . . *auf* **ein Auto sparte** (Ch. Wolf) *Horst Rudolf, who was saving **for** a car*
  Schon mit fünf Jahren wurde Liza Minnelli *auf* **Hollywood getrimmt** (*Zeit*) *When only five Liza Minnelli was already being groomed **for** Hollywood*
  OF:
  Renate ist *auf* **Ulrike(s Erfolg) eifersüchtig** *Renate is jealous **of** Ulrike('s success)*
  er ist stolz *auf* **seine Medaille** *he is proud **of** his medal*
  ON:
  Schließlich einigte man sich *auf* **einen Kompromiss** (*FAZ*) *Finally they agreed **on** a compromise*
  Das Institut soll sich *auf* **Kulturprogramme konzentrieren** (*FAZ*) *The institute is to concentrate **on** cultural programmes*
  TO:
  die Stadt ist jetzt *auf* **Erdgas umgestellt** *the town is now converted **to** natural gas*
  Den Begriff „Engländer" *auf* **die Schotten anzuwenden, diesen Fauxpas begeht man kein zweites Mal** (*Zeit*) *Applying the term 'Engländer' **to** the Scots is a faux pas you don't commit twice*
  das Recht *auf* **Glück** *the right **to** happiness*

6. (*per*) TO:
  solange *auf* **einen Indianer etwa hundert Büffel kamen** (*Spiegel*) *as long as there were approximately a hundred buffalo **to** every (American) Indian*

AUS (+ dative)

1. (indicating motion) OUT OF:

Ich beugte mich *aus* dem Fenster (Penzoldt) *I leaned **out of** the window*
Den Mantel hatte er schon *aus* dem Schrank genommen (Ch. Wolf) *He had already taken the coat **out of** the wardrobe*

2. (indicating origin, source) FROM:

Nachrichten *aus* den USA *news **from** the U.S.A.*
Ölscheichs *aus* dem Nahen Osten (*Zeit*) *oil sheikhs **from** the Middle East*
die Richtung, *aus* der sie die Schüsse hörten (Lenz) *the direction **from** which they heard the shots*
***aus* zuverlässiger Quelle** *from a reliable source*

3. MADE OF:

Schultornister *aus* imitiertem Leder (Grass) *satchels **made of** imitation leather*

OF:

eine Währungsordnung, die *aus* verschiedenen Währungsblöcken zusammengesetzt ist (*Aktuell*) *a monetary system composed **of** various currency blocs*
eine botanische Sinfonie *aus* Buchen und Linden und Eichengruppen (*Spiegel*) *a botanical symphony **of** beeches and lime trees and groups of oaks*

4. (indicating reason) OUT OF:

Ich . . . guckte *aus* lauter Verlegenheit unters Bett (Zwerenz) *I looked under the bed **out of** sheer embarrassment*
***aus* Höflichkeit/Stolz/Verzweiflung** *out of politeness/pride/despair*

AUSSER (außer) (+ dative)

1. APART FROM, EXCEPT:

***Außer* den Bulgaren stieg keiner aus** (Lenz) ***Apart from** the Bulgarians nobody got out*
***außer* uns war niemand da** *nobody was there **apart from** (except) us*

2. BEYOND:

es steht *außer* jedem Zweifel *It is **beyond** all doubt*

3. OUT OF:

sie waren alle *außer* Atem *they were all **out of** breath*
der Aufzug ist *außer* Betrieb *the lift is **out of** order*

AUSSERHALB (außerhalb) (+ genitive)

OUTSIDE:

sie wohnt *außerhalb* der Stadt *she lives outside the town*

außerhalb der Zone, in der interplanetarer Staub die astronomischen Beobachtungen stört *(FAZ) outside the zone in which interplanetary dust interferes with astronomical observations*

Tatsachen, die man *außerhalb* Großbritanniens leicht unterschätzt *facts that are easily underestimated outside Britain*

BEI (+ dative)

1. (indicating place)

(*a*) BY, NEXT TO:

er saß *bei* ihr *he sat by (next to) her*

NEAR:

Bei Trincomalee hielten die Rebellen einen Bus an *(MM) Near Trincomalee the rebels stopped a bus*

Offenbach *bei* Frankfurt *Offenbach near Frankfurt*

(with reference to battle) OF:

die Schlacht *bei* Hastings *the Battle of Hastings*

(*b*) AT (SOMEONE'S) HOUSE:

bei uns (zu Hause) *at our house*

WITH:

er wohnt *bei* seinen Eltern *he lives with his parents*

c/o (in address):

bei Schmidt *c/o Schmidt*

(*c*) AT:

beim Bäcker/Metzger/Arzt *at the baker's/butcher's/doctor's*

wir arbeiten *bei* Woolworth *we work at Woolworth's*

sie kauft ihre Kleidung *bei* C & A *she buys her clothes at C & A's*

IN:

mein Sohn ist *beim* Militär *my son is in the forces*

meine Tochter ist *beim* Film *my daughter is in films*

WITH:

er ist *beim* Ulmer Theater *he's with the Ulm theatre company*

ich versicherte meinen Wagen *bei* der ARAG *I insured my car with ARAG*

(*d*) ON (someone's person):

der Brief wurde *bei* ihm gefunden *the letter was found on him*

ich habe kein Geld *bei* mir *I haven't any money on me*

(*e*) AMONG:

ich lebte jahrzehntelang *bei* den Eskimos *I lived for decades among the Eskimos*

bei seinen Papieren war ein wichtiger Brief *among his papers was an important letter*

(*f*) IN (the works of):
bei **Goethe** *in Goethe*

(*g*) FROM:
Ich lieh *beim* alten Kreft ein Boot für zwei Stunden (Grass) *I borrowed a boat from old Kreft for two hours*
sie nimmt Englischstunden *bei* einem Waliser *she's taking English lessons from a Welshman*

2. (indicating means) BY:

Maria . . . nahm mich *bei* der Hand (Grass) *Maria took me by the hand*
ich nannte ihn *beim* Vornamen *I called him by his first name*

3. ON THE PART OF:

eine Abkürzung sollte nur da verwendet werden, wo *beim* Leser die Kenntnis der Abkürzung vorausgesetzt werden kann *an abbreviation should only be used where a knowledge of the abbreviation can be assumed on the part of the reader*

4. (indicating specific instance)

(*a*) IN THE CASE OF, WITH:

die Reparatur dauert *bei* Puppen zwei Wochen *in the case of (with) dolls the repair takes two weeks*
er hat viel Glück *bei* Frauen *he's very successful with women*

(*b*) AMONG:
bei **Metzgern findet man diese Ansicht häufig** *this view is common among butchers*

5. (indicating time, circumstances)

(*a*) AT:
bei **Sonnenaufgang** *at sunrise*
bei **Kriegsende** *at the end of the war*
bei **seiner Geburt** *at his birth*
beim **Frühstück** *at breakfast*
bei **der Premiere von Tschechows „Drei Schwestern"** (Stern) *at the première of Chekhov's 'Three Sisters'*
bei **ihrem Anblick** *at the sight of her*
bei **dem bloßen Gedanken** *at the mere thought of it*
ON:
bei **seiner Ankunft** *on his arrival*
Wie *bei* allen feierlichen Gelegenheiten stand der Oberst aufrecht (Kafka) *As on all ceremonial occasions the colonel stood erect*
IN:
er hat *bei* einem Autounfall seine Eltern verloren *he lost his parents in a car accident*
der Handy ['hɛndi] **ist *beim* Transport beschädigt worden** *the mobile phone has been damaged in transit*

(with verbal noun) WHEN, AS, WHILE:
bei der Aufteilung Preußens *when Prussia was divided*
die beleibte Sopranistin riss *bei* ihrem Auftritt eine Kulisse um *when making her entrance the stout soprano knocked down a bit of the scenery*
bei der Ausfahrt aus dem Bahnhof *as the train left the station*
beim Anflug auf München (of aircraft) *while approaching Munich*
beim Skilaufen *while skiing*
ON:
der Satellit verglühte *beim* Wiedereintritt in die Atmosphäre *the satellite burnt out on re-entering the earth's atmosphere*
IN:
beim Bewältigen dieser Aufgabe *in accomplishing this task*
(with **sein** etc.) —ING:
wir sind gerade *beim* Aufräumen *we're just tidying up*
sie waren *bei* Rätselraten *they were doing puzzles*
wir sahen den Kindern *beim* Spielen zu *we watched the children playing*
ich erwischte ihn *beim* Lügen *I caught him lying*

(*b*) (indicating prevailing conditions) BY:
bei Kerzenlicht *by candlelight*
IN:
es ist gefährlich *bei* Nebel zu fahren *it's dangerous to drive in fog*
Hans Castorp wuchs auf *bei* miserablem Wetter (Th. Mann) *Hans Castorp grew up in dreadful weather*
WITH:
sie schläft immer *bei* offenem Fenster *she always sleeps with the window open*
OVER:
bei einem Glas Bier / einer Tasse Tee *over a glass of beer / a cup of tea*

(*c*) (indicating simultaneous developments etc.) AS:
Die Emigrantenzahl fiel—*bei* wachsendem Wohlstand der Bundesrepublik—auf 200 000 zurück (*Zeit*) *As the Federal Republic's prosperity increased (so) the number of emigrants went down to 200,000*
WHILE:
Im neuen Telefonnetz sind *bei* unveränderter Gesprächigkeit der Einwohner die Gebühreneinnahmen um 20 Prozent gesunken (*Zeit*) *In the new telephone system receipts have fallen by 20 per cent while the loquaciousness of the inhabitants has remained unchanged*

(*d*) (indicating condition) IF:
bei richtiger Anwendung dieses Verfahrens *if this process is properly applied*
bei Achsenbruch *if an axle breaks*
WHERE:
bei folgendem Akzent *where the stress follows*
bei steigender Produktion *where production is rising*

IN THE EVENT OF:
bei **Nichteinhaltung dieser Bestimmung** *in the event of failure to comply with this regulation*
ON:
bei **näherer Bekanntschaft** *on closer acquaintance*

6. IN VIEW OF:
bei **der Größe des Fundes** *in view of the size of the find*
WITH:
bei **solchen Preisen** *with prices like that*
bei **deinem Aussehen solltest du doch keine Probleme haben** *with your looks you shouldn't have any problems*

7. (*in spite of*) FOR, WITH:
bei **all seinen Fehlern** *for (with) all his faults*
bei **alledem** *for all that*
beim **besten Willen** *with the best will in the world*

BINNEN (+ dative)

WITHIN (period of time):

die **Befürchtungen, dass** *binnen* **vier Jahren bei Opel 7500 Stellen verschwinden** (*Spiegel*) *the fears that within four years 7,500 jobs will go at Opel*

Occasionally used with the genitive in literary usage.

BIS (+ accusative of noun without article, or followed by second preposition, which determines the case)

1. (indicating time)

(*a*) UNTIL, TILL:
bis **Ostern/Ende Juli waren wir verreist** *we were away until (till) Easter/the end of July*
ich bin *bis* **nächsten Montag da** *I'll be here until (till) next Monday*
(with dates) TO (usually represented by –):
F. D. Roosevelt (1882 *bis* **1945)** *F. D. Roosevelt (1882–1945)*
von . . . bis FROM . . . TO:
von **8** *bis* **10 (Uhr)** *from 8 to 10 (o'clock)*
von **Montag** *bis* **Freitag** *from Monday to Friday*

(*b*) BY:
sie ist *bis* **Dienstag zurück** *she'll be back by Tuesday*
Bis **Mittwoch waren die Israelis bis zum Suez-Kanal vorgedrungen** (*Zeit*) *By Wednesday the Israelis had pushed forward as far as the Suez Canal*

(*c*) Frequently used before adverbs and adverbial phrases; UNTIL, TILL:
bis **jetzt** *until (till) now*
bis **dahin** *until (till)/by then*

bis vor einem Jahr *until (till) a year ago*
Compare **bis bald/später/Dienstagabend!** *see you soon/later/on Tuesday evening*

Before an article or a demonstrative, possessive, or interrogative adjective:
BIS ZU

(*i*) UNTIL, TILL:

bis zum **Jahr der ersten Ausgrabung** (C. W. Ceram) *until (till) the year of the first excavation*
bis zu **diesem Augenblick** *until (till) this moment*
bis zu **ihrem Tod** *until (till) her death*
TO:
sie kämpften *bis zum* **bitteren Ende** *they fought to the bitter end*

(*ii*) BY:

Da Neufundland und Manitoba *bis zum* **Stichtag nicht unterzeichnet hatten** (*Aktuell*) *As Newfoundland and Manitoba had not signed by the deadline*

2. (indicating place) AS FAR AS:

der Zug fährt *bis* **Rom** *the train goes as far as Rome.*

(Alternative: **bis nach Rom**. A phrase in apposition is in the dative, e.g. **der Zug fährt bis Rom,** *der* **Hauptstadt Italiens**.)

Before an article etc.: **BIS** + second preposition:

wir gingen *bis an* **die Grenze** *we went as far as the frontier*
er versank *bis an* **die Hüften im Schnee** *he sank up to his hips in the snow*
bis auf **drei Kilometer vom Dorf** *to within three kilometres of the village*
er ist *bis vor* **das Haus gefahren** *he drove (right) up to the house*
sie schlenderten *bis zum* **nächsten Restaurant** *they strolled as far as the next restaurant*
voll *bis zum* **Rand** *full to the brim*

3. (with numerals) OR, TO:

wir werden drei *bis* **vier Tage bleiben** *we'll stay three to (or) four days*
TO:
40 *bis* **50 Leute** *40 to 50 people*
18 *bis* **20 Dollar** *18 to 20 dollars*

BIS AUF

(*a*) (RIGHT) ONTO/TO:

er stieg *bis aufs* **Dach / ** *bis auf* **den Gipfel** *he climbed (right) onto the roof / to the summit*

(*b*) TO WITHIN (see **bis 2**)

(*c*) DOWN TO:

bis auf den letzten Tropfen *down to the last drop*

(*d*) EXCEPT (FOR):

alle Inseln *bis auf* Spiekeroog *all the islands except (for) Spiekeroog*

DANK (+ genitive or dative; in plural usually + genitive)

THANKS TO:

er konnte das Problem *dank* seiner Erfahrung lösen *he was able to solve the problem thanks to his experience*

***Dank* finanzieller Opfer seiner Mutter konnte er studieren** (*PersonenLexikon*) *Thanks to his mother's financial sacrifices he was able to go to university*

DIESSEITS (+ genitive)

ON THIS SIDE OF:

diesseits des Kanals *on this side of the Channel*

DURCH (+ accusative)

1. (of place) THROUGH:

Ich hatte gespürt, wie die Nadel sich *durch* die Haut bohrte (Böll) *I had felt the needle boring through my skin*

[Ich] schlenderte *durch* die kleine Stadt (Penzoldt) *I strolled through the little town*

geschützt vor dem eisigen Wind, der hoch *durch* die Kiefern strich (de Bruyn) *protected from the icy wind, which blew through the tops of the pine trees*

OF:

wir machten eine Rundreise *durch* Neusüdwales *we went on a tour of New South Wales*

ein Querschnitt *durch* die Bevölkerung *a cross-section of the population*

2. THROUGH (the agency of):

ich habe es *durch* einen Freund erfahren *I found out through a friend*

3. (indicating means) BY (MEANS OF):

(*a*)

wir haben die alte Methode *durch* eine neue ersetzt *we've replaced the old method by (means of) a new one*

[Churchill] demonstrierte ihnen *durch* seine Gegenwart, wie sehr es auf sie ankam (Canetti) *Churchill showed them by (means of) his presence how much they mattered*

***durch* die Beobachtung des Himmels** *by watching the sky*

(*b*) (with passive: see p. 80) BY:

das Kongobecken wird *durch* den Kongo entwässert *the Congo basin is drained **by** the Congo*

4. (indicating cause) AS A RESULT OF:

***durch* die Epidemie war die Bevölkerung sehr gelichtet** *as a result of the epidemic the population was greatly reduced*

BECAUSE OF:

***durch* den Regen wurde die Straße unpassierbar** *because of the rain the road became impassable*

FOR:

die Stadt Göttingen, berühmt *durch* ihre Würste und ihre Universität (*Heine*) *the town of Göttingen, famed **for** its sausages and its university*

5. (of time; *Austrian*) FOR:

***durch* zwei Jahre bemühte er sich um ein Visum** *for two years he tried to obtain a visa*

ENTGEGEN (+ dative; may also follow the noun)

CONTRARY TO:

der Biss der Tarantel ist *entgegen* dem Volksglauben harmlos *the bite of the tarantula is harmless, **contrary to** popular belief*

ENTLANG

ALONG:

Used *before* a noun in the dative (sometimes genitive), **entlang** indicates a location:

tückische Sümpfe, die sich *entlang* der iranischen Grenze erstrecken (*Spiegel*) *treacherous marshes, which extend **along** the Iranian border*

Used *after* a noun in the accusative, it indicates motion, either alongside or (in the case of, for example, a road or river) along the surface of:

sie fuhren die Küste/Straße *entlang* *they drove **along** the coast/road*

ENTSPRECHEND (+ dative; usually follows the noun)

IN ACCORDANCE WITH:

sie handelten den Anweisungen *entsprechend* *they acted **in accordance with** instructions*

FÜR (+ accusative)

1. FOR (in various contexts):

das Geschenk ist *für* dich *the present is **for** you*

Aber es war *für* ihn zweifellos notwendig, eine neue Ehe einzugehen (*Brecht*) *But it was undoubtedly necessary **for** him to marry again*

Sie betonen, dass große Buchstaben eine wichtige Orientierungshilfe für die meisten Menschen sind (*Aktuell*) *They stress that capital letters are an important aid to orientation* **for** *most people*

China ist groß genug für viele Autohersteller (*Spiegel*) *China is big enough for many car manufacturers*

Der Bundesgrenzschutz ist zuständig für die Sicherung der Staatsgrenze (*Aktuell*) *The Federal Border Police is responsible* **for** *protecting the nation's borders*

für einen Engländer spricht er sehr gut Deutsch *for an Englishman he speaks very good German*

er wollte für seine Hilfe keine Bezahlung nehmen *he wouldn't take any payment* **for** *his help*

Es war nicht klug von dir, für einen Mantel dein Leben zu wagen (*Hesse*) *It wasn't wise of you to risk your life* **for** *a coat*

Denken Sie sich nur für einen Moment in die Lage von Eltern (*Wohmann*) *Imagine just* **for** *one moment the situation of parents*

ich bin nur für drei Tage hier *I'm only here* **for** *three days*

2. (blind, receptive, etc.) TO:

Diese Partei war blind geworden für rechtsstaatliche Grundsätze (*Zeit*) *This party had grown blind* **to** *constitutional principles*

3. (*as perceived by*) TO:

für norddeutsche Ohren klingt es fremd *it sounds strange* **to** *North German ears*

4. (typical etc.) OF:

das ist typisch/charakteristisch für ihn *that's typical/characteristic* **of** *him*

zwei Beispiele für die ökologischen und ökonomischen Risiken (*FAZ*) *two examples* **of** *the ecological and economic risks*

5. (indicating succession) . . . **für** . . . . . . AFTER . . . :

Jahr für Jahr *year* **after** *year*

Abend für Abend *evening* **after** *evening*

. . . BY . . . :

Schritt für Schritt *step* **by** *step*

• In the combination **was für ein** *what kind of* the case of **ein** is not affected by **für**; it is declined like a normal indefinite article:

was für ein **Mann ist er?** *what kind of man is he?*

mit *was für einem* **Auto fährt er nach Hause?** *what kind of car is he driving home in?*

GEGEN (+ accusative)

1. (indicating place) AGAINST:

[Er] lehnte das Fahrrad gegen einen Baum (*Lenz*) *He leant the bicycle* **against** *a tree*

Goldfische drückten ihre blasierten Gesichter *gegen* die Wände hellgrüner Aquarien (Böll) *Goldfish pressed their blasé faces **against** the walls of light green aquaria*

UP TO:

sie hielt das Dia *gegen* das Licht *she held the slide **up to** the light*

INTO:

er ist *gegen* einen Baum gefahren *he ran **into** a tree*

ich bin *gegen* den Stuhl gestoßen *I bumped **into** the chair*

2.

(*a*) (indicating opposition) AGAINST:

ich bin *gegen* den Plan *I'm **against** the plan*

eine Volkserhebung *gegen* die Türken *a popular uprising **against** the Turks*

nach den *gegen* ihn vorgebrachten Beschuldigungen (*Welt*) *according to the accusations made **against** him*

(*contrary to*):

***gegen* meinen Rat / alle Erwartungen** *against my advice / all expectations*

(*b*) FOR:

hast du Tabletten *gegen* Kopfschmerzen? *have you got tablets **for** a headache?*

3. (indicating time, quantity)

(*a*) ABOUT:

wir treffen uns (so) *gegen* 8 Uhr *we're meeting at **about** 8 o'clock*

es waren *gegen* 100 Leute anwesend *there were **about** 100 people present*

(*b*) TOWARDS:

***gegen* Ende des 17. Jahrhunderts** *towards the end of the 17th century*

4. (*in exchange for*) FOR:

sie hat ihre Wohnung *gegen* eine größere getauscht *she's exchanged her flat **for** a larger one*

***gegen* ein entsprechendes Honorar** *for an appropriate fee*

***gegen* Barzahlung** *for cash*

5. COMPARED WITH:

***gegen* gestern ist es heute kalt** *it's cold **compared with** yesterday*

GEGENÜBER (+ dative; sometimes placed after a noun, always after a pronoun)

1. OPPOSITE:

***gegenüber* unserem Haus (unserem Haus *gegenüber*)** *opposite our house*

Er setzte sich mir *gegenüber* (Bernhard) *He sat down **opposite** me*

2. (indicating manner, attitude, etc.) TOWARDS:

sein Verhalten mir *gegenüber* his behaviour **towards** me
unsere Politik *gegenüber* **Russland** our policy **towards** Russia
die ambivalente Haltung der Menschen *gegenüber* **der modernen**
  Architektur people's ambivalent attitude **towards** modern architecture

TO:

er ist ihr *gegenüber* **besonders höflich** he's particularly polite **to** her

3. VIS-À-VIS:

Gewerkschaften zum Schutz der Arbeiter *gegenüber* **dem Staat** (Weiss)
  trade unions for the protection of the workers **vis-à-vis** the state

4. COMPARED WITH:

seiner Schwester *gegenüber* **war er klein / ein Anfänger** he was small/
  a beginner **compared with** his sister
Die Mitglieder [der Jugendorchester] sind *gegenüber* **vielen Berufsor-**
  chestern privilegiert (FAZ) The members of the youth orchestra are privi-
  leged **compared with** many professional orchestras

GEMÄSS (gemäß) (+ dative; usually follows the noun or pronoun) (esp. in formal usage)

IN ACCORDANCE WITH:

sie handelten ihren Prinzipien *gemäß* they acted **in accordance with** their
  principles
gemäß **Artikel 1 des Grundgesetzes** **in accordance with** Article 1 of the
  Basic Law

HINTER

I. (+ dative; indicating place)

1. BEHIND:

die Reihe der Männer *hinter* **den Sandsäcken** (Grass) the row of men
  behind the sandbags
sie versteckte sich *hinter* **einem Baum** she hid **behind** a tree

2. AFTER:

eine Haltestelle *hinter* **dem Bahnhof** one stop **after** the station
hinter **diesem Wort stand ein Fragezeichen** **after** this word there was a
  question mark

BEYOND:

fünf Kilometer *hinter* **München/der Grenze** five kilometres **beyond**
  Munich/the border

II. (+ accusative; indicating motion into a position behind) BEHIND:

er setzte sich *hinter* den Polizisten *he sat down **behind** the policeman*

Die Sonne war schon *hinter* das Dach des vierstöckigen Hauses getaucht (Ch. Wolf) *The sun had already dipped **behind** the roof of the four-storey house*

• Motion may be involved that is not directed towards a position behind the person or thing referred to; then the dative is used:

sie ging *hinter* ihm die Straße entlang *she walked along the street **behind** him*

(Their relative positions do not change.)

IN

I. (+ dative)

1. (indicating place) IN:

Sein Hausschlüssel lag *im* Briefkasten (Frisch) *His front-door key was **in** the letter-box*

***im* Vordergrund steht eine Birke** *in the foreground stands a birch tree*

***in* Mailand** *in Milan*

***in* Australien** *in Australia*

AT:

***im* Theater / *im* Kino / *in* der Oper** *at the theatre/cinema/opera*

***in* der Schule** *at school*

ON:

***im* Fernsehen/Radio** *on television/the radio*

2. (indicating time)

(*a*) IN:

***in* den letzten Jahren** *in the last few years*

***im* Januar** *in January*

***im* Winter** *in (the) winter*

AT:

***in* diesem Augenblick** *at this moment*

***in* seinem Alter** *at his age*

(*b*) (referring to period within which something occurs) IN:

Der Roman hat *in* dieser Zeit eine Auflage von 225 000 Exemplaren erlebt (*Zeit*) *In this period the novel sold 225,000 copies*

der Computer hat *in* fünf Sekunden alles gelöst *the computer solved everything **in** five seconds*

(*c*) (referring to what will occur) IN . . . 's/ . . . s' TIME:

***in* acht Tagen** *in a week's time*

Und *in* hundert Jahren, dann spielen sie noch (Brecht) *And **in** a hundred years' time they'll still be playing*

Compare **heute *in* einer Woche** *a week today, today week*

3. (in figurative use) IN:

> **er ist *in* Geschäftssachen gut bewandert** *he's well versed in business matters*
> ***in* englischer Sprache** *in English*

In various expressions:

> ***im* Durchschnitt** *on average*
> ***im* Gegenteil** *on the contrary*
> ***in* dieser Hinsicht** *in this respect*
> ***in* gewissem Maße** *to a certain extent*

II. (+ accusative)

1. (indicating motion) IN(TO):

> **Als die Katze . . . *ins* Zimmer schlich** (Frisch) *When the cat slunk into the room*
> **sie stellte den Besen *in* die Ecke** *she put the broom in the corner*
> **Aufjauchzend warf er sich *in* die Brandung** (Penzoldt) *Shouting for joy he threw himself into the waves*
> **Rita lehnte sich *in* ihren Stuhl zurück** (Ch. Wolf) *Rita leant back in her chair*
> **er schrieb seinen Namen *in* die linke obere Ecke der Postkarte** *he wrote his name in the top left-hand corner of the postcard*
> TO:
> **sie ging *ins* Theater / *ins* Kino / *ins* Konzert / *in* die Oper** *she went to the theatre/cinema/concert/opera*
> **ich gehe täglich *ins* Büro** *I go to the office every day*
> Also with the names of countries or regions that have a definite article:
> **er ist *in* die Schweiz / *in* die Vereinigten Staaten gefahren** *he's gone to Switzerland/the United States*

2. (in figurative use) INTO:

> **der Dozent hat das Buch *ins* Japanische übersetzt** *the lecturer translated the book into Japanese*
> **der Prinz wurde *in* einen Frosch verwandelt** *the prince was turned into a frog*
> **er hat sich *in* diesen Zustand hineingesteigert** *he worked himself up into this state*

INFOLGE (+ genitive)

AS A RESULT OF:

> **der Eisenbahnbetrieb konnte *infolge* des Unglücks nicht aufrechterhalten werden** *the rail service could not be maintained as a result of the accident*

Where the genitive plural form is not distinctive, **infolge von** is usual:

> *infolge von* **Straßenumleitungen konnte ich nicht rechtzeitig hier sein** *as a result of traffic diversions I couldn't be here on time*

INNERHALB (+ genitive)

INSIDE, WITHIN:

> *innerhalb* **des Gebäudes** *inside the building*
> *innerhalb* **einer Woche** *within a week*
> *innerhalb* **der Partei galt er als Einzelgänger** *within the party he was regarded as a loner*

Where the genitive plural form is not distinctive, **innerhalb von** is used:

> *innerhalb von* **fünf Jahren** *within five years*

JENSEITS (+ genitive)

ON THE OTHER SIDE OF:

> *jenseits* **des Flusses** *on the other side of the river*

BEYOND:

> *jenseits* **des Ozeans** *beyond the ocean*

KRAFT (+ genitive; in formal usage)

BY VIRTUE OF:

> *kraft* **seines Amtes** *by virtue of his office*

LÄNGS (+ genitive, occasionally dative; indicating place)

ALONG(SIDE):

> **der Weg** *längs* **des Bahndamms mit den Brennnesselstauden** (Wohmann) *the track along(side) the railway embankment with the clumps of stinging nettles*

LAUT (+ genitive or dative; in formal usage)

ACCORDING TO (quoting report, person's words, etc.):

> *laut* **dieses Berichtes, laut diesem Bericht** *according to this report*

When **laut** is used with a name or a noun standing on its own this is not inflected:

> *laut* **Gesetz** *according to the law*
> *laut* **Tony Blair** *according to Tony Blair*

Where the genitive plural form is not distinctive, the dative is used:

> *laut* **Briefen aus Kärnten** *according to letters from Carinthia*

MIT (+ dative)

1. WITH (in various contexts):

sie fuhren *mit* ihrem Onkel nach Sorrent *they went with their uncle to Sorrento*
Würstchen *mit* Kartoffelsalat *sausages with potato salad*
die Wartesäle *mit* ihrem lauen Kaffee (Böll) *the waiting-rooms with their lukewarm coffee*
mit Zustimmung seiner Eltern *with the consent of his parents*
mit diesem Ziel vor Augen *with this goal in view*
mit jedem Tag erholte er sich *with every day he got better*
mit einsetzendem Winter *with the onset of winte*r

2. (indicating instrument, means) WITH:

es ist üblich, *mit* Messer und Gabel zu essen *it is customary to eat with a knife and fork*
er schlug einen Nagel *mit* dem Hammer in die Wand *he knocked a nail in the wall with the hammer*

BY:

mit dem Auto/der Bahn/der Straßenbahn/dem Flugzeug/dem Schiff *by car/train/tram/plane/ship*
mit der Post *by post*
er verdient seinen Lebensunterhalt *mit* Zeichnen *he earns his living by drawing*

IN:

mit leiser Stimme *in a low voice*

3. (indicating age, speed, rate) AT:

mit 15 Jahren *at (the age of) 15*
mit 80 Kilometern in der Stunde *at 80 kilometres per hour*
das Bevölkerungswachstum [Kenias], das *mit* jährlich 3,4 Prozent zu den höchsten in der Welt zählt (*Aktuell*) *Kenya's population growth, which at 3.4 per cent annually is among the highest in the world*

4. (used with an intransitive verb in the case of a physical action involving the use of a part of the body (or object held in the hand); no prepositional equivalent in English, which uses a transitive verb):

Sie . . . stampfte heftig *mit* dem Fuß auf (Penzoldt) *She stamped her foot violently*
der Hund wedelte *mit* dem Schwanz *the dog wagged its tail*
sie knallte *mit* der Peitsche *she cracked her whip*
das Gespenst rasselte *mit* seinen Ketten *the ghost clanked its chains*

MITTELS (+ genitive; in formal usage)

BY MEANS OF:

sie öffneten die Kisten *mittels* eines Brecheisens *they opened the crates by means of a crowbar*

When **mittels** is used with a noun standing on its own, this is not inflected:

mittels Draht *by means of wire*

Where the genitive plural form is not distinctive, the dative is used:

mittels Drähten *by means of wires*

NACH (+ dative)

1. (indicating direction)

(*a*) TOWARDS:

Chorillo . . . sah *nach* dem Meer wie verzaubert (Penzoldt) *Chorillo looked* **towards** *the sea as if enchanted*

Also with points of the compass (also -WARDS):

nach Süden *towards the south, southwards*

AT:

der Lümmel warf den Ball *nach* dem Lehrer *the lout threw the ball at the teacher*

der Dackel schnappte *nach* den Wespen *the dachshund snapped at the wasps*

FOR:

und plötzlich griff er *nach* der Hand des anderen (H. Mann) *and suddenly he reached for the other man's hand*

(*b*) TO (with place-names or names of countries used without an article):

jeden Abend fährt er zurück *nach* Berlin *every evening he drives back to Berlin*

Die Hauptmasse der britischen Armee konnte sich *nach* England retten (*Meyers Standardlexikon*) *The bulk of the British army managed to escape to England*

2. (indicating time)

(*a*) PAST:

zehn Minuten *nach* fünf *ten minutes past five*

AFTER:

in den ersten Nächten *nach* seiner Entlassung (Bernhard) *during the first few nights after his release*

(*b*) (*next in importance to*) AFTER:

er war *nach* dem Kaiser der mächtigste Mann der Welt *after the Emperor he was the most powerful man in the world*

3. FOR:

das Verlangen *nach* sozialer Gerechtigkeit (*FAZ*) *the longing for social justice*

ihre Forderung *nach* einer Lohnerhöhung *their demand for a wage increase*

sie graben *nach* Gold *they're digging for gold*

er fischt *nach* Komplimenten *he's fishing for compliments*

4. (sometimes follows the noun) ACCORDING TO:

nach dem Gesetz *according to* the law
nach Schätzungen der Weltgesundheitsorganisation *according to* estimates produced by the World Health Organization
nach Machiavelli *according to* Machiavelli
nach den neuesten Methoden *according to* the latest methods

BY:

seiner/ihrer Anlage *nach* by disposition
nach meiner Uhr ist es schon halb zwölf *by* my watch it's already half past eleven
es wird *nach* dem Gewicht verkauft it's sold *by* weight
ich kenne sie nur dem Namen *nach* I only know her *by* name

JUDGING BY:

ihrem Akzent *nach* stammt sie aus Schwaben *judging by* her accent she comes from Swabia

IN:

meiner Ansicht/Meinung *nach* (also *nach* meiner Ansicht/Meinung) *in* my opinion

AFTER:

ein Gemälde *nach* Raffael *a painting* after *Raphael*
die Stadt wurde *nach* ihrem Gründer benannt the town was named *after* its founder

NEBEN

I. (+ dative)

1. (indicating place) BESIDE, NEXT TO:

die Bettlerin, die *neben* dem Torbogen saß (Broch) *the beggar woman, who sat* beside (next to) *the archway*

2. IN ADDITION TO:

neben Geschichte studiert er auch Theologie *in addition to* history he studies theology

3. COMPARED WITH:

neben seiner Schwester ist er ziemlich klein *compared with* his sister he is rather small

II. (+ accusative, indicating motion into a position next to)

BESIDE, NEXT TO:

sie setzte sich *neben* ihn *she sat down* beside (next to) *him*
er legte die Stoppuhr *neben* das Buch *he put the stop-watch* beside (next to) *the book*

• Motion may be involved that is not directed towards a position next to the person or thing referred to; then the dative is used:

> **sie ging *neben* ihm die Straße entlang** *she walked along the street **beside** (**next to**) him*

(Their relative positions do not change.)

OB (+ genitive, occasionally dative; in literary or ironical use)

ON ACCOUNT OF:

> **sie nannten ihn *ob* seiner Nase Knolle** *they called him Schnozzle **on account of** his nose*

• Except in Switzerland, the original sense ABOVE is obsolete. It survives in South German and Austrian place-names, e.g. **Rothenburg *ob* der Tauber**, **St. Oswald *ob* Eibiswald** (in Styria).

OBERHALB (+ genitive)

ABOVE:

> ***oberhalb* 2000 Meter geht der Regen in Schnee über** *above 6,000 feet the rain turns into snow*
> ***oberhalb* des Dorfes** *above the village*

OHNE (+ accusative)

1. WITHOUT:

> **er ist *ohne* seine Familie in Urlaub gefahren** *he's gone on holiday **without** his family*

Ohne is normally used without the indefinite article:

> **geht sie immer *ohne* Hut?** *does she always go **without** a hat?*
> **ein Zimmer *ohne* Tür** *a room **without** a door*

2. NOT COUNTING:

> ***ohne* Vororte hat die Stadt 600 000 Einwohner** *the city has 600,000 inhabitants **not counting** the suburbs*

SEIT (+ dative)

1. SINCE (point of time):

> **ich wohne hier *seit* 1998** *I've lived here **since** 1998*

2. FOR (period):

> **ich wohne hier *seit* drei Jahren** *I've lived here **for** three years*
> **die ersten Wahlen *seit* Jahrzehnten** *the first elections **for** decades*

For the use of tenses with **seit** see *Use of tenses*, p. 77.

STATT (+ genitive)

INSTEAD OF:

> *statt* **eines Blumenstraußes brachte er Pralinen mit** *instead of a bunch of flowers he brought chocolates*

Where the genitive plural form is not distinctive, the dative is used:

> *statt* **Eiern haben wir Spargel gekauft** *instead of eggs we bought asparagus*

• When **statt** is used as a conjunction, the case following **statt** is determined by the verb concerned:

> **ich gab das Geld ihm** *statt* **ihr** *I gave the money to him instead of her* (= *instead of to her*)

TROTZ (+ genitive; *South German, Austrian, Swiss* + dative)

IN SPITE OF:

> *trotz* **der drastischen Kürzungen im Wehretat** (*Spiegel*) *in spite of the drastic cuts in the defence budget*

The dative may also be used when there is no article (e.g. *trotz* **nassem Asphalt** *in spite of wet asphalt*), and must be used when the genitive plural form is not distinctive:

> *trotz* **Computern** *in spite of computers*

ÜBER

I. (+ dative)

1. (indicating place) ABOVE, OVER:

> **das Bild hängt** *über* **dem Schreibtisch** *the picture hangs above the desk*
> **Nebel lag** *über* **dem Dorf** *fog hung over the village*
> **sie trug einen Mantel** *über* **ihrem Kleid** *she wore a coat over her dress*

2. OVER:

> **wir besprachen es** *über* **einem Glas Wein** *we discussed it over a glass of wine*

3. (forget, overlook, etc.)

(*a*) IN:

> *über* **all der Aufregung habe ich es nicht bemerkt** *in all the excitement I didn't notice it*

(*b*) BECAUSE OF:

> *Über* **Suez hat die Welt Edens Verdienste um den Weltfrieden fast vergessen** (*Zeit*) *Because of Suez the world has almost forgotten Eden's contribution to world peace*

II. (+ accusative)

1. (indicating motion) ABOVE:

er hängte das Bild *über* **den Schreibtisch** *he hung the picture **above** the desk* (motion into a position above)

OVER:

die Wellen schlugen *über* **den Deich** *the waves broke **over** the dike*
Ich lehnte mich *über* **die Reling** (Penzoldt) *I leant **over** the rail*

ACROSS:

Sie fuhren *über* **eine Brücke** (Lenz) *They drove **across** a bridge*
sie segelten *über* **den See** *they sailed **across** the lake*
schwarze Wolken jagten *über* **den Himmel** *black clouds raced **across** the sky*
die Fahndung dehnte sich *über* **das ganze Land aus** *the search extended **across** the whole country*

ALONG:

er raste *über* **die Autobahn** *he tore **along** the autobahn*

DOWN:

Tränen liefen ihr *über* **die Backen** *tears ran **down** her cheeks*

BEYOND:

sein Einfluss reichte weit *über* **die Grenzen seines Heimatlandes** *his influence reached far **beyond** the frontiers of his native land*

- Motion may be involved that is not directed towards a position above the person or thing referred to; then the dative is used:

  das Flugzeug kreiste *über* **der Stadt** *the plane was circling **above** the city*

2. VIA:

wir sind *über* **Lüttich gefahren** *we came/went **via** Liège*
die Sendung ist *über* **den Fernmeldesatelliten ausgestrahlt worden** *the programme was broadcast **via** the communications satellite*

3. (indicating time)

(*a*) OVER:

über **Ostern fahren wir weg** *we're going away **over** Easter*
kann ich *über* **Nacht bleiben?** *can I stay **over**night?*

(*b*) (used after noun, indicating duration):

er hat die ganze Zeit / den ganzen Abend *über* **getrunken** *he was drinking all the time / all evening*

4. (indicating quantity) OVER:

über **hundert Autofahrer** *over a hundred car drivers*
Kinder *über* **zwölf Jahre** *children over twelve years of age*
es kostete *über* **50 Mark** *it cost over 50 marks*

5.

(*a*) (*concerning*) ABOUT:

nach langen Querelen mit den Deutschen *über* technische Details *after a long dispute with the Germans **about** technical details*

wir müssen *über* die Zukunft nachdenken *we must think **about** the future*

ON:

ein Symposion *über* den Philosophen Günther Anders (*FAZ*) *a symposium **on** the philosopher Günther Anders*

die Zeitung berichtet auch *über* die Innenpolitik *the newspaper also reports **on** home affairs*

AT:

ich staunte *über* seine Überheblichkeit *I was amazed **at** his arrogance*

meine Entrüstung *über* diese Äußerung *my indignation **at** this remark*

(*b*) (bill, cheque) FOR:

eine Rechnung/ein Scheck *über* 500 Mark *a bill/cheque **for** 500 marks*

6. (indicating power, victory, etc.) OVER:

der König herrschte *über* sein Volk *the king ruled **over** his people*

der leichte Sieg der Deutschen *über* Frankreich *the Germans' easy victory **over** France*

7. . . . **über** . . . . . . AFTER . . . :

die Bank machte Fehler *über* Fehler *the bank made mistake **after** mistake*

sie schrieb einen Brief *über* den anderen *she wrote one letter **after** another*

UM (+ accusative)

1. (indicating place) ROUND, AROUND:

die Entdeckung eines elften Ringes *um* den Planeten *the discovery of an eleventh ring **(a)round** the planet*

Sie setzten sich alle *um* den Tisch (Ch. Wolf) *They all sat down **(a)round** the table*

Drei Monate im Jahr reist sie *um* die Welt (*Stern*) *For three months a year she travels **(a)round** the world*

Um is frequently reinforced by **herum**:

sie standen *um* den Tisch herum *they stood **(a)round** the table*

2. (indicating time)

(*a*) AT (specified time of day):

ich stehe jeden Tag *um* 9 Uhr auf *I get up every day **at** 9 o'clock*

(*b*) AROUND, ABOUT:

er wurde *um* diese Zeit abends lebendig *around (about) this time in the evening he came to life*

sie ist *um* 1960 (*herum*) geboren *she was born **around** (**about**) 1960*

sie wollen *um* Weihnachten (*herum*) nach Schottland kommen *they're planning to come to Scotland **around** Christmas*

3. (*to the extent of*) BY:

sie hatte sich *um* zehn Jahre verschätzt *she was out (in her calculations) **by** ten years*
Die Bevölkerung wächst jährlich *um* zwei Prozent (*Aktuell*) *Each year the population increases **by** two per cent*
die Festspiele sind *um* einen Tag verlängert worden *the festival has been extended **by** one day*
Often not translated:
die Haltestelle ist *um* 20 Meter versetzt worden *the bus/tram stop has been moved 20 yards*
sie war *um* vieles jünger als ihr Mann *she was much younger than her husband*
ich glaube, du spielst diese Passage *um* eine Nuance zu laut *I think you play this passage a shade too loud*

4. (*in respect of*)

(*a*) ABOUT:

Meternagel war so blass geworden, dass Rita Angst *um* ihn bekam (Ch. Wolf) *Meternagel had turned so pale that Rita grew worried **about** him*

(*b*) FOR:

Der irische Autofahrer . . . muss ständig *um* sein Leben . . . kämpfen (Böll) *The Irish motorist must constantly fight **for** his life*
OVER:
Zwei Tage lang streikten Frankreichs Eisenbahner—nicht *um* Lohn, sondern um bessere Arbeitsbedingungen (*Welt*) *For two days France's railwaymen went on strike—not **over** pay but better working conditions*

(*c*) FOR:

diese Bitte *um* Hilfe *this request **for** help*
das Mädchen wandte sich an mich *um* Rat *the girl turned to me **for** advice*

5. (*South German, Austrian*) FOR (price):

ein Buch *um* 100 Schilling *a book **for** 100 schillings*

6. (indicating deprivation, loss) OUT OF:

sie haben ihn *um* sein ganzes Geld betrogen *they cheated him **out of** all his money*

7. . . . um . . . . . . AFTER . . . :

Monat *um* Monat *month **after** month*

UNTER

I. (+ dative)

1. (indicating place)

(a) UNDER, BELOW, BENEATH:

der Hund saß unter dem Tisch *the dog sat under the table*
die Familie, die unter uns wohnte *the family which lived below us*
800 Meter unter dem Meeresspiegel *800 metres below sea level*

(b) AMONG:

er fand die Rechnung unter ihren Papieren *he found the bill among her papers*
in Südafrika war er unter Freunden *in South Africa he was among friends*
Spürt man eine neue Rivalität unter den Spielern? (*Stern*) *Does one detect a new rivalry among the players?*

2. (indicating quantity) UNDER:

Kinder unter acht Jahren *children under eight years of age*

3. (indicating circumstances) UNDER:

unter diesen Umständen *under these circumstances*
TO:
unter lautem Beifall *to loud applause*
(with verbal noun) expressed by —ING:
unter Missachtung aller ethischen Gesichtspunkte *disregarding all ethical considerations*
or WHILE —ING:
man bringe das Wasser unter Beigabe von etwas Essig zum Kochen *bring the water to the boil while adding a little vinegar*

II. (+ accusative, indicating motion)

1. (into a position under) UNDER, BELOW, BENEATH:

der Ball war unter den Tisch gerollt *the ball had rolled under the table*
die Sonne ist unter den Horizont getaucht *the sun dipped below the horizon*
Ich . . . guckte aus lauter Verlegenheit unters Bett (Zwerenz) *I looked under the bed out of sheer embarrassment*

• Motion may be involved that is not directed towards a position under the person or thing referred to; then the dative is used. Thus, *if one drives under the bridge* is expressed by **wenn man unter der Brücke durchfährt**; **wenn man unter die Brücke fährt** would mean that one drives to a position under the bridge and stops there.

2. AMONG:

er verteilte sein Geld unter die Armen *he distributed his money among the poor*

UNTERHALB (+ genitive)

BELOW:

unterhalb des Dorfes *below the village*

VON (+ dative)

1. FROM:

das Regenwasser tropft *vom* Dach *the rainwater is dripping **from** the roof*
sie erhoben sich *von* ihren Stühlen *they got up **from** their chairs*
sie kommt gerade *vom* Arzt *she's just come **from** the doctor*
ich habe einen Brief *von* meiner Freundin bekommen *I've received a letter **from** my girl-friend*
die Affen legen keinen Wert darauf, *von* uns abzustammen *the apes attach no importance to being descended **from** us*
OFF, FROM:
er sprang *vom* Dach *He jumped **off** (**from**) the roof*

2. (indicating cause etc.) FROM:

er ist müde *vom* weiten Weg *he's tired **from** the long walk*
WITH:
die Berge sind weiß *vom* Schnee *the hills are white **with** snow*
(with passive—indicating agent—or expressing authorship etc.) BY:
sie ist *vom* Hund gebissen worden *she's been bitten **by** the dog*
das Stück ist *von* Shakespeare *the play is **by** Shakespeare*
ein Bild *von* Tizian *a painting **by** Titian*
sie hat ein Kind *von* ihm *she has a child **by** him*

3. (indicating means)

(*a*) OUT OF:
ich habe das Geschenk *von* meinem Taschengeld bezahlt *I paid for the present **out of** my pocket-money*

(*b*) ON:
Tante Jane lebte nur *von* Tee, schwarzem Kaffee und zwei Tassen Fleischbrühe täglich (Musil) *Aunt Jane lived solely **on** tea, black coffee, and two cups of broth a day*

4. ABOUT:

Von ihrer Ehe sprach sie nie (Bachmann) *She never spoke **about** her marriage*
Auch glaube ich, etwas *von* einem dreijährigen Kind gelesen zu haben (Grass) *I also think I read something **about** a three-year-old child*
von seinem Lebensweg ist wenig bekannt *little is known **about** his life*

5. (in various contexts) OF:

(*a*) Where the genitive is not shown:
   der Geruch *von* Tomaten *the smell of tomatoes*
   der Export *von* Kohle *the export of coal*

(*b*) To indicate a quality:
   eine Frau *von* großer Schönheit *a woman of great beauty*
   ein Edelstein *von* großem Wert *a gem of great value*
   eine Angelegenheit *von* größter Wichtigkeit (Musil) *a matter of the
      greatest importance*

(*c*) In descriptive phrases of the type **ein . . . von**:
   ein Riese *von* einem Mann *a giant of a man*

(*d*) *consisting of*:
   eine Inflationsrate *von* zwei Prozent *an inflation rate of two per cent*

(*e*) *on the part of*:
   das war nett *von* ihr *that was nice of her*

6. (partitive use) OF:

   einige *von* ihnen *some of them*
   kein Wort *von* dem, was du sagst, ist wahr *not one word of what you
      say is true*
   OUT OF:
   in drei *von* zehn Fällen *in three cases out of ten*
   SOME OF:
   er hat *von* der Milch getrunken *he's drunk some of the milk*

7. (as part of a name, functions as the nobiliary particle—cf. French *de*):

   J. W. *von* Goethe

• The genitive is sometimes replaced by **von**, especially in spoken German:

   einige *von* meinen Freunden (also einige meiner Freunde) *some of my
      friends*
   der neue Freund (*von*) meiner Schwester *my sister's new boy-friend*

VOR

I. (+ dative)

1. (indicating place)

(*a*) IN FRONT OF:
   Bewerber . . . standen Schlange *vor* dem Schloss (de Bruyn) *Suitors
      queued up in front of the castle*
   AT (door, gate, etc.):
   Immer länger wurde die Schlange *vor* dem Schalter (Böll) *Longer and
      longer grew the queue at the counter*

OFF (coast etc.):

Das Zentrum möchte die Ölsuche *vor* Norwegen gänzlich untersagen
(*Zeit*) *The Centre Party [of Norway] would like to prohibit completely the
search for oil **off** Norway*

OUTSIDE (town, harbour, building, etc.):

sie trafen sich *vor* dem Bahnhof *they met **outside** the station*

auf einer Straße *vor* Bad Langenschwalbach (C. W. Ceram) *on a road
outside Bad Langenschwalbach*

BEFORE:

Sie müssen *vor* der Kirche links abbiegen *you must turn left **before** the
church*

(*b*) (*in the presence of*) IN FRONT OF:

**als meine Schwiegermutter mir dann *vor* den beiden Mädchen
ungastliches Verhalten vorwarf** (*Brigitte*) *when my mother-in-law then
accused me **in front of** the two girls of inhospitable conduct*

TO (audience):

sie spielten *vor* ausverkauftem Haus *they played **to** a full house*

seine Rede *vor* der Jungen Union (*Zeit*) *his speech **to** the Young Christian
Democrats*

(*c*) (bow etc.) TO:

die Achtung derer . . . , die bisher *vor* mir den Hut gezogen hatten
(Hesse) *the respect of those who had hitherto taken off their hats **to** me*

die ganze Armee kapitulierte *vor* dem Feind *the whole army surrendered
to the enemy*

(*d*) AHEAD OF:

Schmidt liegt zwei Runden *vor* den anderen *Schmidt is two laps **ahead**
of the others*

2. (indicating precedence) OVER:

**die Rettung von Menschenleben hat den Vorrang *vor* allen anderen
Maßnahmen** *the saving of human lives takes precedence **over** all other
measures*

3. (indicating time)

(*a*) BEFORE:

Er ließ unmittelbar *vor* seiner Moskau-Reise den Hafen verminen
(*Spiegel*) *He had the harbour mined immediately **before** his trip to Moscow*

***vor* dem letzten Ausbruch des Vesuvs** (C. W. Ceram) ***before** the last
eruption of Vesuvius*

**Stalin wollte die Reichshauptstadt *vor* den Westalliierten erreichen
und einnehmen** (*Spiegel*) *Stalin wanted to reach and take the capital of
the Reich **before** the Western allies*

TO:

zehn Minuten *vor* sechs *ten minutes **to** six*

(*b*) AGO:

Zwischenfälle, die sich *vor* drei Wochen in Laibach zutrugen (*Zeit*) *incidents which occurred three weeks **ago** in Ljubljana*

Heute *vor* einer Woche wurde Elisabeth . . . ins Krankenhaus eingeliefert (Wohmann) *A week **ago** today Elisabeth was admitted to hospital*

4. (indicating cause) WITH:

Sie zitterte am ganzen Leibe *vor* Zorn und Leidenschaft (Penzoldt) *Her whole body was trembling **with** anger and passion*

weiß *vor* Wut *white **with** rage*

FOR:

sie machte *vor* Freude einen Luftsprung *she jumped **for** joy*

5. (*in respect of*)

(*a*) FROM:

Schutz *vor* dem Verkehrslärm (*Zeit*) *protection **from** traffic noise*

um uns *vor* völligem Verhungern zu bewahren (Kafka) *to keep us **from** total starvation*

solange nichts davon *vor* ihm verborgen wird (Canetti) *so long as nothing of that is kept **from** him*

(*b*) AGAINST:

als Churchill dann begann, *vor* der Befriedungspolitik zu warnen (H. Höpfl) *when Churchill then began to warn **against** the policy of appeasement*

(*c*) FOR:

aus Achtung *vor* seinen Eltern *out of respect **for** his parents*

Man hatte eine gewisse Ehrfurcht *vor* ihr (Musil) *People felt a certain reverence **for** her*

(*d*) OF:

Angst *vor* dem Liebesverlust (S. Freud) *fear **of** the loss of love*

II. (+ accusative, indicating motion into a position in front of) IN FRONT OF:

sie stellte die Blumen *vor* das Fenster *she placed the flowers **in front of** the window*

er setzte sich *vor* die Tür *he sat down **in front of** the door*

OUTSIDE:

er ging *vors* Haus *he went **outside** the house*

sie stellte das gestohlene Auto *vor* die Polizeiwache *she parked the stolen car **outside** the police station*

• Motion may be involved that is not directed towards a position in front of the person or thing referred to; then the dative is used:

sie ging *vor* ihm die Straße entlang *she walked along the street **in front of** him*

(Their relative positions do not change.)

WÄHREND (+ genitive, colloquially also + dative)

DURING:

Die Dramatiker sind *während* des Festivals anwesend (*NZZ*) *The dramatists are present **during** the festival*
***während* der Unterredung mit seiner Schwester** (Bernhard) ***during** my conversation with his sister*

Sometimes expressed by the conjunctions AS or WHILE:

Eine Emsige liest *während* der Wanderung im Brevier (S. Wichmann) *One industrious girl is reading her breviary **as** they walk*

• **Während**, unlike French *pendant*, is not used to refer to duration; *for* in e.g. *she lived abroad for five years* is expressed by the accusative: **sie lebte fünf Jahre im Ausland.**

WEGEN (+ genitive, colloquially also + dative; may follow the noun esp. in formal usage)

BECAUSE OF, ON ACCOUNT OF:

***wegen* des schlechten Wetters sind wir zu Hause geblieben** *because of the bad weather we stayed at home*
Die Leiche . . . beschlagnahmte man *wegen* Seuchengefahr (Grass) *The body was seized **because of** the danger of an epidemic*
weil wir ihn der vielen Russen *wegen* . . . nicht beerdigen konnten (Grass) *because we couldn't bury him **on account of** all the Russians*

FOR THE SAKE OF:

ich mache die Arbeit ihrer selbst *wegen* *I do the work **for** its own **sake***

ABOUT:

Gewiss bestehe kein Anlass, sich *wegen* Elisabeth Sorgen zu machen (Wohmann) *There was, I said, certainly no reason to worry **about** Elisabeth*
wir müssen *wegen* des Liefertermins anfragen *we must inquire **about** the delivery date*

Where the genitive plural form is not distinctive, the dative is used:

***wegen* Magengeschwüren** *because of stomach ulcers*

ZU (+ dative)

1. (indicating place, in set phrases) AT, ON, TO:

zu **Hause** *at home*
zu **jemandes Füßen** *at someone's feet*
zu **beiden Seiten (der Straße** etc.) *on either side (of the street etc.)*
zu **jemandes Linken/Rechten** *to someone's left/right*

2. (indicating direction) TO:

er ging *zum* Fenster *he went **to** the window*
ich fahre dich *zum* Flughafen *I'll drive you **to** the airport*

Missionen *zum* Nachbarplaneten der Erde, dem Mars *missions to Earth's neighbouring planet, Mars*

der Übergang *zur* Marktwirtschaft *the transition to a market economy*

3. (indicating time, occasion)

(*a*) AT:

Lord Carnarvon befand sich *zu* dieser Zeit in England (C. W. Ceram) *Lord Carnarvon was in England at this time*

wir fahren *zu* Ostern nach Dänemark *at Easter we're going to Denmark*

(*b*) FOR:

was hast du *zum* Geburtstag / *zu* Weihnachten bekommen? *what did you get for your birthday / for Christmas?*

4. (indicating purpose) FOR:

Die Sowjetunion verkaufte eine Raumstation an Japan *zu* Forschungszwecken (*Aktuell*) *The Soviet Union sold a space station to Japan for research purposes*

die Vorbereitungen *zur* Uraufführung seiner achten Sinfonie *preparations for the first performance of his eighth symphony*

Stoff *zu* einem neuen Kleid *material for a new dress*

(with definite article) AS:

***zur* Belohnung für ihre Dienste** *as a reward for her services*

Zu + verbal noun frequently = TO + infinitive:

Übungen *zur* Entspannung der Muskeln *exercises to relax the muscles*

Zur Fassung von Beschlüssen ist eine absolute Mehrheit von 35 Stimmen nötig (*Aktuell*) *An absolute majority of 35 votes is required to pass resolutions*

5. (*in respect of*)

(*a*) TO:

er war sehr freundlich *zu* mir *he was very friendly to me*

FOR:

seine Liebe *zu* seiner Frau *his love for his wife*

(*b*) TO(WARDS):

die Haltung Roosevelts *zu* diesem Problem *Roosevelt's attitude to(wards) this problem*

(*c*) ON:

die drei amerikanischen Dissertationen *zu* Fallada *the three American theses on Fallada*

ein Standardwerk *zur* deutschen Sprache *a standard work on the German language*

hat er sich *zu* dieser Statistik geäußert? *has he commented on these statistics?*

(*d*) WITH:

wegen seiner Beziehungen *zu* **einer Geisha** (*Welt*) *because of his relationship* **with** *a geisha*

6. (indicating change of state):

ihm ist Kalifornien *zur* **zweiten Heimat geworden** *California has become his second home*

INTO:

die Kirche hatte sich *zu* **einer politischen Macht entwickelt** *the church had developed* **into** *a political power*

er verzog den Mund *zu* **einem Grinsen** *he twisted his mouth* **into** *a grin*

TO FORM:

die Firmen sind *zu* **einem großen Unternehmen verschmolzen** *the firms have merged* **to form** *a large company*

With a complement in English (but no preposition):

Eisenhower wurde zweimal *zum* **Präsidenten der USA gewählt** *Eisenhower was twice elected President of the USA*

7. TO (someone's surprise, regret, satisfaction, etc.):

zu **meiner großen Verwunderung hat er sofort geantwortet** *to my great surprise he answered immediately*

8. WITH:

nehmen Sie Milch *zum* **Tee?** *do you take milk* **with** *your tea?*

9. (with numerals)

(*a*) (indicating price) AT:

zu **niedrigen Preisen** *at low prices*

sie verkauften Äpfel *zu* **1 Mark das Pfund** *they sold apples* **at** *1 mark a pound*

(*b*) (indicating ratio) TO:

zehn *zu* **eins** *ten* **to** *one*

(*c*) (indicating score):

(Es steht) 5:1 [pronounced **fünf** *zu* **eins**] *(The score is) 5–1*

ZUFOLGE (+ dative; follows the noun or pronoun)

ACCORDING TO:

Umfragen *zufolge* **sprachen sich 56% der Befragten für die politische Souveränität ihrer Provinz aus** (*Aktuell*) *According to opinion polls 56% of those interviewed expressed their support for the political sovereignty of their province*

dem Zeugen *zufolge* **hatte der Radfahrer keine Schuld an dem Unfall** **according to** *the witness the cyclist was not to blame for the accident*

ZULIEBE (+ dative; follows the noun or pronoun)

FOR (someone's) SAKE:

ich habe es dir *zuliebe* **getan** *I did it for your sake*

ZWISCHEN

I. (+ dative)

1. BETWEEN:

er saß *zwischen* **seiner Frau und seiner Nichte** *he sat between his wife and his niece*

es ist *zwischen* **sechs und sieben Uhr passiert** *it happened between six and seven o'clock*

die fundamentalen Unterschiede *zwischen* **christlicher und islamischer Kultur** *the fundamental differences between Christian and Islamic culture*

die offene Konfrontation *zwischen* **Rauchern und Nichtrauchern** (*Aktuell*) *the open confrontation between smokers and non-smokers*

2. AMONG:

der Pass war *zwischen* **den Papieren in der Schublade** *the passport was among the papers in the drawer*

die neuen Wohnsiedlungen *zwischen* **den grünen Hügeln Kuala Lumpurs** (*Welt*) *the new housing estates among the green hills of Kuala Lumpur*

II. (+ accusative, indicating motion into a position between or among)

1. BETWEEN:

er setzte sich *zwischen* **Herrn und Frau Schmidt** *he sat down between Herr and Frau Schmidt*

er parkte das Auto *zwischen* **zwei andere** *he parked the car between two others*

• Motion may be involved that is not directed towards a position between the person or thing referred to; then the dative is used:

sie ging *zwischen* **ihren Brüdern** *she walked between her brothers*

(Their relative positions do not change.)

2. AMONG:

er hat *zwischen* **den Salat Radieschen gesät** *he's sown radishes among the lettuce*

CROSS-REFERENCE LIST OF ENGLISH PREPOSITIONS

Items are cross-referred to the list of German prepositions beginning on p. 117. Prepositions not rendered by a German preposition are also included, with translations.

ABOUT 1. (*concerning*) **über** ACC. (II 5*a*), p. 144; **wegen**, p. 151.
    2. (time) **um** (2*b*), p. 144; [- . . . *o'clock*] **gegen** (3*a*), p. 133; (quantity) **gegen** (3*a*), p. 133; **etwa, ungefähr**.
    3. (quality: e.g. *the important thing* -) **an** DAT. (I 6), p. 120

ABOVE (place) **über** DAT. (I 1), p. 142, **oberhalb**, p. 141; (motion) **über** ACC. (II 1), p. 143

ACCORDING TO **nach** (4), p. 140; **zufolge**, p. 153; **laut**, p. 137

ACROSS (motion) **über** ACC. (II 1), p. 143; - *the street* **gegenüber**

AFTER 1. (time) **nach** (2*a*), p. 139
    2. (place) **hinter** DAT. (I 2), p. 134
    3. (*next in importance to*) **nach** (2*b*), p. 139
    4. [*name* -] **nach** (4), p. 140

AGAINST 1. (place) **gegen** (1), p. 132; [*lean* -] **an** DAT. (I 1*f*), p. 118· **gegen** (1), p. 132
    2. (opposition) **gegen** (2*a*), p. 133

ALONG **entlang**, p. 131

AMONG (place) **bei** (1*e*), p. 125, **unter** DAT. (I 1*b*), p. 146; **zwischen** DAT. (I 2), p. 154; (motion) **unter** ACC. (II 2), p. 146; **zwischen** ACC. (II 2), p. 154

APART FROM **außer** 1, p. 124; **abgesehen von**.

AROUND 1. (place) **um** (1), p. 144
    2. (time) **um** (2*b*), p. 144; [- . . . *o'clock*] **gegen** (3*a*), p. 133; (quantity) **gegen** (3*a*), p. 133; **etwa, ungefähr**.

AT 1. (place) **an** DAT. (I 1*h*), p. 118; [- window] **an** (I 1*b*), p. 118; (in front of) **vor** DAT. (I 1*a*), p. 148; [- *baker's* etc.] **bei** (1*c*), p. 125; [- *theatre* etc.] **in** DAT. (I 1), p. 135; [- *post office, conference*, etc.] **auf** DAT. (I 1*b*), p. 121; [*aim, point* -] **auf** ACC. (II 2), p. 122; [*nibble* etc. -] **an** DAT. (I 1*k*), p. 118; (motion: *sit down* -) **an** ACC. (II 1), p. 120
    2. (time) **zu** (3*a*), p. 152; [- *moment*] **in** DAT (I 2*a*), p. 135; [- . . . *o'clock*] **um** (2*a*), p. 144; [- *sunrise, breakfast*, etc.] **bei** (5), p. 126
    3. [- *age, speed, rate*] **mit** (3), p. 138
    4. [- *price*] **zu** (9*a*), p. 153
    5. (*in response to*:- *request* etc.) **auf** ACC. (II 5*b*), p. 123
    6. [*amazed* etc. -] **über** (II 5*a*), p. 144

BECAUSE OF **wegen**, p. 151

BEFORE (place) **vor** (I 1*a*), p. 148; (time) **vor** (I 3*a*), p. 149

BEHIND (place) **hinter** DAT. (I 1), p. 134; (motion) **hinter** ACC. (II), p. 135

BELOW, BENEATH (place) **unter** DAT. (I 1*a*), p. 146, **unterhalb**, p. 147; (motion) **unter** ACC. (II), p. 146

BESIDE (place) **neben** DAT. (I 1), p. 140; (motion) **neben** ACC. (II), p. 140

BETWEEN (place) **zwischen** DAT. (I 1), p. 154; (motion) **zwischen** ACC. (II 1), p. 154

BEYOND [- *border* etc.] **hinter** DAT. (II 2), p. 135; [- *ocean* etc.] **jenseits**, p. 137

BY 1. (place) **bei** (1*a*), p. 125; [*sit down* -] **an** ACC. (II 1), p. 120; (motion: *past*) **an . . .** DAT. **vorbei**.
    2. (time) **bis** (1*b*), p. 128; **bis zu** (*ii*) (p. 129).
    3. (means) (*by means of*) **durch** (3), p. 130; [*recognize* etc. -] **an** DAT. (I 4), p. 119; [*take, call*, etc. -] **bei** (2), p. 126; [*grab* etc. -] **an** DAT. (I 3), p. 119; [- *car, train*, etc.] **mit** (2), p. 138
    4. (*according to*) **nach** (4), p. 140
    5. (*to the extent of*) **um** (3), p. 145
    6. [- *Shakespeare* etc.] **von** (2), p. 147; --*ing* **indem**, p. 163; **dadurch, dass**.

BY MEANS OF **durch** (3*a*), p. 130; **mittels**, p. 138; [*demonstrate* etc. -] **an** DAT. (I 4), p. 119

BY THE TIME **bis** (2), p. 129

BY WAY OF **an** DAT. (I 7), p. 120

CONTRARY TO **entgegen**, p. 131

DOWN (away from one) . . . **hinab**, . . . **hinunter**; (towards one) . . . **herab**, . . . **herunter**.

DURING **während**, p. 151

EXCEPT (FOR) **außer** (1), p. 124; **bis auf** (*d*) (p. 129).

FOR 1. (various senses) **für** (1), p. 131; (expressing indirect object) dative case or **für** [e.g. *I bought a present for him* **ich habe ihm ein Geschenk gekauft** or **ich habe ein Geschenk für ihn gekauft**].
    2. (time: length of time) . . . ACC. (**lang**) [e.g.- *three days* **drei Tage (lang)**]; (past time continuing) **seit** (2), p. 141; [*go away* etc. -] **für** (1), p. 131; [*elect* -] **auf** ACC. (II 3*a*), p. 122
    3. (occasion: - *Christmas* etc.) **zu** (3*b*), p. 152
    4. (purpose) **zu** (4), p. 152; [*tablets* etc. -] **gegen** (2*b*), p. 133
    5. [*bill, cheque* -] **über** ACC. (II 5*b*), p. 144
    6. (*in exchange for*) **gegen** (4), p. 133
    7. [*request* etc. -] **um** (4*c*), p. 145; [*longing, demand*, etc.] **nach** (3), p. 139; [*fight* -] **um** (4*b*), p. 145
    8. [*respect* -] **vor** DAT. (I 5*c*), p. 150

FROM 1. **von** (1), p. 147; [*hang* -] **an** DAT. (I 1*i*), p. 118
   2. (origin, source) **aus** (2), p. 124
   3. (protection) **vor** DAT. (I 5*a*), p. 150; -. . . *onwards* **ab**, p. 117;
von . . . an.

IN 1. (place) **in** DAT. (I 1), p. 135; [- *field, street, Cyprus,* etc.] **auf** DAT.
(I 1*c*), p. 122; [- *sky*] **an** (I 1*e*), p. 118
   2. (time) **in** DAT. (I 2), p. 135; [- *morning* etc.] **an** DAT. (I 2*a*), p. 119
   3. (circumstances) [- *fog* etc.] **bei** (5*b*), p. 127; [- *accident*] **bei** (5*a*),
p. 126
   4. [- *manner*] **auf** ACC. (II 4), p. 123; [- *low* etc. *voice*] **mit** (2), p. 138
   5. [- *opinion*] **nach** (4), p. 140
   6. [*rich* etc. -] **an** DAT. (I 7), p. 120

IN ACCORDANCE WITH **entsprechend**, p. 131; **gemäß**, p. 134

INSIDE **innerhalb**, p. 137

IN SPITE OF **trotz**, p. 142

INSTEAD OF **statt**, p. 142, **anstatt**, p. 121

INTO 1. **in** (II), p. 136; [*run, bump* -] **gegen** (1), p. 132
   2. (change of state) **zu** (6), p. 153; **in** (II 2), p. 136

IN FRONT OF 1. (place) **vor** DAT. (I 1*a*), p. 148; (motion) **vor** ACC. (II),
p. 150
   2. (in presence of) **vor** DAT. (I 1*b*), p. 149

NEAR **bei** (1*a*), p. 125; **in der Nähe** + GEN./**von**

NEXT TO (place) **bei** (1*a*), p. 125; **neben** DAT. (I 1), p. 140; (motion) **neben**
ACC. (II), p. 140

OF 1. genitive case [e.g. *the solving - difficult problems* **die Lösung
schwieriger Probleme**] or, where the genitive cannot be shown, **von** (5*a*),
p. 148 [e.g. *the solving - problems* **die Lösung von Problemen**]
   2. (consisting of: *inflation rate* etc. -] **von** (5*d*), p. 148
   3. [*jealous, proud* -] **auf** ACC. (II 5*c*), p. 123
   4. [*typical* etc. -] **für** (4), p. 132

OFF 1. (from) **von** (1), p. 147
   2. [- *coast* etc.] **vor** DAT. (I 1*a*), p. 149

ON 1. (place: on top of) **auf** DAT. (I 1), p. 121; (on side of) **an** DAT. (I 1*a*),
p. 117; [- *border, coast,* etc.] **an** DAT. (I 1*c*), p. 118; (on s.o.'s person) **bei**
(1*d*), p. 125; (motion: put, draw, etc.) **auf** ACC. (II 1*a*), p. 122
   2. (time: - *Friday* etc.) **an** DAT. (I 2*a*), p. 119
   3. (about) **über** ACC. (II 5), p. 144; [*comment* etc. -] **zu** (5*c*), p. 152
   4. [- *holiday, journey*] **auf** DAT. (I 2), p. 122

5. [- *arrival, occasion*] **bei** (5*a*), p. 126; [- *closer acquaintance*] **bei** (5*d*), p. 127

6. [- *TV, radio*] **in** DAT. (I 1), p. 135

7. [*demands* -] **an** ACC. (II 2), p. 121; [*agree, concentrate* -] **auf** ACC. (II 5*c*), p. 123

ON ACCOUNT OF **wegen**, p. 151

OPPOSITE **gegenüber** (1), p. 133

OUT OF 1. (motion) **aus** (1), p. 124

2. (reason) **aus** (4), p. 124

3. (means) **von** (3*a*), p. 147

4. [*cheat* etc. -] **um** (6), p. 145

5. (partitive) **von** (6), p. 148

OUTSIDE (place) **außerhalb**, p. 125; [- *town, harbour,* etc.] **vor** DAT. (I 1*a*), p. 148; (motion) **vor** ACC. (II), p. 150

OVER 1. (place) **über** DAT. (I 1), p. 142; (motion) **über** ACC. (II 1), p. 143

2. [- *glass of beer* etc.] **bei** (5*b*), p. 127; **über** DAT. (I 2), p. 142

3. (time: - *Easter* etc.) **über** ACC. (II 3*a*), p. 143

4. (precedence) **vor** DAT. (I 2), p. 149

5. (quantity) **über** ACC. (II 4), p. 143

6. [*power, victory,* etc. -] **über** ACC. (II 6), p. 144

7. [*strike* -] **um** (4), p. 145

PAST 1. (place) **an** . . . DAT. **vorbei**; (beyond) **hinter** DAT.

2. (time: *minutes* -) **nach** (2*a*), p. 139

ROUND **um** (. . . **herum**) (see **um** (1), p. 144).

SINCE **seit** (1), p. 141

THANKS TO **dank**, p. 130

THROUGH 1. (place) **durch** (1), p. 130

2. (through agency of) **durch** (2), p. 130

THROUGHOUT 1. (place) **im/in der ganzen** . . . [e.g. - *the country* **im ganzen Land**]; (with name of country, city, etc.) **in ganz** . . .

2. (time) **den ganzen / die ganze / das ganze** . . . **hindurch** [e.g. - *the war* **den ganzen Krieg hindurch**].

TILL see *until.*

TO 1. (direction) **zu** (2), p. 151; **an** ACC. (II 1), p. 120; (with name of country, city, etc.) **nach** (1*b*), p. 139, (with such name preceded by definite article) **in** ACC. (II 1), p. 136; [- *theatre* etc.] **in** ACC. (II 1), p. 136

2. (expressing indirect object) dative case is used [e.g. *I'll give it - her later* **ich gebe es ihr später**].

3. (time: *minutes* -) **vor** DAT. (I 3*a*), p. 149
4. [*address question* etc. -] **an** ACC. (II 2), p. 121
5. [*three - four* etc.] **bis** (3), p. 129
6. (ratio: *10 - 1* etc.) **zu** (9*b*), p. 153; (*per*) **auf** ACC. (II 6), p. 123
7. [- *applause*] **unter** (I 3), p. 146
8. [- *s.o.'s surprise, dismay,* etc.] **zu** (7), p. 153
9. [*attitude* -] **zu** (5*b*), p. 152
10. [*polite* etc. -] **gegenüber** (2), p. 134, **zu** (5*a*), p. 152

TOWARDS 1. (direction) **auf . . . ACC. zu.**
2. (time) **gegen** (3*b*), p. 133
3. [*attitude* -] **gegenüber** (2), p. 134, **zu** (5*b*), p. 152

UNDER 1. (place) **unter** DAT. (I 1*a*), p. 146; (motion) **unter** ACC. (II 1), p. 146
2. (quantity) **unter** DAT. (I 2), p. 146
3. [- *circumstances*] **unter** DAT. (I 3), p. 146

UNTIL **bis** (1*a*), p. 128; **bis zu** (*i*), p. 129

VIA **über** ACC. (II 2), p. 143

VIS-À-VIS **gegenüber** (3), p. 134

WITH 1. **mit**, p. 138
2. (*in view of*) **bei** (6), p. 128
3. (*in spite of*) **bei** (7), p. 128
4. [*tremble* etc. -] **vor** (I 4), p. 150

WITHIN 1. (time) **binnen**, p. 128; **innerhalb**, p. 137
2. (place) **innerhalb**, p. 137

WITHOUT **ohne** (1), p. 141

Guide to Conjunctions

For abbreviations used see Guide to Prepositions, p. 117.

ABER

BUT:

> sie ist groß, *aber* nicht stark *she is tall **but** not strong*
> er wollte kommen, *aber* er durfte nicht *he wanted to come, **but** he wasn't allowed to*

Aber may also, however, function as an adverb and come later in the clause (sometimes expressed by HOWEVER):

> er wollte kommen, er durfte *aber* nicht
> Im Norden [Schottlands] *aber* kann man stundenlang wandern an ve lassenen Seen (St. Zweig) *In the north, **however**, one can walk for hours on end by solitary lochs*
> Sabine schrieb, Heinrich *aber* spielte Schach *Sabine was writing, **but** Heinrich was playing chess*

When two verbs share the same subject, **aber** is often placed after the second verb:

> sie schreibt gern Romane, baut *aber* ungern Betten *she likes to write novels, **but** dislikes making beds*

ALLEIN (in literary usage)

BUT:

> er rief um Hilfe, *allein* es war zu spät *he cried for help, **but** it was too late*

ALS

1. (followed by noun)

(*a*) AS (A/THE):

> Sie könnten eines Tages *als* Lord Kilmarnock . . . erwachen (Th. Mann) *you could wake up one day **as** Lord Kilmarnock*
> Sie arbeitet *als* Politesse in Stuttgart (*Bunte*) *She works **as** a traffic warden in Stuttgart*
> Not translated in:
> wir gingen *als* gute Freunde auseinander *we parted good friends*
> er ist *als* Held/Bettler/Christ gestorben *he died a hero/beggar/Christian*

(*b*) (with causal nuance) BEING:

> *Als* aufgeklärter Amerikaner glaubte er nicht an Gespenster (*Zeit*) *Being an enlightened American he did not believe in ghosts*

2. (introducing clause)

(*a*) (indicating past time) WHEN:

 als **er nach Hause kam** *when he came home*
 als **der Krieg vorbei war** *when the war was over*
 BY THE TIME:
 als **die Aufführung zu Ende war, war ich total erschöpft** *by the time the performance was over I was completely exhausted*
 AS:
 als **ich in die Stadt zurückfuhr** *as I drove back into town*
 gerade *als* **ich einschlafen wollte** *just as I was going off to sleep*
 Or expressed by —ING:
 Komm, hier, sagte sie leise, *als* **sie hörte, wie er sich in der Dunkelheit vorsichtig hinter ihr hertastete** (Kluge) *'Come on, over here,' she said softly, hearing him feel his way gingerly behind her in the darkness*

Als is also used with the present tense in the 'historic present':

 Als **ich die Namen Edith Piaf und Judy Garland ins Gespräch werfe** (interview in *Brigitte*) *When I casually mentioned the names of Edith Piaf and Judy Garland*

and in the synopsis of literary works:

 als **der Prinz einsieht, dass er Unrecht hat** *when* the prince realizes that he is wrong

(*b*) (with inversion, verb in subjunctive; in literary usage) AS IF/THOUGH:

 Sie spielte, *als* **beachte sie ihn nicht, mit ihrem offenen Haar** (Penzoldt) *She was playing with her loose hair* ***as if*** *taking no notice of him*

3. (expressing comparison) THAN:

 er ist intelligenter *als* **ich** *he's more intelligent* **than** *me*
 sie ist jünger, *als* **sie aussieht** *she's younger* **than** *she looks*

ALS OB

AS IF:

 sie sieht/sah aus, *als ob* **sie krank wäre** *she looks/looked* ***as if*** *she were ill*

BEVOR

BEFORE:

 Sie wollte ihn noch einmal sehen, *bevor* **sie abreiste** (Kluge) *she wanted to see him once more* ***before*** *she left*
 das muss geändert werden, *bevor* **sich noch mehr Unfälle ereignen** *that must be changed* ***before*** *more accidents happen*

BIS

1. UNTIL, TILL:

 ich bleibe hier, *bis* **der Regen aufhört** *I'm staying here* **until** *(till) the rain stops*

2. BY THE TIME:

 bis sie die Schule verlässt, ist sie ein reifer Mensch *by the time* she leaves
 school she'll be a mature person

3. (*Austrian*, in colloquial usage) WHEN

DA (indicating cause)

AS, SINCE:

 da er taub war, hörte er es nicht *as (since)* he was deaf he didn't hear it

DAMIT [daː'mɪt] (indicating purpose)

SO THAT:

 das Mädchen schrieb sich selber Briefe, *damit* man denken sollte, sie
 hätte einen Freund *the girl wrote letters to herself **so that** people would
 think she had a boyfriend*

DASS

THAT:

 es tut mir leid, *dass* ich Sie beleidigt habe *I'm sorry **that** I offended you*
 ich wusste nicht, *dass* er Österreicher war *I didn't know **that** he was Austrian*
 Meine Gefühle sind so national, *dass* ich nur ein deutsches Mädchen
 lieben könnte (A. Hitler) *My feelings are so national **that** I could only love
 a German girl*

THE FACT THAT:

 Dann aber kam noch hinzu, *dass* er ungern nein sagte (Kluge) *But
 then there was also **the fact that** he didn't like to say no*
 ich machte ihn darauf aufmerksam, *dass* es regnete *I drew his attention
 to **the fact that** it was raining*

FOR . . . TO:

 Es ist notwendig, *dass* die Partei wieder zur Avantgarde des Pro-
 letariats wird (Weiss) *It is necessary **for** the Party **to** become once again
 the avant-garde of the proletariat*

DENN

1. (indicating reason, cause) BECAUSE, AS, SINCE, (in formal usage) FOR:

 Das ist gefährlich, *denn* in den nächsten Monaten muss viel geschehen
 (*FAZ*) *That is dangerous **because** in the next few months a lot has to
 be done*
 Ich rückte das Licht in die Mitte des Schreibtisches, dann aber wieder
 weg und löschte es schließlich ganz aus, *denn* er wollte kein Licht
 (Bernhard) *I moved the lamp to the middle of the desk, then moved it
 away again before finally switching it off altogether, **since** he didn't want
 any light*

• **Denn** is used with main clause word order; a sentence may not begin with a **denn**-clause.

2. THAN:

(*a*) (to avoid repetition of **als**):

Die Schriftstellerinnen dieser Zeit sind mehr als Persönlichkeiten *denn* **als Autorinnen interessant** (*SZ*) *The women writers of this period are interesting more as personalities **than** as authors*

(*b*) **denn je (zuvor)** THAN EVER (BEFORE):

es ist kälter *denn je* *it's colder **than ever***

DOCH

BUT:

sie versprach zu kommen, *doch* **ihre Mutter wurde krank** *she promised to come, **but** her mother fell ill*

EHE (esp. in literary usage)

BEFORE:

Dann dauert es noch zwei Jahre, *ehe* **die Russen am Atlantik sind** (Böll) *Then it'll take another two years **before** the Russians get to the Atlantic*

ehe . . . nicht UNTIL:

Ich glaube . . . kein Wort davon, *ehe* **ich es** *nicht* **mit meinen eigenen Augen gesehen habe** (Penzoldt) *I won't believe a word of it **until** I've seen it with my own eyes*

ENTWEDER . . . ODER

EITHER . . . OR:

entweder **hat sie unsere Verabredung vergessen,** *oder* **sie hat nicht kommen können** *either she forgot our date, **or** she couldn't come*
er kann *entweder* **den Apfel** *oder* **die Orange haben, aber nicht beides** *he can have **either** the apple **or** the orange, but not both*

FALLS

1. IF:

Falls **es mir gelingt, die erste kritische Zeit zu überleben** (Kafka) ***If** I (Should I) succeed in surviving the first critical period*

2. IN CASE:

ich nehme das Buch mit, *falls* **er dort sein sollte** *I'll take the book with me **in case** he should be there*

INDEM

BY ——ING:

Eine Sprache erlernt man, *indem* **man sie liebt** (Wohmann) *You learn a language **by** lov**ing** it*

Ich verdiente mir mein Brot, *indem* ich . . . Kanarienvögel, Papageien und Katzen ausstopfte (Th. Mann) *I earned a living by stuffing canaries, parrots, and cats*

- The original sense of the conjunction, namely AS, WHILE, is now obsolete.

NACHDEM

AFTER:

Nachdem ihr Dolmetscher sie ins Bild gesetzt hatte (Lenz) *After her interpreter had put her in the picture*

OB

WHETHER:

Ich . . . wusste noch nicht, *ob* ich in meiner alten Schule war (Böll) *I didn't know yet whether I was in my old school*
Oskar war es gleichgültig, *ob* wir blieben oder gingen (Grass) *It didn't matter to Oskar whether we stayed or went*

(in elliptical construction) expressed by direct question:

ob er es schafft? *will he manage(, I wonder)?*
ob ich Deutscher sei? *was I German(, he asked)?*

OBGLEICH, OBWOHL

ALTHOUGH:

Nach Zwiebeln roch es, *obgleich* Zwiebeln knapp waren (Grass) *There was a smell of onions, although onions were scarce*
Erst bei Metro Goldwyn Mayer erhielt [Clark Gable] seine Chance—*obwohl* man dort an seinen abstehenden Ohren Anstoß nahm (Bunte) *It was Metro Goldywn Mayer that gave Clark Gable his chance—although there they took exception to his protruding ears*

ODER

OR:

ich werde sie anrufen *oder* ihr schreiben *I'll ring her up or write to her*
sollten wir links *oder* rechts fahren? *should we drive on the left or the right?*

SEIT(DEM)

SINCE:

seit(dem) ich in Straßburg wohne, fühle ich mich wie ein Europäer *since I've been living in Strasbourg I've felt like a European*
seit(dem) ich in Straßburg wohnte, fühlte ich mich wie ein Europäer *since I'd been living in Strasbourg I'd felt like a European*
seit(dem) sie ein Haus gekauft hat, kauft sie nicht mehr so viel Kleidung *since she bought a house she no longer buys so many clothes*

SO (introducing concessive clause)

HOWEVER:

> *so* arm er auch ist, ich kann ihm nicht helfen *however poor he is, I can't help him*

SOBALD

AS SOON AS:

> *sobald* ich nach Hause komme, wedelt unser Hund mit dem Schwanz *as soon as I come home our dog wags his tail*

SODASS, SO DASS (indicating result)

SO THAT:

> ihre Mutter ist wieder da, *sodass* (*so dass*) wir gehen können *their mother is back, so that we can go*

SOFERN

PROVIDED (THAT):

> *sofern* das Wetter schön bleibt, machen wir am Montag einen Ausflug *provided (that) the weather stays fine we'll go on an outing on Monday*

SOLANGE

AS LONG AS, SO LONG AS:

> Aber war das möglich, *solange* der letzte Milchzahn fehlte? (Herzmanovsky-Orlando) *But was that possible as (so) long as the last milk tooth was missing?*

SONDERN

BUT (on the contrary):

> Die Juden schreiben Jiddisch nicht in lateinischen, *sondern* in hebräischen Buchstaben (S. Landmann) *The Jews write Yiddish not in Roman but in Hebrew characters*

nicht nur . . . , sondern auch NOT ONLY . . . BUT ALSO:

> sie ist *nicht nur* jung, *sondern auch* intelligent *she's not only young, but also intelligent*

SOOFT

WHENEVER:

> sie besucht ihn, *sooft* er es wünscht *she visits him whenever he wishes*

SOSEHR

HOWEVER MUCH:

> *sosehr* ich sie vermisse, ich gehe zu ihr nicht zurück *however much I miss her, I'm not going back to her*

SOVIEL

AS FAR AS, SO FAR AS:

soviel ich weiß, ist dieses Modell nicht mehr erhältlich *as (so) far as I know, this model is no longer available*

SOWEIT

1. AS FAR AS, SO FAR AS:

soweit ich es beurteilen kann, wird ihr neuer Roman ein großer Erfolg *as (so) far as I can judge, her new novel will be a great success*

2. (IN) SO FAR AS:

ich will gerne helfen, *soweit* ich dazu in der Lage bin *I'd like to help (in) so far as I'm able to*

SOWIE

AS WELL AS:

wir besuchten Kairo, Mombasa und Daressalam *sowie* mehrere Städte in Südafrika *we visited Cairo, Mombasa, and Dar es Salaam as well as several cities in South Africa*

TROTZDEM (colloquial)

EVEN THOUGH:

er ist zufrieden, *trotzdem* er nicht viel Geld hat *he is content, even though he does not have much money*

UND

AND:

ich fühle mich krank, *und* ich bin es auch *I feel ill, and I am*

WÄHREND

1. WHILE, AS:

Während ich mich mit seiner Schwester unterhielt (Bernhard) *While I talked to his sister*
Während er dies sagte, lächelte er ganz durchtrieben (Hesse) *As he said this, he smiled quite craftily*

2. (whereas) WHILE:

während er sehr sparsam ist, kauft sie sich teure Videos *while he is very thrifty, she buys herself expensive videos*

WEIL

BECAUSE:

sie kann nicht kommen, *weil* sie krank ist *she can't come because she's ill*

The **weil**-clause may optionally be anticipated by **darum, deshalb,** or **deswegen** in the main clause; this has the effect of emphasizing the reason given:

> **ich habe ihn** *deshalb* **eingeladen,** *weil* **er ein einflussreicher Politiker ist** *I invited him **because** he's an influential politician* or *the reason I invited him is that he's an influential politician*

WENN

1. WHEN (referring to the present or future, or to a repeated occurrence in the past):

> **Diese Farben des Stichlingmännchens gewinnen noch an Tiefe und Leuchtkraft,** *wenn* **sich ein Weibchen nähert** (K. Lorenz) *These colours of the male stickleback gain in intensity and luminosity **when** a female approaches*
>
> *Wenn* **du nach Pisa kommst, zeige ich dir den Schiefen Turm** *when you come to Pisa I'll show you the Leaning Tower*
>
> *Wenn* **er sie kommen sah, nahm er seine Brille ab** (Ch. Wolf) *When (whenever) he saw her coming he would take off his glasses*

2. IF:

> *Wenn* **der, den ich verdächtige, der Mörder ist** (Dürrenmatt) *If the man I suspect is the murderer*
>
> *wenn* **ich das gewusst hätte, wäre ich zu einem anderen Zahnarzt gegangen** *if I had known that I would have gone to another dentist*

Note, however, that **wenn** can be ambiguous, meaning either *when* or *if*; thus, **wenn sich ein Weibchen nähert** and **wenn du nach Pisa kommst** in 1 may also mean *if a female approaches* and *if you come to Pisa*. The context usually makes it clear which sense is meant.

Wenn . . . einmal ONCE:

> *wenn* **er** *einmal* **ins Erzählen kommt, hört er nie auf** *once he starts telling stories he never stops*

WIE

AS:

> **ich war ziemlich überrascht,** *wie* **du dir vorstellen kannst** *I was rather surprised, **as** you can imagine*

Note the use of **wie** to introduce a clause corresponding to an English parenthesis without a conjunction:

> **eine Maßnahme, die,** *wie* **er hoffte, die Situation verbessern würde** *a measure which would, he hoped, improve the situation*
>
> **das war,** *wie* **wir schnell erkannten, keine Lösung des Problems** *this was, we quickly realized, no solution to the problem*

ZUMAL

ESPECIALLY AS:

> er hat viel Verständnis für Kinder, *zumal* er selbst sechs hat *he has a lot of understanding for children, **especially as** he himself has six*

CROSS-REFERENCE LIST OF ENGLISH CONJUNCTIONS

Items are cross-referred to the list of German conjunctions beginning on p. 160

AFTER **nachdem**, p. 164

ALTHOUGH **obgleich, obwohl**, p. 164

AND **und**, p. 166

AS 1. (followed by noun) **als** (1*a*), p. 160
    2. (introducing clause: e.g. - *you can imagine*) **wie**, p. 167
    3. (time) **während**, p. 166
    4. (cause) **da**, p. 162

AS IF **als ob**, p. 161

BECAUSE **weil**, p. 166

BEFORE **bevor**, p. 161; **ehe**, p. 163

BUT **aber**, p. 160; **allein**, p. 160; **doch**, p. 163; (on the contrary) **sondern**, p. 165

EITHER . . . OR **entweder . . . oder**, p. 163

FOR **denn** (1), p. 162

IF **wenn** (2), p. 167; **falls** (1), p. 163

IN CASE **falls (2)**, p. 163

ONCE **wenn . . . einmal** (see **wenn**, p. 167).

OR **oder**, p. 164; [e.g. *three - four*] **bis** (3), p. 162

SINCE 1. (cause) **da**, p. 162
    2. (time) **seit, seitdem**, p. 164

SO THAT 1. (purpose) **damit**, p. 162
    2. (result) **sodass, so dass**, p. 165

THAT **dass**, p. 162

TILL see *until*.

UNLESS **es sei denn, (dass); wenn . . . nicht.**

UNTIL **bis** (1), p. 161

WHEN (with present tense) **wenn** (1), p. 167; (with past tense) **als** (2), p. 161, (repeated occurrence) **wenn**, p. 167. See also **bei** (5*a, with verbal noun*), p. 127; **bei** is also frequently used to refer to circumstances indicated in English by *when* [e.g. *when the traffic lights are red* **bei Rotlicht**, *when the temperature outdoors is 20°* **bei 20° Außentemperatur**].

(NOTE: As an interrogative adverb *when* is **wann** [e.g. *when were you born?* **wann bist du geboren?**], also in indirect speech [e.g. *I asked her when she was born* **ich fragte sie, wann sie geboren sei**].)

WHETHER **ob**, p. 164

WHILE 1. (time) **während** (1), p. 166. See also **bei** (5*a, with verbal noun*), p. 127.

      2. (*whereas*) **während** (2), p. 166

Conjugation of Strong and Irregular Verbs

Strong Verbs

(grouped according to vowel change)

Only a selection of verbs is given here, to illustrate the various types; details of conjugation are given for all strong verbs in the alphabetical list below.

The parts shown are: (*a*) the infinitive, (*b*) (only shown—in brackets—where vowel change is involved) the 2nd and 3rd persons singular of the present tense, (*c*) the past tense, (*d*) the past participle.

a—(ä)—ie—a

(i) **schlafen** *to sleep*—(schläfst, schläft)—schlief—geschlafen
blasen *to blow*—(bläst, bläst)—blies—geblasen
raten *to advise*—(rätst, rät)—riet—geraten

(ii) **fallen** *to fall*—(fällst, fällt)—fiel—gefallen
halten *to hold* etc.—(hältst, hält)—hielt—gehalten
lassen *to let* etc.—(lässt, lässt)—ließ—gelassen

a—(ä)—u—a

(i) **fahren** *to go, drive*—(fährst, fährt)—fuhr—gefahren
laden *to load*—(lädst, lädt)—lud—geladen
tragen *to carry, wear*—(trägst, trägt)—trug—getragen

(ii) **wachsen** *to grow*—(wächst, wächst)—wuchs—gewachsen
waschen *to wash*—(wäschst, wäscht)—wusch—gewaschen

e—(ie or i)—a—e

(i) **sehen** *to see*—(siehst, sieht)—sah—gesehen
lesen *to read*—(liest, liest)—las—gelesen
geben *to give*—(gibst, gibt)—gab—gegeben
treten *to step* etc.—(trittst, tritt)—trat—getreten

(ii) **messen** *to measure*—(misst, misst)—maß—gemessen
vergessen *to forget*—(vergisst, vergisst)—vergaß—vergessen
essen *to eat*—(isst, isst)—aß—gegessen

(iii) (with **i** or **ie** in infinitive and present):
    bitten *to ask*—**bat**—**gebeten**
    liegen *to lie*—**lag**—**gelegen**
    sitzen *to sit*—**saß**—**gesessen**

e—(i or ie)—a—o

(i) **helfen** *to help*—(**hilfst, hilft**)—**half**—**geholfen**
  sterben *to die*—(**stirbst, stirbt**)—**starb**—**gestorben**
  werfen *to throw*—(**wirfst, wirft**)—**warf**—**geworfen**

(ii) **sprechen** *to speak*—(**sprichst, spricht**)—**sprach**—**gesprochen**
  treffen *to hit, meet*—(**triffst, trifft**)—**traf**—**getroffen**

(iii) **stehlen** *to steal*—(**stiehlst, stiehlt**)—**stahl**—**gestohlen**
  befehlen *to order*—(**befiehlst, befiehlt**)—**befahl**—**befohlen**

(iv) **nehmen** *to take*—(**nimmst, nimmt**)—**nahm**—**genommen**

i—a—o or u

(i) **schwimmen** *to swim*—**schwamm**—**geschwommen**
  beginnen *to begin*—**begann**—**begonnen**

(ii) **finden** *to find*—**fand**—**gefunden**
  klingen *to sound*—**klang**—**geklungen**
  trinken *to drink*—**trank**—**getrunken**

ei—i—i, ei—ie—ie

(i) **reiten** *to ride*—**ritt**—**geritten**
  beißen *to bite*—**biss**—**gebissen**
  pfeifen *to whistle*—**pfiff**—**gepfiffen**

(ii) **bleiben** *to remain*—**blieb**—**geblieben**
  schweigen *to be silent*—**schwieg**—**geschwiegen**

ie—o—o

(i) **schießen** *to shoot*—**schoss**—**geschossen**
  riechen *to smell*—**roch**—**gerochen**

(ii) **fliegen** *to fly*—**flog**—**geflogen**
  frieren *to freeze*—**fror**—**gefroren**
  ziehen *to pull, draw*—**zog**—**gezogen**

FOUR MAJOR VERBS

(past in **ie**; same vowel or diphthong in infinitive and past participle)

    heißen *to be called*—**hieß**—**geheißen**
    laufen *to run*—(**läufst, läuft**)—**lief**—**gelaufen**
    rufen *to call*—**rief**—**gerufen**
    stoßen *to push* etc.—(**stößt, stößt**)—**stieß**—**gestoßen**

ALPHABETICAL LIST

NOTE: When a prefix is added to a strong or irregular verb, the conjugation forms normally remain the same. It should, however, be noted that there are certain verbs whose last element happens to be identical with a strong verb but which are conjugated *weak*, being formed on the pattern prefix + noun + -en (e.g. **beauftragen, veranlassen** incorporating **der Auftrag, der Anlass**).

INFINITIVE (with 2nd, 3rd singular present where *vowel change* is involved)	PAST (with subjunctive in brackets where *vowel change* is involved)	PAST PARTICIPLE (with auxiliary, if **sein**, also **haben/sein** in special cases)
backen to *bake* (2nd, 3rd singular also **bäckst, bäckt**)	**backte**, obsolescent **buk (büke)**	**gebacken**
befehlen to *order* (**befiehl(s)t**)	**befahl (beföhle/befähle)**	**befohlen**
beginnen to *begin*	**begann (begänne**, also **begönne)**	**begonnen**
beißen to *bite*	**biss**	**gebissen**
bergen to *rescue* etc. (**birg(s)t**)	**barg (bärge)**	**geborgen**
bersten to *burst* (**birst, birst**)	**barst (bärste)**	**(ist) geborsten**
bewegen to *induce*	**bewog (bewöge)**	**bewogen**
In the sense *to move* (also figuratively) conjugated weak		
biegen to *bend*; (intr.) to *turn*	**bog (böge)**	**(intr. ist) gebogen**
bieten to *offer*	**bot (böte)**	**geboten**
binden to *tie, bind*	**band (bände)**	**gebunden**
bitten to *ask*	**bat (bäte)**	**gebeten**
blasen to *blow* (**bläst, bläst**)	**blies**	**geblasen**
bleiben to *remain*	**blieb**	**(ist) geblieben**
braten to *roast*; to *fry* (**brätst, brät**)	**briet**	**gebraten**
brechen to *break* (**brich(s)t**)	**brach (bräche)**	**(intr. ist) gebrochen**
brennen to *burn*	**brannte (brennte** rare)	**gebrannt**
bringen to *bring*; to *take*	**brachte (brächte)**	**gebracht**
denken to *think*	**dachte (dächte)**	**gedacht**
dreschen to *thresh*; (coll.) to *thrash* (**drisch(s)t**)	**drosch (drösche)**	**gedroschen**
dringen: with various prepositions, e.g. **auf** to *insist on*, **in** to *penetrate*	**drang (dränge)**	**(hat/ist)**[37] **gedrungen**
dürfen to *be allowed to* (for conjugation see p. 76)		
empfehlen to *recommend* (conjugated like **befehlen**, above)		

[37] **Hat** with **dringen auf**, otherwise **ist**.

INFINITIVE (with 2nd, 3rd singular present where *vowel change* is involved)	PAST (with subjunctive in brackets where *vowel change* is involved)	PAST PARTICIPLE (with auxiliary, if **sein**, also **haben/sein** in special cases)
erlöschen *to go out* (of fire) (**erlisch(s)t**)	erlosch (erlösche)	(ist) erloschen
erschallen *to ring out*	erscholl (erschölle)/ erschallte	(ist) erschollen/ erschallt
erschrecken *to be frightened* (**erschrick(s)t**)	erschrak (erschräke)	(ist) erschrocken
As a transitive verb *to frighten* conjugated weak		
essen *to eat* (**isst, isst**)	aß (äße)	gegessen
fahren *to drive* (a vehicle); (intr.) *to go* (in a vehicle) (**fähr(s)t**)	fuhr (führe)	(intr. ist) gefahren
fallen *to fall* (**fäll(s)t**)	fiel	(ist) gefallen
fangen *to catch* (**fäng(s)t**)	fing	gefangen
fechten *to fence* (**fichtst, ficht**)	focht (föchte)	gefochten
finden *to find*	fand (fände)	gefunden
flechten *to weave; to plait* (**flichtst, flicht**)	flocht (flöchte)	geflochten
fliegen *to fly*	flog (flöge)	(intr. ist) geflogen
fliehen *to flee*	floh (flöhe)	(intr. ist) geflohen
fließen *to flow*	floss (flösse)	(ist) geflossen
fressen *to eat* (of animal) etc. (**frisst, frisst**)	fraß (fräße)	gefressen
frieren *to freeze*	fror (fröre)	(hat/ist)[38] gefroren
gären *to ferment*	gor (göre)/gärte	(hat/ist)[39] gegoren/ gegärt
Weak in figurative use		
gebären *to give birth to* (obsolescent: **gebier(s)t**)	gebar (gebäre)	geboren
geben *to give* (**gib(s)t**)	gab (gäbe)	gegeben
gedeihen *to thrive*	gedieh	(ist) gediehen
gehen *to go; to walk*	ging	(ist) gegangen
gelingen *to succeed* (impersonal)	gelang (gelänge)	(ist) gelungen
gelten *to be valid* etc. (**giltst, gilt**)	galt (gälte/gölte)	gegolten
genesen *to recover*	genas (genäse)	(ist) genesen
genießen *to enjoy*	genoss (genösse)	genossen
geschehen *to happen* (3rd singular only: **geschieht**)	geschah (geschähe)	(ist) geschehen

---

[38] **Das Wasser ist gefroren** (completed action), but **heute Nacht hat es gefroren** *it was freezing last night*, also **ich habe gefroren** *I was cold.*

[39] Only **hat** in the figurative sense.

INFINITIVE	PAST	PAST PARTICIPLE
(with 2nd, 3rd singular present where *vowel change* is involved)	(with subjunctive in brackets where *vowel change* is involved)	(with auxiliary, if **sein**, also **haben/sein** in special cases)

gewinnen to win; to gain	gewann (gewönne/ gewänne)	gewonnen
gießen to pour	goss (gösse)	gegossen
gleichen (+ DAT.) to resemble	glich	geglichen
gleiten to glide; to slide	glitt	(ist) geglitten
glimmen to glow	glomm (glömme)/ glimmte	geglommen

In figurative use conjugated strong

graben to dig (**gräb(s)t**)	grub (grübe)	gegraben
greifen to grasp; to seize	griff	gegriffen
haben to have (for conjugation see p. 74)		
halten to hold; (intr.) to stop (**hältst, hält**)	hielt	gehalten
hängen to hang (intr.)	hing	gehangen

As a transitive verb to hang conjugated weak

hauen to hit etc.	haute/hieb[40]	gehauen
heben to lift	hob (höbe)	gehoben
heißen to be called	hieß	geheißen
helfen (+ DAT.) to help (**hilf(s)t**)	half (hülfe, also **hälfe**)	geholfen
kennen to know (be acquainted with)	kannte (kennte rare)	gekannt
klimmen to climb	klomm (klömme)/ klimmte	(ist) geklommen/ geklimmt
klingen to sound	klang (klänge)	geklungen
kneifen to pinch	kniff	gekniffen
kommen to come	kam (käme)	(ist) gekommen
können to be able to (for conjugation see p. 96)		
kriechen to creep; to crawl	kroch (kröche)	(ist) gekrochen
laden to load; to invite (**läd(s)t**)	lud (lüde)	geladen
lassen to let etc. (**lässt, lässt**)	ließ	gelassen
laufen to run; to walk (**läuf(s)t**)	lief	(intr. ist) gelaufen
leiden to suffer	litt	gelitten
leihen to lend	lieh	geliehen
lesen to read (**liest, liest**)	las (läse)	gelesen
liegen to lie	lag (läge)	gelegen
lügen to (tell a) lie	log (löge)	gelogen
mahlen to grind	mahlte	gemahlen
meiden to avoid	mied	gemieden

[40] The form **hieb** occurs chiefly when a blow is aimed at someone, e.g. **er hieb mit dem Schwert auf den Angreifer** *he hit out at the attacker with his sword.*

INFINITIVE (with 2nd, 3rd singular present where *vowel change* is involved)	PAST (with subjunctive in brackets where *vowel change* is involved)	PAST PARTICIPLE (with auxiliary, if **sein**, also **haben/sein** in special cases)
melken to *milk*	melkte, obsolescent molk (mölke)	gemolken, also gemelkt
messen to *measure* (**misst, misst**)	maß (mäße)	gemessen
misslingen to *fail* (of attempt etc.) (conjugated like **gelingen**, above)		
mögen to *like; may* (for conjugation see p. 76)		
müssen to *have to* (for conjugation see p. 76)		
nehmen to *take* (**nimm(s)t**)	nahm (nähme)	genommen
nennen to *name*	nannte (nennte rare)	genannt
pfeifen to *whistle*	pfiff	gepfiffen
preisen to *praise*	pries	gepriesen
quellen to *swell; to well (from)* (**quill(s)t**)	quoll (quölle)	(ist) gequollen
raten to *guess;* (+ DAT.) to *advise* (**rätst, rät**)	riet	geraten
reiben to *rub*	rieb	gerieben
reißen to *tear*	riss	(intr. ist) gerissen
reiten to *ride*	ritt	(intr. hat/ist)[41] geritten
rennen to *run; to race*	rannte (rennte rare)	(ist) gerannt
riechen to *smell*	roch (röche)	gerochen
ringen to *wrestle*	rang (ränge)	gerungen
rinnen to *run, flow*	rann (ränne, also rönne)	(ist) geronnen
rufen to *call*	rief	gerufen
salzen to *salt*	salzte	gesalzen
saufen to *drink* (of animal) etc. (**säuf(s)t**)	soff (söffe)	gesoffen
saugen to *suck*	sog (söge)/saugte[42]	gesogen/gesaugt[42]
schaffen to *create*	schuf (schüfe)	geschaffen
In the senses to *manage (to do)*; to *do, get done* conjugated weak		
scheiden to *separate;* (intr.) to *part*	schied	(ist) geschieden
scheinen to *shine; to seem*	schien	geschienen
scheißen (vulgar) to *shit*	schiss	geschissen
schelten to *scold* (**schiltst, schilt**)	schalt (schölte)	gescholten

[41] See p. 73.
[42] The weak form is always used in **Staub saugen** to *vacuum-clean.*

INFINITIVE	PAST	PAST PARTICIPLE
(with 2nd, 3rd singular present where *vowel change* is involved)	(with subjunctive in brackets where *vowel change* is involved)	(with auxiliary, if **sein**, also **haben/sein** in special cases)

scheren to crop; to clip; to shear	schor (schöre)	geschoren
schieben to push	schob (schöbe)	geschoben
schießen to shoot	schoss (schösse)	(intr. **ist**) geschossen
schinden to ill-treat; to sweat (labour)	schindete	geschunden
schlafen to sleep (schläf(s)t)	schlief	geschlafen
schlagen to hit; to beat (schläg(s)t)	schlug (schlüge)	geschlagen
schleichen to creep	schlich	(ist) geschlichen
schleifen to sharpen	schliff	geschliffen

The separate verb **schleifen** to *drag* is conjugated weak

schließen to close	schloss (schlösse)	geschlossen
schlingen to tie (knot) etc.	schlang (schlänge)	geschlungen
schmeißen (coll.) to chuck	schmiss	geschmissen
schmelzen to melt (schmilzt, schmilzt)	schmolz (schmölze)	(intr. **ist**) geschmolzen
schneiden to cut	schnitt	geschnitten
schreiben to write	schrieb	geschrieben
schreien to shout; to cry out	schrie	geschrien [-ˈʃriːən]
schreiten to stride	schritt	(ist) geschritten
schweigen to be silent	schwieg	geschwiegen
schwellen to swell (schwill(s)t)	schwoll (schwölle)	(ist) geschwollen

As a transitive verb to *swell* (sails etc.) conjugated weak

schwimmen to swim; to float	schwamm (schwömme, also schwämme)	(hat/ist)[43] geschwommen
schwinden to dwindle; to vanish	schwand (schwände)	(ist) geschwunden
schwingen to swing; to brandish	schwang (schwänge)	geschwungen
schwören to swear (affirm solemnly)	schwor (schwüre)	geschworen
sehen to see (sieh(s)t)	sah (sähe)	gesehen
sein to be (for conjugation see p. 74)		
senden to send; to broadcast	sandte/sendete (sendete rare)	gesandt/gesendet

In the sense to *broadcast* only **sendete, gesendet**

sieden to boil	sott (sötte)/siedete	gesotten/gesiedet

Only weak when intransitive; **kochen** is the usual word for both transitive and intransitive senses

---

[43] See p. 73.

INFINITIVE	PAST	PAST PARTICIPLE
(with 2nd, 3rd singular present where *vowel change* is involved)	(with subjunctive in brackets where *vowel change* is involved)	(with auxiliary, if **sein**, also **haben/sein** in special cases)
singen to *sing*	**sang (sänge)**	**gesungen**
sinken to *sink*	**sank (sänke)**	(ist) **gesunken**
sinnen to *ponder*	**sann (sänne)**	**gesonnen**
sitzen to *sit*	**saß (säße)**	**gesessen**
sollen to *be supposed to* (for conjugation see p. 76)		
spalten to *split*	**spaltete**	**gespalten/gespaltet**
speien to *spit*; to *vomit*	**spie**	**gespien** [-'ʃpiːən]
spinnen to *spin*	**spann (spönne/spänne)**	**gesponnen**
spleißen to *splice*	**spliss**	**gesplissen**
sprechen to *speak* (**sprich(s)t**)	**sprach (spräche)**	**gesprochen**
sprießen to *sprout*	**spross (sprösse)**	(ist) **gesprossen**
springen to *jump*	**sprang (spränge)**	(ist) **gesprungen**
stechen to *prick*; to *stab*; to *sting* (**stich(s)t**)	**stach (stäche)**	**gestochen**
stecken to *be* (in a certain place, state)	**steckte**, literary **stak (stäke)**	**gesteckt**
As a transitive verb to *put, stick* only weak		
stehen to *stand*	**stand (stünde, also stände)**	**gestanden**
stehlen to *steal* (**stiehl(s)t**)	**stahl (stähle)**	**gestohlen**
steigen to *climb*; to *rise*	**stieg**	(ist) **gestiegen**
sterben to *die* (**stirb(s)t**)	**starb (stürbe)**	(ist) **gestorben**
stieben to *fly* (of sparks) etc.	**stob (stöbe)/stiebte**	(hat/ist) **gestoben/gestiebt**
stinken to *stink*	**stank (stänke)**	**gestunken**
stoßen to *push* etc.; (intr.) with various prepositions, e.g. **auf** to *come across / up against* (**stößt, stößt**)	**stieß**	(intr. **ist**)[44] **gestoßen**
streichen to *stroke*; to *spread*; to *cross out*; (intr.) to *sweep* (across) etc.	**strich**	(intr. **ist**)[45] **gestrichen**
streiten to *quarrel*; to *argue*	**stritt**	**gestritten**
tragen to *carry*; to *wear* (**träg(s)t**)	**trug (trüge)**	**getragen**
treffen to *hit*; to *meet* (**triff(s)t**)	**traf (träfe)**	**getroffen**
treiben to *drive* etc.; (intr.) to *sprout*; to *drift*	**trieb**	(intr. **hat/ist**)[46] **getrieben**

[44] Except in the case of **stoßen an** to *adjoin*.
[45] Except when an act of stroking is referred to, e.g. **sie hat ihm über den Kopf gestrichen** *she stroked his head*.
[46] **Hat getrieben** when the verb means to *sprout*, **ist getrieben** when it means to *drift*.

INFINITIVE (with 2nd, 3rd singular present where *vowel change* is involved)	PAST (with subjunctive in brackets where *vowel change* is involved)	PAST PARTICIPLE (with auxiliary, if **sein**, also **haben/sein** in special cases)
treten to *kick*; (intr.) *to step*; *to tread* (**trittst, tritt**)	trat (träte)	(intr. ist) getreten
trinken to *drink*	trank (tränke)	getrunken
trügen to *deceive* (by nature)	trog (tröge)	getrogen
tun to *do*; (coll.) *to put*	tat (täte)	getan
verderben to *spoil*; *to ruin*; *to corrupt*; (intr.) *to go bad* (**verdirb(s)t**)	verdarb (verdürbe)	(intr. ist) verdorben
verdrießen to *vex*	verdross (verdrösse)	verdrossen
vergessen to *forget* (**vergisst, vergisst**)	vergaß (vergäße)	vergessen
verlieren to *lose*	verlor (verlöre)	verloren
verschleißen to *wear out*	verschliss	verschlissen
wachsen to *grow* (**wächst, wächst**)	wuchs (wüchse)	(ist) gewachsen
wägen to *ponder* (someone's words)	wog (wöge), also **wägte**	gewogen, also gewägt
waschen to *wash* (**wäscht, wäscht**)	wusch (wüsche)	gewaschen
weben to *weave*	webte / figuratively wob (wöbe)	gewebt/figuratively gewoben
weichen to *ease* (of pressure etc.); (+ DAT.) *to give way to*	wich	(ist) gewichen
weisen to *point* (at etc.)	wies	gewiesen
wenden to *turn*	wandte/wendete[47] (wendete rare)	gewandt/ gewendet[47]
werben to *win* (customers etc.); *to recruit* (**wirb(s)t**)	warb (würbe)	geworben
werden to *become* (for conjugation see p. 74)		
werfen to *throw* (**wirf(s)t**)	warf (würfe)	geworfen
wiegen to *weigh*	wog (wöge)	gewogen
The verb **wiegen** to *rock*; *to sway (hips)* is conjugated weak		
winden to *wind*; *to winch*	wand (wände)	gewunden
wissen to *know* (fact etc.) (for conjugation see p. 76)		
wollen to *want (to)* (for conjugation see p. 76)		
wringen to *wring*	wrang (wränge)	gewrungen

---

[47] In certain senses, only **wendete, gewendet** are used, notably when a change of direction is involved (e.g. **sie hat das Auto gewendet**) and—in reflexive use—when a change in the weather or someone's luck is referred to.

INFINITIVE (with 2nd, 3rd singular present where *vowel change* is involved)	PAST (with subjunctive in brackets where *vowel change* is involved)	PAST PARTICIPLE (with auxiliary, if **sein**, also **haben/sein** in special cases)
zeihen (+ GEN.) *to accuse of* (obsolescent)	**zieh**	**geziehen**
ziehen *to pull; to draw* (intr.) *to move, go*	**zog (zöge)**	(intr. **ist**)[48] **gezogen**
zwingen *to force*	**zwang (zwänge)**	**gezwungen**

[48] **Hat** is, however, used with certain intransitive senses, including *to move* (in chess); *to pull* (of vehicle); *to stand* (of tea); (coll.) *to work* (of excuse etc.).

A Note on Dictionaries

MONOLINGUAL DICTIONARIES

G. Drosdowski (ed.), *Duden: Deutsches Universalwörterbuch A-Z* (3rd edition: Mannheim, 1996)

A comprehensive treatment of the German lexis; uses the new spelling.

D. Götz, G. Haensch, H. Wellmann (eds.), *Langenscheidts Großwörterbuch: Deutsch als Fremdsprache* (6th edition: Berlin & Munich, 1997)

Specifically aimed at foreign learners; provided with excellent examples.

G. Wahrig, *Deutsches Wörterbuch* (new edition: Gütersloh, 1997; ed. R. Wahrig-Burfeind)

Uses the new spelling.

Two useful Duden Taschenbücher documenting vocabulary specific to Austrian and Swiss German are:

J. Ebner, *Wie sagt man in Österreich?: Wörterbuch der österreichischen Besonderheiten* (2nd edition: Mannheim, 1980)

K. Meyer, *Wie sagt man in der Schweiz?: Wörterbuch der schweizerischen Besonderheiten* (Mannheim, 1989)

BILINGUAL DICTIONARIES

P. Terrell et al., *Collins German-English, English-German Dictionary* (3rd edition: Glasgow, 1997)

With its impressively extensive coverage of the German and English vocabularies and rich documentation of contemporary usage, this dictionary might seem the ideal tool for the student of German. Its authors have, however, shown a disturbing indifference to the need for accuracy—to such an extent that it can only be regarded as seriously flawed. Only a handful of examples of errors noted (a number of which also appear in the *Collins German Concise Dictionary*) can be given here: wrong gender (**Asbest** n. [should be m.]), wrong plural (**Tief, -e [-s]**), wrong case (**fern** + gen. [+ DAT.]), wrong type of prefix (**anerziehen** insep. [sep.]—and **antizipieren** is given as insep.!), wrong auxiliary (**zerbröckeln** h. [sn.]), wrong category of verb (**herumflegeln** v.i. [v.r.]), sense labelled subjunctive (**sollen** f); wrong pronunciation (**Erz-** *arch-* with long [short] **e**); German words misspelt (at **Stunde: acht-Stunden-Tag [Achtstundentag]**), English words misspelt (at **kribbeln**: *teaming with ants*); mistranslations (**Raumklang** *stereoscopic [stereophonic] sound*, **Überraschungsmoment** *moment [element] of surprise*, **Volksbefragung** *public opinion poll [referendum]*, **nachdatieren** *to postdate [to antedate]*).

W. Scholze-Stubenrecht, J. B. Sykes (eds.), *The Oxford-Duden German Dictionary* (revised edition: Oxford, 1997)

This dictionary does not provide the same depth of treatment as the Collins. In the first ten pages of English-German, for example, the following items are absent: *abasement, abnegate, abreact, abusiveness, accordionist, accoutrements, action-packed, activism, adamantine, admonitory, adopted* (son etc.), *advance booking/party/warning, aerobatic.* But the reliability of the dictionary is not in doubt.

Index